HIS WAYS

A Monastic Journey of Life and Light

Br. Victor-Antoine d'Avila-Latourrette

Introduction by Michael Centore

Liguori
Liguori, Missouri

Imprimi Potest:
Harry Grile, CSsR, Provincial
Denver Province, The Redemptorists

Published by Liguori Publications
Liguori, Missouri 63057

To order, call 800-325-9521
www.liguori.org

Cataloging-in-Publication Data is on file with the Library of Congress

p ISBN: 978-0-7648-2285-8
e ISBN: 978-0-7648-6895-5

The quotations in this book, except those from Scripture, were collected by and are the responsibility of the author.

Liguori Publications, a nonprofit corporation, is an apostolate of The Redemptorists. To learn more about The Redemptorists, visit Redemptorists.com.

Printed in the United States of America
18 17 16 15 14 / 5 4 3 2 1

First Edition

CONTENTS

IN MEMORIAM

† Pere Pierre Minard of Liguge and Pere Yves Chaussy of Paris
† Mere Marie and Soeur Telchilde of Jouarre
† Mere Marie-Elizabeth of Dourgne
† Mere Ida and Mere Marie-Assumpta of Bethlehem, Connecticut

In thanksgiving to God for their faithful and humble monastic witness.

INTRODUCTION

Blessed are all who fear the L*ORD*,
and who walk in his ways.
PSALM 128:1

The image adorning this book, of what appears to be an anonymous road winding through an autumnal forest, is actually the entranceway of Our Lady of the Resurrection Monastery in Lagrangeville, New York. While all roads imply a journey, knowing the location of this particular road lends the scene an added depth. In leading us into the monastic enclosure from the world beyond, it invites us to embark on an inward journey of spiritual contemplation.

As is the image, so follows the text. *Walk in His Ways* is a yearlong journal documenting a life "en route" to Christ through small, often overlooked daily events. Each day's selection generally includes a title for Br. Victor-Antoine's reflection, the saint(s) or honored person being recognized on that day, a quotation, and the author's reflection.

This book is infused with the Holy Spirit and is deeply felt throughout these pages. Br. Victor-Antoine writes as a monk but addresses us as fellow strugglers in the faith. His concerns will not be remote to anyone seeking an authentic life in accord with the Gospel. The direct, diaristic tone of the writing presents the reality of the monastic experience without sentiment. Like many monastic texts, it was written as an extension of the author's prayer life, as much to cultivate an interior stillness as to communicate something to an audience.

A theme that runs throughout this book is the unity of Eastern and Western Christianity. As a foundational principle of life at Our Lady of the Resurrection, the dialogue between East and West is not an abstract concept. It is a tangible thing, heard in the psalmody of the offices and seen in the iconography adorning the walls. A visitor thus feels a kinship to an earlier, pre-schismatic Christianity centered entirely on the divine mystery.

The constant return to this mystery at the heart of Christian life is the book's refrain. Even when addressing topics of contemporary relevance, Br. Victor-Antoine does so in light of an ancient faith. Like the Desert Fathers and Mothers whom he quotes and in whose lineage this book rests, he conveys a life stripped of superfluities, pointing always to Christ. The experience of reading guides us toward our own encounter, that we may also "walk in his ways."

MICHAEL CENTORE

BROOKLYN, NEW YORK
NOVEMBER 7, 2013
FEAST OF ST. DIDACUS

JANUARY

JANUARY 1 · *The Holy Mother of God*

A MOST ADMIRABLE EXCHANGE

A marvelous wonder has this day come to pass: nature is made new and God becomes man. That which he was, he remains: and that which he was not, he has taken upon himself without suffering confusion nor division.

SYNAXIS OF THE MOST HOLY *THEOTOKOS*

Today is the beautiful octave of Christmas. It seems as if winter at its worst has only just begun. We have three whole months ahead of us in the Northeast to reconcile and make peace with our usual harsh and coldest of seasons. Today is also the beginning of the new year. Most people, myself included, want to know: What will it bring new? The upcoming year is upheld in the mystery of time. We don't know what it will bring, how it will go, or how it will end. I get inner strength and fortitude from the fact that the new year begins under the protection of the *Theotokos*, the holy Mother of God. She shall watch over us, take care of our needs, and grant us her maternal protection. She shall also inspire us by the example of her genuine humanity and exquisite charity. She certainly is the Virgin most humble, a Virgin most compassionate and charitable. Her *Magnificat* and the few life examples of her given in the Gospels attest vividly to this. I think our Lady, humble as she is, doesn't wish us to idealize her but rather imitate those virtues by which she herself so pleased God. Most Holy *Theotokos*, save us!

JANUARY 2 · *St. Basil the Great, St. Gregory Nazianzen, St. Macarius of Alexandria, and St. Seraphim of Sarov (the Wonderworker)*

THE FATHERS: OUR TEACHERS IN THE FAITH

As we begin the new year, we celebrate today the memory of two great Fathers and pillars of the early Church. It is a curious fact to keep their memorial together on the same day, but not totally illogical, since both St. Basil and St. Gregory Nazianzen were great and close friends during their earthly life. It is true, the two were as different from each other as we can imagine, and yet it was precisely their differences that enriched their friendship and helped balance their individual personalities. Throughout the years, they shared the same concerns to safeguard the purity of the early Christian faith. They both loved to study philosophy, language, writing, and poetry, and they used their linguistic and writing talents for the service of the true God. St. Basil, called the Great by his contemporaries, was a bishop and a monk, a pastor of great measure, and a dialogist. He had a great influence on St. Benedict, who lovingly called him "our father, St. Basil." St. Basil was a strong proponent and practitioner of the cenobitic form of monastic life. He preferred it as a most practical life that was closer to the ideals of the early Christian community, in contrast to the eremitical solitary life in the desert. Nevertheless, both forms of monastic life survived side by side throughout the centuries to this day, and it goes without saying that in both God is glorified.

BROTHER FIRE

I gird myself today with
the might of heaven.
The rays of the sun,
The beams of the moon,
The glory of fire,
The speed of wind,
The depth of the sea,
The stability of earth,
The hardness of rock.

ST. PATRICK

During this seemingly long, uninterrupted winter darkness, there is a stimulating and comforting feeling emanating from the heat in our kitchen's wood-burning stove. During these long months of our winter hibernation, one could almost feel imprisoned by the limited warm space in the monastery, most of which remains unheated. And yet there, in a small quiet corner, the radiant fire from the kitchen stove offers us comfort and renewed energy to soothe us, to heal us from the frosts contracted in the outdoor's bitter cold. It is as if the fire agreed to treat us with its utmost gentle care. St. Patrick describes it as "the glory of fire," and St. Francis of Assisi refers to him as simply "Brother Fire." Our four cats—Margot, Walter, Nicole, and Pompom—relish the comfort found in proximity to "Brother Fire." We all do. Fire and heat, bless the Lord.

A SPECIAL WINTER JOY

Fireside happiness, to hours of ease
Blest with that charm, the certainty to please.

JOHN WILT, EARL OF ROCHESTER

Tending the monastery stoves provides me another of those joys in which I delight wholeheartedly, the occasion to enjoy blissful quiet time by the fireside. On certain days when the temperature is below zero, the monastic buildings are covered by inches of snow, and fierce, gusty winds can be heard in the background. It is indeed a peaceful, stimulating feeling to spend time around the stoves, watching the fire rising straight upward in the chimney, listening to its crackling sound in the deep silence, and, of course, being comforted by its warmth. I find the period of time spent each evening by the fireplace to be restful and extremely soothing to my inner spirit. There is great peace, deep tranquility, and a particular quality of soul delight during the quiet moments of prayer, reading, and utter silence by the fireplace. During those soothing moments I am reminded of the Lord's mysterious words: "I have come to set the world on fire, and how I wish it were already blazing!" (Luke 12:49).

THE MYSTICAL SYMBOLISM OF FIRE

Brother Joseph said to Brother Lot, "One can't be a monk unless one becomes like a consuming fire."

ABBA JOSEPH OF PANEPHYSIS

The mysterious, complex reality that a fire embodies speaks volumes to me, sometimes concretely and sometimes abstractly. A roaring fire has a way of insinuating something about the eternal truths in which the life of a monk is plunged. The Apostle Paul describes God as a consuming fire, a mystical image that readily resonates in the monastic heart. Fire, one of the most basic elements of nature, has its own vivid way of revealing to those who wish to see, something utterly indefinable about the presence of God.

Praise be, my Lord, for Brother Fire,
By whom thou lightest up the night;
He is beautiful, merry, robust, and strong.

ST. FRANCIS OF ASSISI,
CANTICLE OF THE CREATURES

THE EPIPHANY OF THE LORD

The moment I realized that God existed, that moment I knew I couldn't do otherwise but live for him alone.

BLESSED CHARLES DE FOUCAULD

The twelve days after Christmas are completed today, and we are invited by the Church calendar to feast on the great event of God's manifestation to the Gentiles, that is, to the whole wide world. The salvific event of God's Incarnation is not only for the benefit of the Jews, God's Chosen People, but for the salvation of all humankind, of the whole world. Thus today we see a humble baby, God's manifestation of himself in the flesh, warmly welcoming the Gentiles to the stable in Bethlehem and showing his very self to them. St. Paul, in his First Letter to Timothy, expresses today's mystery as no other:

[He] was manifested in the flesh,
vindicated in the spirit,
seen by angels,
proclaimed to the Gentiles,
believed in throughout the world,
taken up in glory.

1 TIMOTHY 3:16

In one of the Byzantine texts of the feast, an inspired composer proclaims: "The Magi falling before You they adored You: for they saw you, the Timeless One, lying as a babe in the cave." *Venite adoremus!*

EPIPHANY DAYS

God's promises are like the stars;
The darker the night the brighter they shine.
DAVID NICHOLAS

Yesterday was Epiphany, the summit of our Christmas celebrations, the day the Lord manifested himself to all peoples: Jews, pagans, Gentiles. He is our Savior, and he came to save all humankind. Everyone is included in his plan of salvation. As I meditate on this mystery, well beyond all human comprehension, I come to the realization there is only one simple explanation for all this: God's boundless love. God loves each and every one of his creatures, without distinction, infinitely, passionately, boundlessly....All of us—saints, sinners, and all those in between—fit into the category of those who are loved by him. As I glance upon the crêche in our community room where our visitors are usually received and welcomed, I see the Infant with his outstretched arms. He has a tender smile as he welcomes everyone. It feels good to be welcomed into his tiny arms; indeed, I find it heartwarming to realize how much each of us is loved by him. It is hard to leave that blessed scene. To think that a poor, simple stable, similar to barns and stables everywhere, can contain so much fire, so much love within.

OUR LADY

The fourteenth-century English recluse Julian of Norwich wrote about Mary, the Mother of God: "I saw our Blessed Lady, grounded in humility. She was filled with grace and all virtues and is thus higher than all other creatures."

We can't help but rejoice in Julian's clear statement about the Mother of God. It is totally in concert with the Byzantine *Magnificat* antiphon we sing daily at Vespers: "More honorable than the Cherubim, and more glorious beyond compare than the Seraphim. Remaining a Virgin you gave birth to God, true *Theotokos*, we magnify you." And also we rejoice with one of the cherished quick, short prayers, one which I daily alternate with the Jesus prayer: *"Most Holy* Theotokos, *save us!"*

JOURNEYING TOWARD THEOPHANY

O blessed Jordan stream! You received within yourself the Creator at his baptism and thus you were made a fountain of life-giving water for our salvation. Therefore we sing: "O God our Deliverer, blessed are You, O Lord."

OFFICE FOR THE FOREFEAST OF THE THEOPHANY

These past Epiphany days were fiercely cold—however, the air is dry and the sky is clear. The snowy countryside beams radiantly with sunshine during the daylight hours; but again, once the sun sets, the gloom of winter returns with its low nighttime temperatures.

The winters here in the Northeast are unique in their own peculiar way, and it takes a certain temperament to adjust to its daily eccentricities. In the monastic offices we continue to sing the beautiful Epiphany Gregorian hymns and antiphons all through the octave, all the way to the feast of the Theophany, a great feast here in this small corner of the world. It is a feast I await every year with joyous anticipation.

The theophany icon, created by our friend and neighbor, the artist Olga Poloukhine, already takes its place on our lectern, and it is venerated each time one enters or leaves the oratory, as well as during the daily singing of the *Magnificat* at Vespers. The monastic chants during the season feed and replenish our inner prayer with love, compassion, and a profound sense of God's beauty. It also brings consolation and comfort to those in doubt, in sorrow, or in distress. We must thank the Lord for the gift of such simple plain music, a true vehicle of prayer that possesses such a mysterious power to lead us into his mysteries.

ANOTHER CAPPADOCIAN FATHER

Faith ought in silence to fulfill the commandments, worshiping the Father, reverencing with him and the Son, abounding in the Holy Spirit....These truths ought to be hidden in the silent veneration of the heart.

ST. HILARY OF POITIERS

The monastic calendar today honors the memory of one of three Cappadocian Fathers, St. Gregory of Nyssa. We keep his holy memorial a week after that of St. Basil and St. Gregory Nazianzen, the two other Cappadocian Fathers. These men are truly our fathers in the faith. With their writings and wisdom, they nurture our faith, opening wide our inner eyes, helping us to recognize the mystery of God's revelation: the Father, the Son, and the Holy Spirit. An icon of these three hierarchs hangs in our chapel, and their quiet presence is interiorly felt. As we approach the culmination of our Christmas cycle and reach the glorious feast of the Theophany, the first occasion when the presence of the Trinity is revealed in the New Testament, we adhere once more to the ancient faith of our fathers and confess: Glory to you, O Lord, O one and undivided Trinity!

THE HOLY SPIRIT

[Strive] to preserve the unity of the spirit through the bond of peace.

EPHESIANS 4:3

The Holy Spirit's presence in the depths of our being is the soul's true rest, strength, and joy. It is this Holy Spirit who guides the soul into the quiet ways of prayer. He is its only teacher. With unspeakable sweetness, the Holy Spirit leads us also into the practice of true charity toward others. Prayer and charity are intimately connected. They both have their origin in God himself, they both were taught by the Lord in the Gospels as essential for a true, sincere, Christian life. Prayer and charity are powerful signs in our world of the presence of God's kingdom in our midst. The kingdom of God does not exist in the abstract; rather, it is present in the world through those who allow the Holy Spirit to possess them and act in them according to his designs. And what are his designs? The Gospels give us the answer: "Pray always," and "love God above all else and your neighbors as yourself." The work of prayer and charity are at the heart of Gospel messages. They are also visible signs of the Holy Spirit's divine indwelling in the soul.

Making Bread

Give us this day our daily bread.

THE OUR FATHER

The practice of bread making is as ancient as humanity itself. History tells us that the ancient Egyptians invented the first ovens in their open fields for the sole purpose of baking their daily bread. The Greeks contributed their own talents to this ancient practice by discovering how to carefully mill and grind flour for baking. In the meantime, the old Romans—always avid bread consumers—updated the process of bread making in other ways and introduced their methods to the whole of the Roman Empire. Throughout the centuries, monasteries developed their own traditions and particular recipes for making and baking bread. The monks created certain recipes for ordinary days and others for more festive occasions such as Christmas, Epiphany, Easter, and Pentecost. Nothing is so appealing in the monastic kitchen as the fragrance of simple, fresh-baked bread. In the past, for years, I used to bake bread weekly, not only for consumption at the monastery but to sell at one of the local health-food stores where our fresh organic breads were deeply appreciated by some of the clientele.

There is no doubt in my mind that the making of delicious fresh bread is a cultivated art form. It demands time and patience to learn to do it properly. Obviously, the time, preparation, and effort put into it brings rewards: quality of the bread, solid nutrition, and the pure delight that comes from tasting such a good and authentic product, the fruit of our own labors! As James Beard is quoted as saying: "Good bread is the most fundamentally satisfying of all foods; and good bread with fresh butter, the greatest of feasts."

Bread making using the inexpensive regular yeast one finds in the local supermarket is not necessarily a difficult task. And it doesn't consume endless amounts of time, either. A good baker must simply be careful in mixing the exact measures of ingredients, be patient in the kneading process and in the shaping of the loaves, and pay close attention to the rising and baking time so that the end result coincides exactly with what one had in mind from the beginning. There are hundreds of recipes to choose from, for bread itself comes in many varieties, types, shapes, and sizes. I usually choose basic, simple recipes that are easy to prepare and a pure delight to the palate. In my humble view, there is really nothing comparable to the allure of homemade bread. It feeds both the body and the soul.

THE THEOPHANY OF THE LORD

When you were baptized in the Jordan, O Lord, the mystery of the Trinity was made manifest; for the voice of the Father bore witness to you, calling you his beloved Son. And the Spirit in the form of a dove confirmed the truthfulness of his Word. O Christ, our God, who has appeared and enlightened the world, glory to you!

TROPARION OF THE FEAST

The Theophany of the Lord is one of the loveliest feasts in the Christian calendar. It is a very personal feast for me, very dear to my heart. I look forward to it all year-round. Though the Western Church prefers to call it the feast of the Baptism of the Lord, I am more at home with its ancient title and meaning, as it has been kept in the Eastern Church throughout the centuries, and where the feast actually originated. The Eastern Church emphasizes this feast as the manifestation of the Holy Trinity to the whole world during the Lord's baptism in the Jordan. Historically speaking, it is the first time that the three divine persons reveal themselves together in the New Testament. During this glorious manifestation, the Father gives witness to the Son: "This is my beloved Son, with whom I am well pleased" (Matthew 3:17). And the Holy Spirit gives witness to the Son by descending as a dove upon him and anointing him as the Holy One, the chosen One of God. In turn, Jesus, our Lord and Savior—witness to the Father and the Holy Spirit—reveals to us the intimate God-life that unites the three of them. From all eternity, God the Father chooses the humble moment of Christ's baptism to reveal to the world the mystery hidden from before time began. Glory to you, O Lord our God, glory to you!

CONTACT WITH THE OUTDOORS

LORD, my God, you are great indeed!
You are clothed with majesty and splendor,
robed in light as with a cloak.

PSALM 104:1–2

Unless we find ourselves in the middle of one of those blinding blizzards rather common here in the Northeast, it is important during our winter days to get outdoors and go for a small walk or hike. Just breathing the fresh winter air reinvigorates our lungs, renews our insides. It is also a healthy change for our eyes, which are so used to perceiving surrounding physical reality through artificial light. I find it soothing to our eyes to contemplate nature with all its bright colors, as it is, without the assistance of artificial lighting. I also find that a brief, brisk walk outdoors often helps me to clear the mind and rejuvenate my inner spirit. This daily walk, a sort of daily contact with nature, allows us to keep a certain balance during our dark winter days. Even a short half-hour walk can do wonders for our well-being, especially during this long winter hibernation. The light we perceive outdoors and the cold, fresh air we breathe, are all such quiet gifts from the Almighty.

ST. BENEDICT' YOUNG DISCIPLES

Three things are most helpful for our spiritual growth: fear of the Lord, prayer, and doing good to our neighbor.

ABBA POEMEN, DESERT FATHER

Our father, St. Benedict, like Christ his Master, was someone of a large and generous heart. He had room for everyone in that wide-open heart of his. He loved all his followers, all those who sought his guidance, both young and old. Among his young disciples were little Placid and young Maur, both entrusted by their parents to the care and guidance of St. Benedict. These two adolescents came from high Roman society, the nobility of the times. Their parents were concerned about the children's education, as many parents are in our own times. They wished a solid upbringing for the children and a wise master and guide who could impart this solid education to them. St. Benedict, because of his holy and impeccable reputation, became their choice.

The two young disciples loved their new master and father, and there was nothing they wouldn't do to please him. Maur assisted St. Benedict in many of the daily monastery tasks. It is not surprising, therefore, that one day, when in a vision St. Benedict saw that poor little Placid was drowning in the nearby lake, he immediately sent Maur to rescue him from the peril. St. Benedict was always a true father to his disciples, and in a special way to the young ones, so totally depending on him for example and guidance.

Today's feast, an intimate one within the confines of the monastic family, warms our hearts, for we also are disciples of our cherished father, St. Benedict. Like Placid and Maur, we are called to open the ears of our hearts and listen to the wise counsels of a master. And our father in monastic life never tires of exhorting us: "Prefer nothing to the love of Christ."

THE NOURISHMENT OF JOURNALING

We are pilgrims who have as the goal of our journey the city of peace.

DOROTHEUS OF GAZA, DISCOURSE 10

One of the winter activities I particularly enjoy is a daily recourse to writing. I have a certain affinity for journaling. There is something holistic about daily writing, a daily putting-down of everyday thoughts and experiences. I think most people should try to keep a personal spiritual journal. Daily journaling allows us to focus on the essentials of the day.

The practice of keeping a daily spiritual journal enables us to nourish the inner self. It fuels us with lots of personal insights and positive thoughts. Daily writing is like daily meditation. It is a powerful tool to expand and nurture the inner journey. Daily writing explores, inspires, and strengthens our resolve to move forward in our spiritual quest. It instigates reflections on our daily practice of *lectio divina.*

"Your word is a lamp for my feet."

PSALM 119:105

THE FATHER OF MONKS

It was said of St. Antony that he was "Spirit bearer," that is, filled with and carried along by the Holy Spirit, but he would never speak of this to people. Such men see what is happening in the world, as well as knowing what is going to happen.

ABBA ANTONY, *APOPHTHEGMATA PATRUM*

During our long winter, our prolonged desert solitude, the feast of St. Antony arrives in mid-January in the West. Somehow this seems appropriate, for Antony, the father of monks, was a lover of the solitary desert life. I am particularly fond of him and feel a close affinity to him since he is my patron saint and model in monastic life.

St. Antony lived in Egypt between 251 and 356. As a young man, at the age of eighteen, he heard the Gospel invitation: "There is still one thing left for you: sell all that you have and distribute it to the poor.... Then come, follow me" (Luke 18:22). Antony, touched by grace, was so moved and changed at that moment that he immediately retired to the wilderness solitude, answering God's invitation without creating any noise or calling attention to himself. From the beginning of his journey into the desert, he understood that all basic Christian life is based on these two principles: the love of God and the love of neighbor. He worked to live daily by these two commandments. He instinctively knew that his intimate relationship with the Lord was tested by how he interacted with others and by the way he loved and treated every human being he encountered. Antony knew what Abba Apollo points out elsewhere: "A person who sees his brother sees his God."

More on Journaling

No foul language should come out of your mouths, but only such as is good for needed edification, that it may impart grace to those who hear.

EPHESIANS 4:29

A useful part of journaling practice is the choice of words we make while writing and relating the day's events. Of themselves, words carry concrete meaning, and thus we are challenged in their proper selection and aim for words that articulate best what lies deep within us—words with sufficient clarity and simplicity.

By spending a few moments each day keeping up with our journals, we are given the unique opportunity to uncover the inner nature of words. For instance, in our daily writing, we sometimes uncover words that convey all that is true, good, and beautiful. Some of these words help us achieve personal and practical insight into the matter at hand. Sometimes, as I do, one must make recourse to an old dictionary in search of the proper word. The dictionary, then, like a map, becomes a treasury for those lost and in search of the right destination. The truth is that the more we write, the more comfortable we become with writing.

DESERT SOLITUDE

A man who remains in his one place throughout life will not undergo tribulations.

ABBA POEMEN, DESERT FATHER

I often find that in the seasons of monastic life, there are degrees of solitude. For instance, in winter, when one sees almost no one except at the weekly liturgy, our solitude seems almost complete. Monastic solitude is not an avoidance of company *per se*, but rather the opening of a wide-open space for God alone. If a monk can find humble contentment in solitude, it is because there he can perceive the face of God. I was deeply moved once when I read what a medieval Carthusian monk wrote of his journey into solitude. As he journeyed deeper into God, the pain of love became more intense, like an unending crescendo, culminating in mystical ecstasy. When the journey ended, he was unable to speak a single word but "Ah."

It is the pure and sole desire for God alone that sustains us in our desert solitude, be it in a humble cell or a rustic remote, hermitage. *O bonitas, Deus soli!*

JANUARY 20 · St. Euthymius the Armenian Hermit

DESERT WISDOM ON PRAYER

Abbot Macarius was asked, "How should one pray?" The old man said, "There is no need to waste time in long discourses; it is sufficient to stretch out one's hands and say, "Lord, do as you will, and since you know me, have mercy." And if the conflict continues to bother one and grows ever fiercer then say, "Lord, help!" God knows very well what we need and he always shows his mercy.

Prayer is so simple, so basic, as basic as the exercise of breathing. Even when one is not in the mood to pray we can simply return to it by repeating slowly the Lord's holy name. Slowly, invariably, it leads us back to our inner center.

JANUARY 21 · St. Agnes, Martyr

A FEAST OF LIGHT AND JOY

Sometimes during our bleak, cold wintry days, I think we tend to see the rest of the world in a negative, gloomy way. The darker days, the soggy snow, the fierce cold all seem to contribute to and encourage a certain pessimism in most people. I think all of us need to fight this attitude and look for positive things to do and read, to find a certain resilience and simple contentment for our hearts.

I find daily inspiration, as I am sure others do, in my daily readings and in the feasts and cycles of the liturgy. Today, for instance, we celebrate a feast full of light and joy, St. Agnes' day. Today we honor a young martyr of Rome, someone who was both an adolescent and a cherished bride of Christ. The office for the feast sings poetically of her soul full of love for the divine Bridegroom awaiting her at the doors of paradise. St. Agnes would have been happy uttering the words of Richard of Chichester: "O most merciful Redeemer, friend and brother, may I know thee more clearly, love thee more dearly, follow thee more nearly, day by day!"

JANUARY 22

Vigilance

We are in need of nothing else but a vigilant spirit.

ABBA POEMEN, DESERT FATHER

Be watchful inwardly, be watchful outwardly.

ABBA POEMEN, DESERT FATHER

A monk's day starts with the Office of Vigils in the early hours. In monastic life, this long tradition of keeping vigils originates in the Gospels, in the Lord's constant counsel for his disciples to remain vigilant at all times. The beautiful parable of the wise and foolish virgins is essentially a teaching on the necessity of vigilance for a true spiritual life. The Lord feels so strongly about vigilance that he rebukes his disciples in the Garden of Gethsemane when he finds them deep in slumber: "So you could not keep watch with me for one hour? Watch and pray that you may not undergo the test" (Matthew 26:40–41).

The Desert Fathers and Mothers, our mentors in the spiritual life, never ceased insisting to their disciples on the true place of vigilance in their quest for God. Daily vigilance allows us to spend our earthly days attentively in the expectation and preparation for the Lord's coming. We pray and keep vigil for, as the Lord tells us, we don't know the hour or day of his coming; all we know is that he may come one day when least expected "as a thief in the night."

ANTHONY BLOOM

During the 1970s, I was privileged to keep correspondence for a while with the well-known orthodox thinker and spiritual writer, Anthony Bloom. He wrote, "We should always approach God knowing that we do not know him. We must approach the unsearchable, mysterious God who reveals himself as he chooses; whenever we come to him, we are before a God we do not yet know."

During the quiet moments of deep prayer, the Lord allows us to taste something of himself, yet deep down we realize we don't really know him. For what may seem a second or an eternity of seconds, the Holy Spirit gives us an inkling, a hint of what is later to come. Truthfully, at the end we realize our hearts cannot contain his omnipotence, and our minds cannot grasp his infinity. "My thoughts are not your thoughts, nor are your ways my ways—oracle of the LORD" (Isaiah 55:8).

A TREAT ALL YEAR

Soup as a main course,
Soup to begin the meal,
And when it is homemade,
It is soup to nourish the soul.

JULIA CHILD

From primitive times, soups have always held a conspicuous place in the daily fare of families and monasteries. This is still true in many parts of the world, and it continues to be so in most of the Mediterranean countries, such as Italy, Spain, France, Greece, and so on. The monasteries located near the Mediterranean today continue this custom, as did their early ancestors. Soup appeal is universal! There is something so fundamental about soups that our basic instincts readily identify and feel drawn naturally to the magic of soups. Once I made a point of writing a cookbook about soups. It took me five years to complete it and then it went on to become a bestseller, selling out inconceivable numbers worldwide. The success had nothing to do with the author, but more with the popularity of soups and the fact that the recipes were easy to follow.

Soups are welcome any time of the year: hot during the cold weather months and cold during the steamy, hot periods. Throughout the years, I have always noticed how comforted guests feel at the monastery when a bowl of homemade soup is offered to them upon their arrival. In many ways, that bowl of soup symbolizes to them the warmth and comfort they expect to find during their stay in the monastery. Something as simple as a bowl of soup sometimes has the power to speak volumes to others!

TRUE CONVERSION: TURNING TO CHRIST

There is a voice that cries out to each person until his last breath: "Be converted today."

ABBA POEMEN, DESERT FATHER

The liturgical calendar reminds us that today we honor the event of St. Paul's conversion, and what an event that is in itself! It shows how dramatically God's grace deals with some of his children. St. Paul's conversion to Christianity, his discovery and acceptance of Christ as his Lord and Savior, was certainly a great event and much more. The history of our personal ongoing conversions (hopefully daily) is rather ordinary and dull in comparison. It is a fact that sometimes there are several stages to our personal conversions, as there are stages in all of our spiritual lives. Each day we begin anew the spiritual journey, and as we proceed in the journey, we are called to consider the dynamics of our personal conversion as a continuum of steps and stages leading us to the final act of conversion that will occur only at the end, as we all face the crucial moment of death. True conversion instigates us to let go of ourselves and turn wholly to Christ, our Lord and Savior. Conversion makes us realize that Christ is the only one worth holding onto at the end. In the view of St. Benedict, the purpose of *conversatio*—that is, true conversion—is the discovery of a new all-transforming life in Christ, a life we inherit when we accept to become his true disciples.

THE CÎTEAUX FOUNDERS

There was in the desert an old monk named Apollo. If someone came to him about doing some work, he would set out joyfully, saying: "I am going to work with Christ today for the salvation of my soul, for that is the reward he offers."

Today the monastic family celebrates the memory of the three great abbots who were at the origins of the Cistercian Reform in the eleventh century. The documents relating the early days of Cistercian history speak warmly of the influence of Abbot Robert, first at his monastery in Molesmes and later at Cîteaux. Abbot Robert seems to have emphasized a return to *The Rule of St. Benedict* (hereafter, *Rule*) that comprised austere discipline, agricultural labor, and strict poverty. During the second period of the reform, Abbot Albéric, to safeguard the purity of the early Cistercian ideals, made further recourse to the authority of St. Benedict, insisting that monasteries must be established far from cities and towns in distant seclusion from the world.

During the third period of the reform, Abbot Stephen of Harding consolidated the work done before by creating a new code of "usages" that affected every aspect of the monastic life at Cîteaux. These "usages" intensified the then well-established principles of the new Cistercian Reform: seclusion, silence, simplicity, poverty, manual labor, and constant prayer. These holy abbots and the early Cistercian Fathers who followed them are to be commended for restoring the sound balance found in St. Benedict's *Rule*: the harmony between prayer and work, silence and community, in the daily life of the monk.

RECOLLECTION

The arrows of the enemy cannot touch someone who loves quiet recollection. But those who wander among crowds will often be wounded by them.

ABBA NILUS

The desert monks and nuns were fiercely attached to, and protective of, the practice of quiet recollection among themselves. They usually and simply referred to it as "quiet." It was that simple and significant for them. The quiet of their cells and surroundings generally disposed their inner beings, especially their hearts, toward that needed attitude for growing ever more deeply into an intimate friendship with God, their only goal at all times. They understood the meaning of Jesus' words: "The kingdom of God is within you." That is, the innermost of our hearts is God's special dwelling place. Hence, these desert monks made every effort to remain and persevere at all times in their innermost, keeping loving company with him who dwelt in their souls.

The more faithfully they observed their own inner quiet, the more steadfast their recollection, the freer and less constrained was their access to the divine presence dwelling within them. This deeply recollected attitude was a free grace in itself, but they also knew they had to constantly make every effort to remain faithful to God's free gift. The deeper they traveled into the landscape of profound recollection, the greater and deeper the divine presence manifested itself in the center of their hearts.

THE WORK OF PRAYER

So far this has been a very snowy winter season. It snows day after day, and it snows ceaselessly. The continuous snow brings in me a certain contemplative feeling, reminding me that the life of the Christian monk is one that aims at continual ceaseless prayer—just as it snows and snows and doesn't stop snowing, so too must we pray and pray and never stop praying. This is the work of prayer, no matter what, and at all times, our hearts and minds must be occupied with the one single occupation of prayer. Jürgen Moltmann, the German Lutheran theologian, once wrote: "Prayer and the hearing of prayer are the marks of man's friendship with God and God's friendship with man."

St. Sulpicius Severus, Monk and Disciple of St. Martin of Tours

MONASTIC HOSPITALITY

Later, seeing his patience, he opened the door and received Abba Macarius with joy, saying to him, "I have wanted to see you for a long time, having heard much about you." He then rendered him all the duties of hospitality and made him rest, for he was very tired.

ABBA ANTONY TO ABBA MACARIUS

Today, in the midst and depths of our winter solitude, when I barely hear from others or see anyone, I am nevertheless caught mentally with reflecting on the theme of monastic hospitality. It is an ancient monastic practice, deeply rooted in the Gospels. The Desert Fathers practiced it assiduously, seriously. And those of us who live under *The Rule of St. Benedict* know the importance he gave to it in the daily life of a monastery.

Basically, hospitality is a blessing, for in welcoming the guest we welcome Christ himself. Hospitality allows monks and nuns to humbly serve others in the selfless giving of themselves. Somehow the giving of ourselves to others is what basic Gospel monastic living encompasses. Jesus gave of himself to the world when he came to save us. This giving of himself was completed ultimately during his sacrifice on the cross. We, too, complete ourselves when we give of ourselves to others, when we welcome and embrace the guest the Lord sends our way and, when we allow him or her to experience life to the fullest under God's roof.

THE GOSPELS

Practice fasting a little later; meditate on the Gospel and the other Scriptures, and if a strange thought rises within you, never look at it but always look upwards, and the Lord will come at once to help you.

ABBA MACARIUS THE GREAT

One of the special joys I experience while attending the weekly liturgy—or "synaxis," as the early monastic fathers called it—takes place during the reading aloud of the Gospel. The joy becomes even greater when the Gospel is sung as in the Byzantine tradition, not just read. I am totally consumed by listening to the reading and transported to another realm, especially if the reading is done slowly, meaningfully, thoughtfully, reverently. To me it is like the Gospel event is happening right there and then, all over again, and I am present to it. Every word uttered means something, and I somehow feel a concrete spiritual taste for it. My great disappointment comes after the Gospel reading, during the sermon. It is usually a letdown, not because the preacher might not be good, but simply because he cannot replace or surpass on what was just read. The holy Gospels are simple, straightforward, and to the point. Not a single word is wasted. I often yearn for a long, silent pause after the reading to properly absorb it. Only silence can help us distill the mysterious wisdom we just heard.

JANUARY 31

TIME'S MYSTERY

Dost thou love life? Then do not squander time,
for that's the stuff life is made of.

BENJAMIN FRANKLIN, *POOR RICHARD'S ALMANACK*

A new year has barely started, and we are already at the conclusion of its first month. *Where did January go?* I asked myself this morning, while walking the snow-covered path to the barn. As the years and seasons, months, weeks, and days succeed each other, I become perplexed by the mystery of time. I know time places a limitation on life's trajectory, yet time itself is not limited. It goes on and on, long beyond our experience or awareness of it. St. Augustine, with that technical, precise mind of his, describes its mystery aptly: "Time is a threefold present: the present as we experience it, the past as a present memory, and the future as a present expectation."

Whatever definition or description of time one accepts, we can all agree that time is a precious gift from God, a special grace not to be wasted. The mystery of time contains in itself a seed: the beginning of eternity.

FEBRUARY

FEBRUARY 1

A MONTH OF UNCERTAINTIES

...Yet February suns' uncertain shine,
For rain and frost alternately combine
To stop the plow, with sudden wintry storms
And often fearful violence the month deforms.
EDMUND SPENSER

The month of February has an interesting history. Its origins in antiquity are fascinating. For the ancient Romans it was the month of purification: the time of the year when the people repented for their past misdeeds and offered expiation to their gods. It is not surprising to see the resemblance between this ritual period and our present observance of Lent. In fact, when the Roman Empire became Christian, Lent was probably placed around the same time as a substitute for the old pagan custom of purification.

Here in the Northeast, February is always considered a month of uncertain weather and temperatures. Some of the most severe winter storms seem to occur in February. Leigh Hunt describes some of the peculiar month's features: "If February were not the precursor of spring, it would be the least pleasant season of the year, November not excepted. The thaws now take place, and a clammy mixture of moisture and cold succeeds, which is the most disagreeable of wintry sensations."

Like other months, February has its special days and celebrations. Tomorrow we complete the forty days of the Christmas cycle and celebrate the lovely feast of the Presentation of the Lord in the Temple, previously called the Purification of Our Lady. Tomorrow is truly a family feast. With our Lady and St. Joseph we shall take the Child Jesus into the Temple, and there with the blessed Elder Simeon and the Prophetess Anna, we shall all receive a blessing from the Lord.

THE PRESENTATION OF THE LORD

The Elder Simeon bent down and reverently touched the footprints of the Mother of God who knew no wedlock, and he said: "O most pure Lady, thou dost carry Fire. I am afraid to take God as a babe in my arms, he is the Lord of the light that knows no shadows, the King of peace."

BYZANTINE MATINS OF THE FEAST

Today is the feast of the *Hypapante*, as it is called in Greek, and Candlemas in the West, the feast of the meeting or encounter of the Lord with his servants Simeon and Anna in Jerusalem, in the Temple of the Lord. It is one of the most tender, lovely feasts of the calendar year. Let us meditate on some of the beautiful texts of the Byzantine office. The Ikos text at Matins expresses beautifully the exquisite charm of the feast:

> Let us run to the *Theotokos* who wishes to see her Son brought to Simeon. The angelic powers, looking at him from above, were filled with amazement saying: "Now we behold wondrous and marvelous things beyond understanding and past telling."
> He who created Adam is carried as a babe.
> He who cannot be encompassed is contained in the arms of the Elder.
> He who rests uncircumcised in the bosom of the Father voluntarily accepts circumcision in the flesh but not in his divinity.
> He who alone loves mankind.

Simeon, beholding the little child, calls him "a light for revelation to the [nations]" (Luke 2:32). The theme of light permeates the liturgical feast and our entire monastic day. Jesus is the true Light of the World. By receiving the blessed candles before the eucharistic celebration and then forming a procession with lighted candles into the church, we are reminded that we symbolically receive Christ and carry him into the temple of our hearts, as once did Simeon and Anna.

SPIRITUAL DIRECTION

A monk came to see Abba Poemen during the second week of Lent and told him about his thoughts: he obtained peace, and said to him, "I nearly did not come here today." The old man asked him why. The monk responded: "I said to myself, 'Perhaps he will not let me in because it is Lent.'" Abba Poemen said to him, "We have not been taught to close the wooden door but the door of our tongues."

THE DESERT FATHERS, ABBA POEMEN THE SHEPHERD

Occasionally someone who frequents the monastery asks if someone here would be willing to provide spiritual direction. Almost always my response is no. I tell the person that it is one vocation I don't particularly feel called to. Furthermore, although I have good training as a psychologist from Columbia University's graduate school, I don't see myself as called to undertake such a form of service. It is a huge responsibility. However, I tell people who ask, as a Christian I am open to listen to them and their concerns, and if an insight pops up here and there, I wouldn't mind sharing it with them.

Listening itself seems an almost disappearing art. I am mindful that a good spiritual direction, such as the ones practiced by the Desert Fathers, cultivates a deeper awareness of God's action in our lives. The Desert Fathers' practice of discernment was directed to help focus the disciples to recognize the action of the Holy Spirit in the depths of their souls. Whatever the problems, conflicts, or symptoms were, the Desert Fathers would listen quietly to the person and then perhaps utter a word, leading the disciple to discern a divine intervention in that particular experience. Learning to listen to others with great peace, quiet, and reverence—and always without passing judgment—is part of the compassion and charity others expect from us.

A SCHOOL IN THE LORD'S SERVICE

The paths leading to the monastery are diverse. But one day they will converge and form a single way, meeting in him who said, "I am the Way." And "No one can come to the Father except through me." The Christian who becomes a monk is seeking no other way than this.

DOM ANDRE LOUF, *THE CISTERCIAN WAY*

St. Benedict, in his *Rule*, gives a particular purpose to a monastery: to be "a school in the Lord's service." He conceives the monastery as a school of life, where the monk or nun is taught to live "guided by the Gospel" and through that special training undertake the narrow path to salvation.

In the monastic tradition, the monastery is also a "school of love": a school where daily the monk learns to die himself, where he surrenders his entire life to the heavenly Father for the sake and love of Christ. In chapter four of the *Rule*, among the instruments of good works, St. Benedict emphasizes two in particular: "to deny oneself in order to follow Christ" and "to love Christ above all else."

For the sake of Christ, the "Bridegroom," the monk accepts to die to one's false self and surrender his life, his will, his own ego, and all his mental and material possessions. He is reminded by the Apostle John that "no one has greater love than this, to lay down one's life for one's friends" (John 15:13). And if the monastic works daily at this laying down of his or her own life, it is in order to follow Christ more closely. Nothing is more precious to the monastic heart than to be totally possessed, absorbed, by the love of Christ.

HESYCHIA

My eyes greet the night watches
as I meditate on your promise.
Hear my voice in your mercy, O Lord.
PSALM 119:148–149

Daily monastic life, like all human life, has its ups and downs. We try to live in the present moment, doing the task at hand, be it prayer, work, reading, or any other activity dictated by a particular need. And while being engaged in a specific action, we try to keep the *memoria Dei*, that is, to remain conscious of God's presence in that particular moment. But the monk, like everyone else, must battle with the forces of distraction, excessive busyness, a vivid imagination, and sometimes even the disdain for spiritual matters. Humans that we are, this is a daily struggle, a constant and ever-demanding battle. Sometimes one is tempted by the thought, *Is this undertaking really worth it?* It is then the time to remain humble, persevere in the task filled with utter confidence, and trust in a God who loves us deeply. Eventually we shall be consoled by a presence in our innermost that dispels all our darkness. Ever so slowly, the tyranny of our own minds and its earthly concerns somehow recede and we come to rest in God alone. The mind and the heart then remain occupied with only one thing: the constant remembrance of God. We let go of our trivial concerns and daily vicissitudes to enter into a quiet inner state, the state of constant prayer, where our undivided attention is given solidly to him who inhabits our souls.

FEBRUARY 6

Sts. Barsanuphius, John, Dorothée, and Dosithée, Palestinian Monks

THE SOUND FROM THE SNOW

I remember the days of old,
I ponder all your deeds;
works of your hands I recall.
PSALM 143:5

It has snowed throughout the night. I awakened in the dark to feed the wood stoves and thus keep the heat in the kitchen. Our four cats— Walter, Margot, Nicole, and Pompon—love to sleep near the stove, basking it its warmth. Later on when I returned to the comfort of a simple bed, I laid there, in the night stillness, listening to the quiet, gentle sound of the snow coming down. There is something unique to that steady, natural rhythm. I was happy listening to it. It was as if Mother Nature had drawn a long sigh and had begun to weep steadily, copiously. As the snow continued, accompanied by the wind, I heard it tapping on the roof ever so gently. One doesn't usually notice or hear the sound from the snow, but I did hear it last night. It came straight down over the monastery roof and the entire property, filling the night with an ambience of complete solitude. As the old Carthusian monks loved to say, "O blessed solitude, O only blessedness."

THE "TEN COMMANDMENTS" OF HEALTH

Our dark winter days, with their long, prolonged nights, sometimes affect many people's health deeply. Often they instill depression or the "winter blues" in some, as an article in the local newspaper pointed out. It is vital to remember, then, that all of us can do something about fostering a healthy attitude in our daily lives. God our Father is the healer of our infirmities, but he also wishes us to take care of ourselves and learn to live in harmony with the laws of nature, which he created. There are some healthful practices that do not cost a cent and yet they can do wonders for our individual health if observed daily. Recently a friend provided me a basic list of them. He calls them the "Ten Commandments of Health":

> *"You shall love the Lord your God with all your heart, with all your soul, with all your mind, and with all your strength"* (Mark 12:30).

Thou shalt not defile—with any manner of impure thought or act—thy body, which is the Temple of the Holy Spirit.
Thou shalt drink pure water.
Thou shalt breathe pure air.
Thou shalt eat God's ideal foods.
Thou shalt secure adequate rest, relaxation, and sleep.
Thou shalt practice cleanliness.
Thou shalt partake of natural sunlight.
Thou shalt exercise and keep fit.
Thou shalt continually strive to keep these commandments as thou becomest a faithful steward of the earth and God's abundances.

FEBRUARY'S SOLITUDE

Yet February suns uncertain shine,
For rain and frost alternately combine.

EDMUND SPENSER

On days like today, there is no doubt in the mind of local folks that we are having an authentic northeastern winter. January is now behind us, but let's face it, in this part of the country there is not much difference in the weather between January and February. Often the nighttime temperatures fall below zero. During the day the temperature registers between twelve and twenty degrees. The sky is clear, even sunny, and the air is pure, sharp, invigorating. The snow is deep enough to create some hardships while I do my farm chores outdoors.

Somehow, these cold winter days suit me perfectly. I enjoy our beloved monastic solitude, its majestic, profound, long silences. They seem deeper now than during other cycles of the year. Besides, I take advantage of these secluded and solitary winter days to promote some writing, some quiet reading by the fireplace, and to listen to some serene music such as Bach cello suites during our long, still evenings. Deep within I say a short *Deo gratias* for the gift of being here, alone, isolated, in this quiet corner of the earth. I am here alone with him who dwells in the perfect and inaccessible solitude of his divinity.

MORE ON MONASTIC SOLITUDE

When we were in deep solitude and no one else besides, it was God who was our helper. Now that we are in the world, it is man.

ABBA APPHY

People who visit here from time to time during days of decent weather sometimes ask me, "How do you endure your solitude? Aren't you bored? Don't you feel lonely?" and other similar questions. By now I am quite used to these types of questions. Sometimes I try to answer them, and sometimes I just let them stand. Once I replied to a young man that the word monk, *monachos* in Greek, means essentially "he who is alone." I do think—actually, I am convinced—that when the Lord calls someone to a life of solitude and silence, he provides the desire and special grace to undertake such a life.

Through the years, I have learned to love and become increasingly more comfortable in such a solitude. At the beginning, about forty years ago, I did find solitude puzzling, almost scary. I needed lots of help from above, tons of grace to sustain me in what seemed the Lord's chosen path for me. Since then, I feel more at home and comfortable with solitude, and through the years I have learned to appreciate its surpassing loveliness. The Lord, who is ever faithful, never abandons us but always consoles us with his loving presence. Now I know what a gift this monastic solitude is: It is a necessary emptiness always filled with a presence.

THE MOTHER OF NUNS

I pleaded with you, brother, and you did not hear me.
I prayed to my Lord, and he listened to me.

DIALOGUE BETWEEN ST. SCHOLASTICA AND ST. BENEDICT

The monastic family honors today one of its most quiet saints, St. Scholastica, the twin sister of our father, St. Benedict. She was deliberately quiet, for she embodied the monastic charisma portrayed in the *Rule* by her holy brother. St. Benedict expects his monks to be quiet people, lovers of silence, attentive at all times with the "only one thing necessary." St. Scholastica lived her monastic life quietly, without making much fuss or noise around her. The daily work of prayer and the work of love were her daily occupation. They consumed her totally. St. Gregory the Great, who wrote the little we know about her, mentions, "Greater was her power before the Lord, because greater was her love."

St. Scholastica, the beloved mother of nuns, has much to show us in the ways of the spiritual life, not only to those who embrace monastic life, but to all who are open to follow her example. To everyone, she upholds the exemplary life marked by the virtue of a quiet, ordinary life, one that is not centered on oneself, but instead expands our inner thoughts while occupying ourselves wholly doing the work of love.

LOURDES: A VISITATION

Today, right in the middle of our winter journey, we remember the Mother of God under her title Our Lady of Lourdes. To me it brings so many personal memories: memories of past visits to Lourdes, memories of my family rooted in that region of France and, in particular, the remembrance of our Lady's visitation to little Bernadette Soubirous. What a wonderful moment it was when the Mother of God showed herself to Bernadette in the rock of the grotto. On one of those typical cold, gray, winter Pyrenees days, our Lady brought warmth, light, and beauty into the life of a simple shepherdess. In the midst of a somber, dark winter and almost cruel family poverty, our Lady's visitation nurtured true hope in Bernadette. She also provided her guidance on how to go about pleasing and serving her divine Son. Today is as good a day as any for us to do so as well. We should really do it daily, beg the Mother of God for her maternal guidance in our everyday lives. From the example of her own earthly life she can teach us to follow her Son by showing us how to live our lives in the spirit and attitude of the Beatitudes. Nothing would please the Lord more, or our Lady, for it would show them our true determination to follow the ways of God.

MONASTIC SPIRITUALITY

He is rich enough who is poor with Christ.

ST. JEROME

Monastic spirituality is all about a presence, the presence of the Holy Spirit in us, instigating our inner growth into the full measure of Christ. When a future monk knocks at the door of a monastery or hermitage, he comes as he is, poor and dispossessed, eager to realize his potential for full union with God. Spiritual growth is not always visible or easy to detect, for indeed the monastic adventure is a lifelong process, often hidden to human eyes. Nurtured by faith and daily observances of the monastic life, the monastic walks in humility the Gospel path that leads to spiritual maturity. The daily monastic routine, the *Rule*, the communal Hours of the Office, the silence and solitude, the manual work, the fraternal life, the daily *lectio,* and constant prayer are the ordinary means at his disposal for growth into spiritual maturity. Ultimately, the goal of our spiritual journey is to reach that point where we get to taste something of what the Lord promised to his followers. That is, life in abundance. This inner abundant life is possible because the God who called us to undertake the journey is also the God who loved us first and loved us abundantly to the end.

ON NOISE AND SILENCE

For many, the humble silence of a monastery is the ultimate relief from the noise and bustle of a busy, agitated world. Thomas Merton aptly observes, "There is a note of supreme injustice in noisemaking; the noise made by one person can compel another person to listen."

The many young people (and those not so young) who frequent our small monastery from time to time treasure the humble quality of silence they find here. One of them remarked to me recently, "The monastic silence I find here is of immense value to me, not only spiritually, but also when I return back to school and have to face the ever-increasing pressures of classes and studies."

THE BEATITUDES

Blessed are the poor in spirit, for theirs is the kingdom of heaven.
Blessed are they who mourn, for they will be comforted.
Blessed are the meek, for they will inherit the land.
Blessed are they who hunger and thirst for righteousness,
for they will be satisfied.
Blessed are the merciful, for they shall be shown mercy.
Blessed are the clean of heart, for they will see God.
Blessed are the peacemakers,
for they will be called children of God.
Blessed are they who are persecuted for the sake of righteousness,
for theirs is the kingdom of heaven.

MATTHEW 5:3–10

Today we celebrate the memory of two great fathers of the East and West, two brothers in the flesh, Cyril and Methodius, who perhaps more than anyone have done so much to preserve the unity of the Church founded by Christ. They struggled in this pursuit, and their way to win everyone to Christ was to follow the way of the Beatitudes, the straight and narrow road traced by the Lord himself. Again and again, the Beatitudes have been preached to us, with particular colors and nuances, practical implications for our times, right in the here and now. The Desert Fathers were serious about abiding in the true spirit of the Beatitudes daily. They found freshness and freedom in their utterance, such depth, such a true and authentic Gospel simplicity in the structure of each sentence that to them it almost seemed as if they were hearing them pronounced by the Lord himself at that moment!

I always rejoice when I hear the Beatitudes sung in the Eastern Divine Liturgy or when they are sung before a meal blessing as they do in some monasteries in France and Belgium, or when this particular Gospel is proclaimed on the feast of All Saints on November 1. The Gospel way of the Beatitudes tells us that God abides in a permanent state of blessedness, and it is to that eternal blessedness that we are all invited to share the mysterious life of God, with the Father and the Son, in the Holy Spirit.

FEBRUARY 15

MONASTIC INDUSTRIES

The more we count the blessings we have,
the less we crave the luxuries we haven't.
WILLIAM A. WARD

During the cold months we try to use our time adequately, occupying ourselves with diverse indoor activities. One somehow feels freed by the winter weather of certain tasks and responsibilities, such as the care and cultivation of our various gardens. I take advantage of the season and put my time to good use by getting involved daily in the making and preparation of our various vinegars. Our artisanal vinegars demand several months to a year of fermentation. Our annual Monastery Vinegar Festival takes place each year in July on the weekend following the feast of St. Benedict, and we must have sufficient vinegar available. It may still seem a bit distant—after all, it is hard to imagine July's sunny days when we are surrounded by snow. But as I mentioned before, the fermentation period is usually one of several months, and the vinegar prepared now will barely be ready come July. Our artisanal monastic vinegars are known locally for a certain quality, the sort of quality one does not find in the industrially produced types. We continue to labor intensely to keep up the quality and reputation of our products. We don't do this for pride or financial gain but for one reason only: "That God may be glorified in all things," as St. Benedict compels us in the *Rule.*

ICE AND SNOW BLESS THE LORD

My days are like a lengthening shadow, [...] but you, O Lord, are enthroned forever: your renown is for all generations.

PSALM 102:12–13

I woke up this morning, early as usual, and looked outside through the kitchen windows. It had snowed all night, and the whole countryside looked like a wonderland. I opened the outside door for a second and breathed in deeply the fresh, cold air. Gazing into the quiet, magical beauty before my eyes, I could only murmur, "Heaven and earth are full of your glory!" The snowfall has been forecast in the news here in the Northeast and more concretely in the Hudson Valley. The winter forecast is the daily bread of the region. Being barely awake, my head not yet completely clear, I began paraphrasing Psalm 103, sung every evening in the Byzantine Vespers and here on the eve of solemnities:

> Bless the Lord, my soul!
> Lord God, indeed, how great You are,
> You are clothed in majesty and glory…
> wrapped in light as in a mantle!…
> You structured the earth at its base,
> to stand firm throughout the ages.
> You wrapped it with snow (ocean) like a cloak
> the waters stood higher than the mountains.

For a monk, the psalms provide natural responses to any situation. They are as much a part of us as the air we breathe.

ASH WEDNESDAY: THE ACCEPTABLE TIME

Let us persevere in our longing for God so as to be worthy upon the completion of the forty days to behold the most solemn passion of Christ and to feast with spiritual joy in the most holy Passover of the Lord.

BYZANTINE LENTEN OFFICE

Throughout the many years of monastic life, during which the liturgy has always played a prominent role, it has never ceased to amaze me the skillful mingling of the seasons of nature and those of the liturgy. There is an inspiring convergence there, at least for those of us who inhabit the Northern Hemisphere. For could we imagine Lent without winter? Easter without spring? God, who created time, the seasons, and made all things must have had in mind when the time of the passion and resurrection of his Son would occur. After all, St. Paul tells us that "in the fullness of time," God had sent his Son into the world for our redemption. Our Lenten pilgrimage, which starts today, is all about the mystery of time, about using it properly, measuredly. It is the acceptable time to take account of our spiritual lives and the appropriate time to renew our relationship with God. Lent is a time of grace, given to us by God so that the light of repentance may shine deeply within our wearied souls.

A HUMBLE SHEPHERDESS

O my Mother, it is deep inside your heart that I leave my anguishes, my pains, and find the strength and courage I need.

ST. BERNADETTE SOUBIROUS

In our chapel there is an icon that distills a special joy and devotion in my heart. It is the icon of St. Bernadette, written (painted) by our close neighbor and friend, Olga Poloukhine. Olga depicts Bernadette as the simple Pyrenees peasant she was. Before the saint's famous apparition, she was a humble mountain shepherdess. She was deeply attached to her sheep and their little lambs, to which she tended lovingly. She worked daily at the farm tending her flock and spending quiet hours in prayer. In her deep humility, she remained totally open to God's special designs for her. In February 1858, an extraordinary event occurred that changed Bernadette's life. A beautiful young lady, the Holy Mother of God, appeared to her in the Grotto of Massabielle. The apparitions went on for several months, with our Lady making intimate confidences to the little shepherdess. Bernadette submitted herself completely to God's plans for her, and by this submission she opened her heart to receive the extraordinary graces the Lord had in store for her. St. Bernadette, humble shepherdess, pray for us.

LENTEN PREPARATION

The Lenten spring has arrived.
The light of repentance is being offered to us.
Let us enter the holy season with joy.

BYZANTINE LENTEN OFFICE

According to the centuries-old monastic tradition, monks prepare themselves spiritually to undergo the discipline of the Lenten season by reminding themselves of the essence of true monastic life, which St. Benedict teaches must always have a Lenten character. Ancient monastic writer Thomas à Kempis, in his book *The Imitation of Christ,* describes it as such:

> If you wish peace and harmony with others, you must learn to break your own will in many things. To live in a monastery or hermitage, and to persevere faithfully there until death is not a small matter. Happy indeed is he who remains there and ends his days in peace. If you wish to persevere in seeking perfection, you must consider yourself a humble pilgrim, a poor exile on this earth. If you really wish to become a true monk, you must be content to seem a fool for the sake of Christ. The habit and the monastic tonsure does little to change a man. It is the change of life, the complete mortification of passions that fashions a true monk. He who seeks anything else besides God alone and the salvation of his soul will only find trouble and grief. He who does not try to become the least and the servant of all, will not achieve peace. In the monastery, men are tried as gold in a furnace. No man remains there unless he desires with all his heart to humble himself before God and seeks to please him alone.

SOBRIETY

Be sober, and vigilant. Your opponent the devil is prowling around like a roaring lion looking for [someone] to devour. Resist him, steadfast in faith.

1 PETER 5:8–9

In chapter 49 of the *Rule*, St. Benedict states in a clear manner that "the life of a monk ought to have at all times the character of a Lenten observance," thus conveying to the monk that Lent is not just a mere liturgical season among others but one that portrays vividly what the monastic life should be all about at all times. St. Benedict, with that usual tactical wisdom of his, took the Lenten observance to heart, so much so that he invites his monks to see it as a program and model for the whole of their monastic life.

One particular monastic practice, cherished by St. Benedict and apt at all times—especially during Lent—is the virtue of sobriety. The concept of sobriety is closely allied with that of moderation. In fact, the two often intermingle and are exchanged one for the other. The concept of sobriety—being sober, moderate, even frugal—comes directly from the teachings of the Gospel and the example of Christ's own life. When St. Benedict counsels monks to strive for moderation in all things, he is telling them to live with sobriety, to reject consumerism, to accept to live with less, and thus renounce the slavery of materialism and overconsumption.

QUARTETS

All people that on earth do dwell,
Sing to the L*ORD with cheerful voice;*
Serve him with fear, his praise forth tell;
Come ye before him, and rejoice.

OLD PSALM 100

It is an unusual treat during these rough winter days when one has the occasion to attend a gem of a concert such as the one I attended last night at Vassar's music hall. It was all about the sort of music in which I delight the most: quartets. The musical program included Mozart's String Quartet No. 22 in B-flat Major and Beethoven's String Quartet No. 14 in C-sharp Minor.

As always, Mozart reveals his extraordinary genius in his quartets. Those wonderful canon renditions are full of tender feelings, gracious, peaceful, oscillating here and there. Among all the instruments in the quartet, I tend to have a great deal of identification with the cello, so it was with profound attention that I followed the inner voices expressed by the cellist. Only silence could parallel that sublime beauty.

The Beethoven quartet, as expected, has a more dramatic quality than does the Mozart. It contains seven movements, more than the usual three or four. There is a strong line that pervades as a motif throughout the piece and provides unity. Suddenly, it comes to a head in the last movement, where Beethoven masterfully resolves and transforms all the previous motifs. Each theme plays its role in the quartet, and at the end all tell a story.

FEBRUARY 22

THE CHAIR OF ST. PETER

No disciple is above his teacher, no slave above his master. It is enough for the disciple that he become like his teacher, for the slave that he become like his master.

MATTHEW 10:24–25

I have always deeply admired and loved the Apostle Peter. Through the icon that represents him, he is very present in our small chapel. He is also found in the transfiguration icon on our wall, ecstatic, an inexorable witness to the divine event before his eyes. Dear St. Peter, how much the Lord loved him and put up with some of his nonsensical remarks. The St. Peter I love, however, is the straightforward, somehow rough, real person we find in the Gospels, not the figure fabricated later on by some throughout the centuries. For instance, one often hears St. Peter being referred as the "Prince of the Apostles." I abhor that expression and all its implications, for there is nowhere to be found in the Gospels any basis for it. Can anyone imagine the Lord calling Peter by that designation or something similar? It was not proper to think of him as such then, and neither is it right to do it now. The Lord never intended to institute a dynasty, an aristocracy, or form of monarchy among his disciples and followers, and he went as far as to refuse to be called king himself.

Today, as we honor St. Peter's memory, let us think of him as he was and still is: a humble disciple who recognized his own sinfulness, an apostle with rough edges in his personality, a servant chosen by the Lord because of his own unworthiness. These days I am reading a fascinating book by three reputable Orthodox theologians, two of whom I knew personally: *The Primacy of Peter.* The book consists of a series of essays on the role St. Peter played in the early days of the Church. This is much in contrast with certain views developed much later in the West to serve a particular purpose. May St. Peter, whom we honor today and every day in our prayers, continue to guide Christ's flock on earth by his example, and may he also protect all those who humbly follow in the steps of the Master he so loved.

An Apostolic Father

O fairest ear of wheat
Which grew among hateful fares
And gave the Bread of Life
Without labor to the hungry,
And makes the curse pass from him.

ST. EPHREM THE SYRIAN

Today we keep the yearly memorial of St. Polycarp, one of the remarkable fathers of the early apostolic Church. His feast is a source of intimate joy for those of us anchored as we are in the teachings and witness of our early fathers in the faith. What would our faith be today if it wasn't for them who paid with their own blood to safeguard intact the integrity of the faith? These early Apostolic Fathers were the immediate followers to the apostles, and they assured the continuity of the Gospel/apostolic tradition in their local churches, the Church of God, so that the true faith could be handed down blameless, intact, for future Christian generations. All of us owe so much to these intrepid early fathers!

The Christian vocation, according to St. Polycarp and the other Apostolic Fathers, consists in participating in the mystery of Jesus Christ. This is the true faith adventure, one that begins at baptism when we are incorporated and sealed into the death and resurrection of Jesus, and are later nourished by the Lord's Body and Blood in the sacrament of the Eucharist which is celebrated weekly by every Christian community. For St. Polycarp, St. Ignatius of Antioch, as well as for those early Apostolic Fathers, each eucharistic celebration was both the symbol and sign of unity of each local church. For them then, as also for us now, it is the Eucharist, the Body and Blood of Christ, that builds and holds together each local eucharistic assembly or community, which in turn becomes fully the Church, ecclesia—that is, the true body of Christ. The Holy Spirit is totally present in each local church, and it is his role to see that each eucharistic congregation, even the tiniest one, becomes the full body of Christ. This is part of God's plan which St. Paul explained so well when he wrote to the Ephesians (1:8–10):

> In all wisdom and insight he has made known to us the mystery
> of his will in accord with his favor that he set forth in Christ.
> As a plan for the fullness of times,
> to sum up all things in Christ, in heaven and on earth.

FEBRUARY'S WEATHER: THE SNOW

Now shifting gales and milder influence blow,
Cloud over skies, and melt the falling snow;
The softened earth with fertile moisture teems
And, freed from my bonds, down rush the swelling streams.

ANONYMOUS

It has snowed all week again. Looking back to the beginning of the month, which started with lots of snow on the ground, this particular February seems one of the more snowy ones I remember. There is well over thirty inches of it on the property. Even the local weathercaster mentions this winter as one of the most ferocious, snow-wise, since 1888. The drifting snow has more or less paralyzed Dutchess County, since many of our neighbors are without electric power. The numbers vary from day to day: 100,000 homes, 150,000, even 180,000, and on both sides of the Hudson. It will take a while before all gets repaired.

The snow does not keep me from trips outdoors, to the barn to feed the animals or to the shed to get wood for the stoves. It is a bit more difficult to make a path to the barn, but the animals themselves help in the task by coming to greet me, thus creating a path. Since it is Lent, I don't let the weather inconvenience my quiet spirit—I admire the breathtaking, savage beauty of the countryside in silence. One never regrets the virtue and power of silence.

LENTEN JOY

Some are deceived by too much abstinence from meat and drink and sleep. That is a temptation of the devil, to make them fall down in the middle of their work so that they do not bring it to an end as they would have done if they had known reason and maintained discretion.

RICHARD ROLLE (1290–1349)

In chapter 49 of the *Rule*, St. Benedict ascertains the monk's life must always be like a Lenten observance, and thus monks must make a point of conducting their lives with the greatest possible purity. Furthermore, he recommends the monks devote themselves to tearful prayer, sacred reading, repentance, and abstinence. All of this would seem to strangers a rather gloomy approach to Lent. One forgets sometimes that St. Benedict, in his usual wisdom, tempers this observance with his typical moderation. While he recommends certain ascetical practices for self-denial, he mentions that these must be done with the abbot's permission and in the joy of the Holy Spirit. St. Benedict, therefore, expects the monk's Lenten journey to be tempered by the experience of spiritual joy. There is no room for gloom in the thought of St. Benedict; on the contrary, he reminds the monk to look forward to Easter with the joy of spiritual desire.

THE SNOWING CONTINUES

Foul weather is no news; hail, rain, and snow are now expected, and esteemed no woe.

THE COUNTRY ALMANAC

The snowflakes continue descending almost at a faster pace. Seemingly, according to the weathercaster, this would go on for a few days. February, from ancient times, has always been considered a month of unpredictable weather and temperature. Who could have really predicted how the month would end?

This last snowstorm is of some real consequences locally: Thousands of homes in the Northeast (and on both sides of the Hudson) are deprived of electric power, and thus of heat and water. The local newspaper relates that people who had to leave their homes for the lack of power have taken every hotel and motel room in the area. Weather like this is what makes northeasterners (New Yorkers, New Englanders) hard, sturdy people. The weather may be harsh, irritatingly cold, and uncomfortable at times, but it is all taken in stride quietly in this part of the country. When one sees people on the road, they may complain about the inconvenience brought by the weather, but they smile and are encouraged by the welfare of neighbors. The piles of snow all around us give rise to feelings of sympathy and concern for others.

OUR SILENT, WINTRY WOODS

The trees of the LORD drink their fill, the cedars of Lebanon which you planted. There the birds build their nests: the stork in the junipers, its home.

PSALM 104:16–17

It is quite a sight to behold the trees in the monastic enclave. Here on the top of the hill, our wintry woods—in a state of passivity and utter silence—are totally dressed in snow. Early in the morning, through the kitchen windows, I glance at them. The first rays from the sun seem to filter through them, creating an almost magic scene. Our trees are totally silent, but they do speak quietly to me with a language all their own, with their arm branches lifted up in constant prayer.

Later in the evening, when I glance at them from another window looking west, I shall witness that almost daily sight: a pink, deep-orange sky with the sun's last rays filtering through the tree branches. These last rays from the sun seem to insinuate something about their bonding and friendship with the trees. It is as if with their last touch of the day, a soft kiss is placed on each of the trees, wishing them well for the night until the light reappears the following day.

A SNOWSTORM IN HIGH LOCATIONS

How varied are your works, Lord! In wisdom you have made them all.

PSALM 104:24

Our small monastery is situated on a rather high hill. This is not altogether a case of chance, since we know St. Benedict built both the Subiaco and the Monte Cassino monasteries in high places. St. Benedict had a definite preference for mountains and hills. It is wonderful for us here to follow this small detail of the monastic tradition, but I must confess that keeping this centuries-old custom also brings about a series of physical inconveniences, especially during our long northeastern winters.

During this past week's lengthy snowstorm it was vividly demonstrated what a difference the elevation of a particular place makes. Places just a few hundred feet above sea level became almost paralyzed. It is true this particular storm was one of the most extreme in the memory of local folks and meteorologists. Many of the local inhabitants lost power for almost a week, and it was reported in the news that homes and buildings at 1,000 feet or more above sea level suffered the most. To those who consider altitude a relatively irrelevant factor, our quirky week proved the contrary. High elevations have advantages, especially during the summer, where they provide a certain relief from heat and humidity. But during the winter, it is altogether a different story. While people in the valley are treated to a foot or two of fresh snow, people in high elevations can get from five to six feet of snow during the same storm. The snow accumulation here on our property was between five and six feet. And since it is cold enough, it melts slowly. In the view of many locals, we shall have snow for a while longer.

MARCH

MARCH 1

THE LAMB

Tossing his mane of snows in wildest eddies and tangles...
Lionlike March cometh in, hoarse.

WILLIAM DEAN HOWELLS, "IN EARLIEST SPRING"

March, the third month of the year, has always been noted for its varied temperatures and weather. There is still snow on the ground from our last storms, so something of our frigid winter remains. At evening time I still light the wood-burning stove and keep the heat going throughout the night. In spite of the cold, the blustery winds, and the daily changes in the weather, I am also confident of the approaching spring. The signs are all there.

One of the most visible signs of spring in the small monastery is the arrival of the first lamb into our midst. Early this morning I peeked into the barn and suddenly heard a distinct crying, a repeated "blah" from a young lamb. The new lamb, a male named Albino, was probably born in the middle of the night; and in spite of the bitter cold, he was healthy and in good shape. The ewe mother, proud of her firstborn, was gently allowing him to nurse, drinking her rich milk.

Today it may officially still be winter and it certainly feels like it, but the first signs of spring are being felt, seen, and heard in the humble monastic barn. There is a new lamb in the old barn; our lambing season has started steadily. All creatures of the Lord, bless the Lord.

MARCH 2

MARCH'S PERSONALITY

We are hemmed round with mystery, and the greatest mysteries are contained in what we see and do every day.

HENRI-FRÉDÉRIC AMIEL

Deeply rooted in the monastic experience is the daily living out of what I call an intertwining of the rhythm of the seasons and that of the liturgical calendar. The cycles of nature and cycles of the liturgy often coincide and converge, at least here in our Northern Hemisphere, as I point out somewhere else in this journal. As we begin the month of March, we find ourselves plunged seriously, I hope, into the ins and outs of our personal Lenten journey. Each journey toward Easter is personal, for conversion itself is personal, something intimate between God and each of us.

While I ponder quietly the reality of Lent and its timely intertwining with the month of March, I discover that as Lent has its own character, its own personality, its own features, so does March possess its own personality, its specific, peculiar feelings.

On certain March days, we feel a bit confused by the weather. On a given day, after the long winter thaw, one may feel tempted to spend several hours outdoors soaking up a warm sun in a blue sky, only to reverse its course the following day, presenting us with a rough, raw wind and with more wet snow on the way. Someone once referred to March as a fickle, almost deceitful month. Sometimes during our Lenten journey we too experience certain fickle, almost deceitful moments, such as the one the Lord experienced in the desert. It is the time then to remain vigilant and watch out for our fickle ways, time also to refocus our eyes on the Lord alone.

DAILY LENTEN PRAYER

The following prayer, composed by St. Ephrem the Syrian, a faithful monk and great Church father, is recited during the weekdays of the Lenten season, from Monday through Friday. The prayer expresses perfectly the true spirit of Lent, and it is an incentive to continue seriously on the road of conversion and repentance.

O Lord and Master of my life,
Take from me the spirit of laziness,
Meddling, ambition, and idle talk.
Grant me instead a spirit of prudence,
Humility, patience, and love.
Yes, Lord and King,
Grant me to see my own sins and faults
And not to judge my brother.
For you are truly blessed
Forever and ever. Amen.

While the world looks negatively on Lent as a time of gloom, deprivation, and sadness, the Christian sees it paradoxically as a time of healing, inner cleansing, restoration, and joyful repentance. It is all worth it if through humility and self-denial we can grow into deeper intimacy with God.

MARCH 4

THE DISCIPLINE OF WRITING

Words are vehicles which incite the spirit to a self-active reproduction of truth by participation in God.

MOTHER MARIA: HER LIFE IN LETTERS

During these Lenten days, I am reminded of the small daily actions that are part and parcel of the discipline of Lent: fasting, the reading of a particular book as prescribed by St. Benedict, assiduousness to prayer, less entertainment (there is not much of that in our monastic life anyhow), certain prayers and prostrations in our daily ritual, and other such exercises in restraint.

Adding to all this, I include the discipline of daily writing. With the amount of work around this place, it is easy to dismiss it or skip it altogether. Somehow I must take the time for it early in the day before the dawn arrives or in small chunks of time here and there throughout the day. Writing, like prayer, allows our minds to focus on the essentials. It is also a form of retraining the mind, allowing it to center itself on the task at hand. As I write daily, nothing specific is required of me, except to relate the flowing of my thoughts in the context of the succession of the days and seasons. And as I make time to apply myself to the work and discipline of writing, I cherish the intimate joy that springs from it.

MARCH 5

TRANSFIGURATION

Having revealed, O Savior, a little of the light of your divinity to those who went up with you onto the mountain, you made them lovers of your heavenly glory. Therefore they cried in awe: "It is good for us to be here!" With them we also sing to you, O Savior Christ, who was transfigured and ineffably shone forth with light.

BYZANTINE MATINS OF THE TRANSFIGURATION

As the harsh cold and bleakness of winter begin to wane, the sun's salutary rays are felt, bringing cheer and joy in our hemisphere. Poor Mother Nature, dormant until now, begins to show her renewed strength, gained in part by the increasing daylight and warmth from the rain. Here and there in Dutchess County, New York, we begin to notice tiny signs of new life. As I stroll through the property, my thoughts turn to the transfiguration Gospel. It is a Gospel story pre-eminently monastic, for the mystery of the transfiguration lies at the heart of the monastic vocation. As a matter of fact, many monasteries of both the East and the West bear the transfiguration title in their name. In the Gospel account of the event, we hear the Father's voice glorifying his Son before undergoing the sufferings of his passion. For a moment in time, the veil covering his divinity is lifted and suddenly Jesus appears, luminous, wrapped in the unsurpassed beauty of his divinity. The disciples present at the event are amazed, speechless at God's glory shining from the Lord's face. All one can mutter is: "Lord, it is good that we are here" (Matthew 17:4).

THE LENTEN-DESERT EXPERIENCE

If we are not able to keep up with the tasks of the desert, let us live patiently in our cells, weeping for our sins, without wandering all over the place. For the eye of God sees the works of a man and nothing escapes him and he knows those who do strive to do good.

ABBA GELASIUS, DESERT FATHER

In the Northeast where we live, Lent usually arrives during a time when the weather itself feels penitential. February and March, as the winter prolongs itself, tend to be the dreariest months of the year. The temperature continues to be cold, the snow continues to fall, the sky is often gray, portraying a feeling of gloom and bleakness. It is a bit like the experience of being in a desolate place such as the desert. Actually, we could all take advantage of the gloominess of the season and transform it into a positive thing. Mother Nature herself, a great teacher, can give us a few cues as to how to approach our Lenten observance.

The long, dark, and often harsh winter season, with all its consequences, could be used as an image of the almost impenetrable inner desert we are invited to enter into after the example of Jesus. In the desert we must learn to confront ourselves with the forces of evil. The desert barrenness and hardship, similar to that of the land during winter, challenge us to look deeply into ourselves and search out the obstacles that hinder God's actions in our souls. The desert experience is purifying and illuminating. The desert strips us of the nonessentials in our ordinary lives to confront the most central questions: Are we living the way Jesus taught us to live, and are we seeking to please God alone?

RAINY WEATHER

When we turn our spirit from the contemplation of God, we become the slaves of our passion.

ABBA THEONIAS, DESERT FATHER

Spring is, officially, still about two weeks away. The weather has been rather reluctant to advance forward in the past few days. The present temperatures are certainly raw and cold; worse yet, for the past few days it has been raining nonstop. It is a true deluge, with flood emergencies all throughout the Northeast. The ground looks again like the dead of winter. This morning, while feeding the animals, I said to myself that a snowstorm might have been preferable to this intense, almost cruel torrential rain. After all, it is easier to walk in the snow than on these water puddles. It seems strange to see the forsythia in bloom in this type of weather, almost an anachronistic sight. I was not planning to light the wood-burning stove, but I am forced to eliminate the raw chill indoors. Rainy weather is usually good for planting the gardens, but we are not there yet. In four weeks or so, I assume the ground and the weather shall be amenable for sowing and encouraging our earliest plantings: salad greens, peas, beets, onions, and leeks.

During these Lenten days, I keep reflecting on the recurrent theme of patient endurance. Certainly the Lord endured his sufferings patiently, and we must all learn a lesson from that humble attitude.

A HINT OF SPRING

A good beginning makes a good ending.

ENGLISH PROVERB

The weather has improved a bit. The first hints of spring are felt here in the Northeast as we notice the gradual warming of the air. During the blessed hours of daylight, it feels good to work outdoors and enjoy these warm rays from the sun. With the help of two Vassar students involved in the monastic land-conservation program, we begin preparing for the upcoming gardening season. We are still almost two months away from the planting season, but now is the time when I need to roll up my monastic sleeves and plunge into the task at hand. I thank the Lord for the students' help. My coworkers and I concentrate today on the cleaning up of the winter debris around and inside the gardens. There are dead branches scattered over the garden beds, the result of past storms. Slowly we break down the branches and, with the help of a wheelbarrow, transport them to a place where they will be burned. Other debris, such as the dead leaves, are taken and incorporated into the compost pile. Later in the day, the students begin the tedious job of digging the sheep manure buried inside the barn and spreading it all over the vegetable garden, especially in those spots most in need: the potato and Jerusalem artichoke fields. The manure, a natural organic matter, shall provide the necessary nutrients to enrich the quality of our vegetables. Our Lenten spring is a time of renewal, both inside and outside ourselves.

LENT: A FAITH JOURNEY

Consider it all joy, my brothers, when you encounter various trials, for you know that the testing of your faith produces perseverance. And let perseverance be perfect, so that you may be perfect and complete, lacking in nothing.

JAMES 1:2–4

The Lenten journey we undertake by following Christ into the desert is basically a faith journey. Faith enlightens our minds and hearts. It opens our inner eyes to recognize the journey will be difficult and demanding, but at the end it shall be totally worthwhile. Faith illumines us to see that throughout all the challenges, including some missteps and mistakes made along the journey, the Lord remains at all times by our side. The aridity and temptations experienced in the desert must never lead us to despair, for the Lord is the faithful one, and he is with us all along this journey to the Promised Land. Let us be grateful for the blessings of faith, for without it we would not have the support we need to endure the hardships of the journey. As St. James says, faith produces endurance, perseverance; it is only by enduring and persevering until the end that we shall reap the fruits of the journey. Through patient endurance, God's power is manifested and glorified in our weakness.

Each day during Lent, as I do daily all year, I tell myself the words of Abba Apollo, "I am going to work with Christ today for the salvation of my soul, for that is the reward he gives." Each day, that is my daily program. I have no other goal or objective but to spend the entire day with Christ, doing whatever he and the day demands. I usually wake up early and pray the *Veni Sancte Spiritus* and then the Angelus. As I beseech the Holy Spirit's guidance, I pray to him to make Christ present to me during each instant of the day, while I pray, read, toil, eat, rest, recite the Jesus prayer, or welcome a visitor. At all times, no matter what, I am accompanied by Christ, our Savior and Master, and thus the hours of the day are enriched by the pleasure of his company. Throughout the years of monastic life I have always found renewed energy and motivation in the fact that each day is concretely spent working with Christ. Even the most tedious of occupations become lighter to bear while keeping his company. During the day, I often look at the icon of the Lord, present all throughout the monastery, breathe deeply, and say to him: "Thank you, Lord, for being here with me, for never disappointing me."

St. JOSEPH'S NOVENA

Our father, St. Joseph, grant that we may always rejoice under your protection.

MONASTIC DAILY PRAYER

Today begins our yearly novena to the father and protector of this small monastery, the good St. Joseph. I do not particularly consider myself a practitioner of novena prayers or anything similar, for all in all, the monastic offices and other daily prayers such as the Angelus, the rosary, and the Jesus' prayer are enough in our otherwise regulated life of prayer. But St. Joseph is special in this little monastic enclave, thus I must prepare myself for his upcoming solemnity by keeping daily a specific schedule of prayers to honor him. I usually choose a different prayer addressed to the saint every year. This year I am reciting in French a prayer to St. Joseph composed by Blessed John XXIII, who was also closely bonded with St. Joseph. This is my translation:

Dear St. Joseph,
To you who the Son of God called father and the Virgin Mary honored as a spouse.
You saw realized in yourself Jesus' promise:
"He who humbles himself shall be exalted,"
therefore, your holiness and power are proclaimed everywhere,
and so we join all those who admire your virtues and beseech your help.
Eagerly, we ask of you this particular grace…
Deign, O glorious St. Joseph, to welcome our prayer lovingly
And to grant our petition.
Following your example and guided by your protection,
We wish to continue our journey toward eternal happiness with God. Amen.
O good St. Joseph,
May your interior example of inner peace, silence, work, and faithful prayer continue to inspire us always. Amen.

OUR LADY OF LENT

Most Holy Theotokos, *intercede for our salvation.*

BYZANTINE PRAYER

During the forty days of our Lenten journey, of our wandering into the wilderness of the desert, one feels the compelling need for moral and spiritual support; even more so, for the loving company of someone who can nurture us along the journey. No one can better play this role than our Lady, the Most Holy *Theotokos.* It is a natural role for her, for at the foot of the cross she adopted each one of us as her own child. During this Lenten journey we address her appropriately with the words of the inspiring hymn:

Our most gracious Queen,
Our hope, O *Theotokos.*
You welcome the orphan
And are the protector of strangers.
You are the joy of those in sorrow,
And loving Mother of the poor.
Look at my distress and see my affliction.
Help me, for I am helpless.
Feed me, for I am a pilgrim and wanderer.
You who know my sinfulness, my offences,
Obtain for me forgiveness and great mercy.
For I know no other help but you,
No other intercessor or gracious consoler.
Only you, O *Theotokos,*
To guard and protect me
For ever and ever. Amen.

LEARNING TO ASSIMILATE CHRIST

We could say, particularly during these cleansing rugged days of Lent, that the sole purpose of our journey is to allow the Holy Spirit to form Christ in each of us. We daily strive for true conversion with the help of prayer and tears of repentance. We desire this inner conversion so that Christ may be free to grow in us. As we undertake the route that leads to holy Easter, we seek to relive with Christ all the moments of his earthly life, the extraordinary as well as the ordinary events: his birth; his growing up in Nazareth; his teaching in the Temple; his quiet life as a carpenter, son, and apprentice; his baptism in the Jordan and solitude in the desert; his ministry and community life with the disciples; his teaching moments; his miracles; his transfiguration; his encounters with the poor, the lowly, the sick, and the dying; and ultimately his passion and death that preceded his glorious resurrection. All we have to do is to open the Gospels and follow him step by step. And during these periods of deep, silent, trusting prayer, we humbly beseech him to show his face to us.

MOTHER NATURE WEEPS

O Lord, listen to my prayer
For my days are vanishing like smoke.
I cry with all my strength
And my skin clings to my bones.

PSALM 102

Heavy, steady rain. Thunderous, powerful winds. This is a real storm, and a very noisy one. Tons of tree branches are scattered throughout the property. Entire trees have fallen, some right in the middle of our small, narrow road. This unusual storm is to continue until Monday and is creating lots of damage in the region: floods, power outages, closed roads, difficulty in driving. It is dangerous weather. I venture out just to perform our daily farm duties and to fetch wood for the stove. The wood is wet, and I place it near the stove in the hope that it shall dry quicker. One of the paradoxes of living here in the country is the daily change in the weather. This past week we had some early intimations of spring; today, instead, there is a certain regression and return to winter. Today Mother Nature is weeping as with a broken heart. This imagery reminds me of the crucifixion icon showing the sun, moon, indeed the whole cosmos, weeping and mourning the death of their Lord and Creator.

LENT'S GOSPEL READINGS

Abba Paul often repeated to his disciples, "Remain close to Jesus."

ABBA PAUL THE GREAT

One of the high points of the Lenten season is the attentive reading of and listening to the Gospel passages chosen for each day, in particular those read in church on Sundays. Every one of the passages is a concrete scene of Christ's earthly life, and they make him very present to us, as if that particular event was happening at that moment in our lives. I must confess, I often feel totally transported to the Gospel-described scene during those moments, and it takes me a while to walk away from them. Christ, through his life's events, is so present at those moments. He ceases to be a remote personage, a fleeting concept, or even an absent friend living elsewhere. As we listen to or do the reading ourselves, he becomes alive in the reading and mysteriously present to us. In fact, he is right in front of us and next to us, and we can simply call him "Lord" as his disciples and friends did during those precious encounters with him.

The Gospel readings are not points of reference to a distant past or just a superficial reading of history. On the contrary, when we listen to them with the ears of faith, we enter into the *kairos*, the very time of God, the acceptable time when he manifested himself in those particular events. In the book of the Gospels, we always find the living Christ; in its pages we learn to read and decipher him. If we allow the mystery contained in the Gospels to grow in us, we shall discover Christ's loving presence in each of us as he takes total possession of our being so that we can say with St. Paul, "For to me life is Christ" (Philippians 1:21).

CONVERSION: CHANGE OF LIFE

Repent and believe in the Gospel. Turn back to the Lord and do penance. Be renewed in heart and spirit.

A LENTEN COUNSEL

On Ash Wednesday, when the Church imposes the ashes on our heads, it is inviting us at the same time to enter the path of repentance and to embrace true conversion of life. Our Lenten pilgrimage takes us across the desert for forty days, time that we aim to spend in contrite prayer, reading, fasting, and active good works, as St. Benedict and the Desert Fathers counsel us. Conversion, contrition, repentance, and prayer with tears are not signs of a negative attitude, but rather a refreshing, liberating experience of a new life growing in us. Conversion creates the new man and the new woman, created in the image and likeness of God, called to live in true intimacy with him and according to the Gospel standards. Conversion takes place in the depths of the human heart, the heart visited by God, the place where he makes his dwelling. Then, in the words of St. Benedict in the prologue of his *Rule*, "The heart expands and runs the way of God's commandments with the unspeakable sweetness of love, so that by sharing in the sufferings of Christ, the monk (the Christian) might also merit a share in his kingdom."

THE CHANGE IN WEATHER AND ITS SIDE EFFECTS

For the LORD is the great God, the great king over all gods.

PSALM 95:3

One of the side effects of the good weather we are presently enjoying seems to be a certain expansion of the mind. As one looks at the luminous sky, one feels our sense of perception expanded to a place where there are no limits. Pleasantly, almost humorously, I ponder about this since I am the one always remarking about the mind's limitations. Somehow I know there is no real contradiction in what I am experiencing at the moment and my usual assertion about the limitations of the human mind. This form of perception is more like an undefined feeling, one that keeps extending itself and seemingly never reaches its boundaries. The other, the logical exercise of the mind, is more of a mechanical maneuver, and it always feels its constraints, its rational confines, its limitations. The Lord, somehow, provides us with these two forms of apprehension to help us learn something about him, about his mystery. God is eternal, outside and beyond time, and we must approach him in faith within the confines of time, which of itself limits our understanding of his divine nature. O Holy One! O Eternal One! O Immutable One! O Incomprehensible One, illumine our minds and hearts with your divine light, and have mercy upon us.

MARCH LESSONS

Let the heavens be glad and the earth rejoice:
let the sea and what fills it resound:
let the plains be joyful and all that is in them.
Then let all the trees of the forest rejoice
before the LORD *who comes*
who comes to govern the earth.

PSALM 96:11–13

Two weeks ago we had some seemingly milder days. In spite of the cool breeze, one could enjoy the rays of the sun for hours. I do this while performing my daily chores at the farm—feeding the animals, bringing them water, and seeing that all their needs are cared for. The weather was pleasant enough (in contrast to that of our severe winter) that one could think spring was arriving early, that indeed it was knocking at the doors. Subsequent weather changes then proved this was not totally true. It was only a false spring alarm, as I like to call it. Winter has not yet surrendered its mighty force, and we still have a while longer to wait.

Since yesterday, we are enjoying genuine springlike weather and remarkable days, full of crisp, brisk air and lovely sunshine. As I write, I hear the birds passing through, singing. They are back from their southern sojourn. This past weekend some of the local folks dedicated two entire days to extracting the sap running deep inside the maple trees. That is a distinctly local spring activity. I look at the sky so high and clear, and as I breathe deeply the sweet springlike air, I mutter silently a thanksgiving prayer for the miracle of spring. "Bless the Lord, oh my soul Lord God, how great you are."

JERUSALEM: MOTHER OF GOD'S CHURCHES

With nature's help, humankind can set into creation all that is necessary and life sustaining. Everything in nature, the sum total of heaven and earth, becomes a temple and an altar for the service of God.

ST. HILDEGARD OF BINGEN

Today we are blessed with another beautiful spring day. Most of the snow seems to have vanished from the Hudson Valley, except perhaps in the Catskills and places of high altitude. Even the early-morning frost is gone, at least for the time being. Close to the monastic building, the daffodils are growing taller, ready to burst open any day now. The crocuses planted by the entrance are in full bloom now for a few days, and so are the snowdrops. The birds are lively and active throughout the property.

Today, liturgically speaking, we celebrate the memory of a great father of the early Church: St. Cyril of Jerusalem. I profess a particular attachment to the Church of Jerusalem. It is the mother Church of all other local churches. It is in Jerusalem that Christ died for our salvation—and it is in Jerusalem that he rose from the dead and that his tomb still lies. For me, part of the Lenten journey consists in the mental and spiritual traveling we undertake annually toward our destination: Jerusalem. In Jerusalem, great events shall take place shortly, and we are all invited to witness them. St. Cyril lovingly guided for many years the original mother Church, the cradle of Christianity. With the wisdom and the example of his own holiness, he vividly preached the teachings of the Gospel to the people of Jerusalem and to the many pilgrims who made their way there.

SOLEMNITY OF ST. JOSEPH

God made him the master of his household. He gave him charge over all his possessions.

A MEDIEVAL TRIBUTE TO ST. JOSEPH

The Lord, appropriately, gave us a splendid day to honor St. Joseph. The beautiful clear skies, the warmth from a radiant sun, the cool, crisp air—they all contribute to the special charm of this early spring day. This weather renewal, after our long winter, has reenergized me. I feel stronger and better motivated to perform both my indoor and outdoor chores. I am particularly enjoying anything to do with the outdoors. Today I also spent a great part of my day cleaning and putting order in the oratory, our small chapel. As I worked, every so often I glanced at the poignant and beautiful icon of St. Joseph with a small oil lamp burning the entire day in his honor. The icon is a small replica of a larger one that stands at St. Julien le Pauvre, Paris' oldest little church, or so it claims.

The liturgical texts of today's offices are a true depiction of our beloved quiet saint. They are worth pondering in the silence of our hearts:

God has made him father to the King
and master of all his household
And he has raised me up that he might save many people.

In the words of St. Bernardine of Siena, St. Joseph was chosen by the eternal Father to be the trusted, worthy guardian and protector of his greatest treasures: namely, his divine Son and Mary, his Mother. And we know well that good St. Joseph knew how to please God, for he carried out this vocation with complete fidelity until the end.

MARCH 20 · *St. Cuthbert, Monk*

A LENTEN PROGRAM

The study of inspired Scripture is the chief way of finding our duty.

ST. BASIL THE GREAT

In the *Rule*, St. Benedict emphasizes the imminent place the sacred Scriptures must be given in the daily schedule of the monk. The time allotted for *lectio divina* is the portion of the day the monk must consecrate exclusively to the reading of and meditation on the sacred Scripture. It is understood that, during Lent, this precious time must be prolonged.

Today, during one of the early monastic offices, I found a text from the prophet Isaiah that seems to summarize perfectly the whole Lenten intent. It is indeed a program for all sincere Lenten journeys:

> Wash yourselves clean! Put away your misdeeds before my eyes; cease doing evil; learn to do good. Make justice your aim: redress the wronged, hear the orphan's plea, defend the widow. Come now, let us set things right, says the LORD: Though your sins be like scarlet, they may become white as snow: Though they be red like crimson, they may become white as wool.
>
> ISAIAH 1:16–18

TRANSITUS OF ST. BENEDICT

Into your hands, O Lord, I commend my spirit.

OFFICE OF COMPLINE

St. Benedict is an apt companion to have by our side as we step into our Lenten journey. He has much to teach us about Lent. In the *Rule*, his chapter dedicated to the observance of Lent is truly a compendium on how the Lenten fervor must be preserved throughout the whole year, even long after Lent has come to its conclusion. St. Benedict leads us gradually into a progression during the journey and counsels us to wait for the paschal feast with the joy of spiritual desire. The source of this joy, he reminds us, is the Holy Spirit, the Comforter, and the Spirit of God that makes all things new. Being docile to the action of the Holy Spirit in our innermost is our best preparation for our yearly paschal celebration.

Coincidentally, every year during our Lenten observance, the monastic family celebrates the holy death of our beloved father and mentor St. Benedict. This is appropriate, for it places St. Benedict's presence in the midst of our Lenten journey. St. Gregory, St. Benedict's biographer, tells us in his *Dialogues*, that six days before his death the saint ordered his monks to dig his tomb. He was seized by a severe illness that he bore with constancy. On the sixth day, he asked the monks to carry him into the oratory, where he received the Body and Blood of his Savior to gain fortitude for the final step of the journey. Upheld by his monks, he remained standing with his arms outstretched toward heaven until he breathed his last. How beautiful in the sight of God was the death of his servant Benedict. Like Christ, his Master, St. Benedict died with his hands in prayer, outstretched in the form of a cross.

Psalm 14

The other day while praying the Daily Office (Vespers for Monday, week 1), I was struck by how Psalm 14 was perfectly suitable and applicable to convey Lent's true spirit, and what our Lenten behavior should be all about. Psalm 14 is a good code of conduct for the Christian. As we pray it, it challenges us at the deepest level of our beings to live and act in accordance with Christ's teachings. Here is my own paraphrased translation from the French:

> Lord, who shall dwell under your tent?
> And who shall inhabit your holy mountain?
> He whose conduct is blameless,
> He who acts with justice,
> And who tells the truth from his heart.
> He who controls his tongue from slander,
> And does not criticize or reproach his neighbor.
> In his eyes the wicked are held in disdain,
> But he reverences those who fear the Lord.
> He who lends his money without interest,
> And never accepts bribes against the innocent men.
> Whoever conducts thus in this manner
> Shall remain firm forever.

And while praying the psalm, I could not help but notice its strong similarities with St. Ephrem's Lenten prayer, which we recite three times daily and which also serves as a true Lenten program of conduct and conversion.

LAMBING SEASON

For the Lamb who is in the center of the throne will shepherd them and lead them to springs of life-giving water, and God will wipe away every tear from their eyes.

REVELATION 7:17

The late winter months and early spring ones see the arrival of new life into the quiet of the monastery. We have always maintained throughout the year a small flock of sheep. *"Le petit troupeau de Bethlehem,"* I call them. They pasture and help maintain our fields, and we are grateful for it. When the lambs arrive, as they have been doing for the last three weeks, they demand our continual attention. Monks usually care lovingly for their animals, as they do for their land and gardens. And lambs occupy a special place in our hearts since they are a vivid reminder of the *Agnus Dei*, the Paschal Lamb, who sacrificed his life for our sake. Often, the new lambs may require hand nursing, either because the mother ewes reject them or they have too little milk. As we help nurse the new lamb, we notice how the little ones react sweetly to these gestures of human kindness. I am so content we are able to show respect and care and kindness to our animals. They are truly gifts from the Lord, and they belong in the new creation where all living things sing God's praises day and night. O all creatures of the Lord, bless the Lord!

USEFULNESS OF THE DESERT EXPERIENCE

Waters will burst forth in the wilderness, and streams in the Arabah. The burning sands will become pools, and the thirsty ground, springs of water; the abode where jackals crouch will be a marsh for the reed and papyrus. A highway will be there, called the holy way.

ISAIAH 35:6–8

While in Rome living in a rich mansion, Abba Arsenius prayed to God with these words: "Lord, lead me in the way of salvation." And he heard a voice answering his request: "Arsenius, flee to the desert and you will be saved."

ABBA ARSENIUS, DESERT FATHER

During our Lenten journey, just as during the Advent one, we are invited to make a sojourn into the desert. During Lent, we have the living example of Christ himself, our Savior, sojourning deep into the desert for forty days. If the Lord took the desert experience so seriously, must not we also? We know Christ never wasted time unnecessarily during his lifetime, and yet he didn't hesitate to take this prolonged time in the wilderness, apparently doing nothing else but praying, fasting, and preparing for his upcoming ministry.

Time in the desert, be it at home, on a retreat, in a monastery, or in a real wilderness solitude, is primarily for the purpose of profound conversion, for cleansing our minds, indeed our inner eyes, from all that is frivolous, from cloudy ideas, from unnecessary cares, returning finally and wholeheartedly to the Lord, our God. The desert is not a romantic place to dream about. There is no place to hide in the desert. The desert is barren, and in it we are invited to face our own emptiness. It is desolate, and in it we face our human misery. It is austere, and in it we face our own limitations, our fragility, our weakness. It is depressing, and in it we confront our total dependency on God for survival, our need for redemption and God's mercy.

We Christians do need to heed the example of the Lord and follow him from time to time to the emptiness of the desert, to the barren wilderness, where we can tackle the reality and nakedness of our worldly existence. I don't idealize the desert experience, I simply see the need for it. Imagine if our political, civic, business, educational, and ecclesiastical leaders could submit themselves to the bare reality, the inner cleansing that comes from the desert experience. What would our world be like? What would the churches be like? What would society at large be like? There is a hidden wisdom yet to be discovered in the depths of the desert, for the desert experience sharpens one's vision of reality in a unique way. The desert always presumes an eventual renunciation of power, a submission to an unknown yet totally real God. Doing this could have far-reaching consequences never dreamed of before. The realism of the desert, both bare and empty, helps all of us realize that God alone is in charge.

MARCH 25

THE ANNUNCIATION

Today is the birthday of our salvation and the manifestation of the mystery which was from the beginning, the Son of God becomes the Virgin's Son, and Gabriel proclaims the good tidings of grace. Therefore with them we greet the Mother of God: Rejoice, you are full of grace, the Lord is with you!

TROPARION OF THE FEAST

The Word of God became man that you also may learn from a man how a man becomes God.

ST. CLEMENT OF ALEXANDRIA

Today we commemorate an ancient feast in the Christian calendar, the cherished feast of the Annunciation, in a way also the feast of the Incarnation. In nine months we shall celebrate Christmas, the official feast of the Incarnation. The early fathers wrote with such unction about this mystery that I couldn't help but to quote a few of them here. After the Scripture, the fathers' writings are my daily spiritual food. A great twentieth-century spiritual writer, also daily fed by the fathers, Olivier Clement, writes something so appropriate for today and also for next week, the week of the passion and the resurrection:

> The Word is the gift of God. We must know how to perceive the giver through the gift. More precisely, since the time of the Incarnation, the Passion and Easter, we can see the earth as an immense memorial, the tomb/womb in which Christ was buried and to which he gave resurrected power through the power of his own resurrection....The Word both hides and reveals himself in visible forms as much as in the words of Scripture.

THE GREAT CANON OF ST. ANDREW OF CRETE

The Canon of St. Andrew of Crete is a liturgical treasure of the Eastern Church. It is usually prayed in its entirety during the Morning Office on Thursday of the fifth week of Lent. Unfortunately, to our own impoverishment, there is nothing similar in the Western Church. The canon is a prayer of deep faith, expressing beautifully, tearfully, what the Christian attitude of repentance is meant to be, especially during these final days of our Lenten journey. The imagery in the canon is precise, strong, and it portrays an attitude of mind and soul that must be ours as we approach the presence of Christ, our God and Savior. The theme of repentance permeates the whole canon; again and again the soul mourns its sinful condition and is plunged into a spirit of constant repentance. We repent from minute to minute, from day to day. We repent as individuals and as a whole people as we face the dreadful day of judgment and face alone he who is Judge and Savior. Here are some excerpts:

> Where shall I start to mourn the deeds of my wretched life? What first-fruits shall I lay down, O Christ, to this my present weeping? But, since You are the Merciful One, grant me forgiveness of sins.
>
> I fall down, Jesus, at Your feet, for I have sinned against you; be merciful to me, take from me the burdensome collar of sin. And since You are the Compassionate One, grant me tears of true compunction.
>
> I bring You, O Savior, the tears from my eyes and the groans from the depths, crying aloud from my heart: O God, I have sinned against You, be merciful to me a sinner.

MARCH 27

SPIRITUAL DESIRES

Let us persevere in our longing for God
So as to be worthy upon the completion of the forty days
To behold the most solemn Passion of Christ,
And to feast with spiritual joy
In the most holy Passover of the Lord.

BYZANTINE LENTEN OFFICE

Our Lenten days are quickly winding down; coincidentally, so are also the rest of our March days. *Tempus fugit!* Only a few remaining days and we shall approach—indeed, enter into—the solemn days of Passiontide. Our father, St. Benedict, having artfully mastered the spirit and practices of the Lenten observance during his lifetime, encourages the disciple to do the same in the joy of the Holy Spirit. Guided by the Spirit during the Lenten desert journey, the Christian monastic looks forward to Passiontide and Holy Easter with a unique, intimate joy, the joy of spiritual desire, as St. Benedict describes it. Holy Week and then Easter become the culmination and fulfillment of all of one's spiritual desires, those intense desires nurtured and cultivated along the Lenten journey that suddenly burst into a new abundant life by the power of Christ's resurrection.

MARCH 28

PASSION SUNDAY

Riding upon the heavenly throne, and seated upon an earthly foal, O Christ our God,

You received the praises of angels and the hymns of men,

Exclaiming before You: Blessed is he who comes to restore Adam back to life.

KONTAKION OF PALM SUNDAY

Yesterday, just before arriving to our Palm Sunday celebration, we accompanied the Lord to Bethany, where he raised his friend, Lazarus, from the tomb. The extraordinary event that took place in Bethany boggles the mind, and it is certainly a most-needed preparation for the events of the week to come. Internally, I always remain fixated on Bethany and anticipate eagerly every year the arrival of Lazarus Saturday. Only after that can I begin the journey into the holiest of weeks. The Byzantine Triodon for today's liturgy describes beautifully our sentiments at our entrance into Holy Week:

> O Christ God, before you undertook your voluntary sufferings, You wished to explain and confirm the mystery of the eternal resurrection in Bethany by raising Lazarus from the tomb with your almighty power after he had been dead for four days. And to the blind You gave sight, for You are indeed the Giver of light, O Savior. Today, You enter the city of Jerusalem with your disciples, sitting on an ass, thus fulfilling the preaching of the Prophets, as though riding upon the cherubim, and the Hebrew children acclaimed You with palms and branches. Therefore, we also carry olive branches and palms, crying out to You with gratitude: Hosanna in the highest, Blessed is he who comes in the name of the Lord.

MONDAY OF HOLY WEEK: THE BRIDEGROOM

Behold, the Bridegroom comes in the middle of the night.
Blessed is the servant whom he shall find watching.
But unworthy is he who is careless and not ready.
Let us, then, be vigilant and put aside the works of darkness,
Lest we fall into heavy sleep,
For the Lord shall come as a thief in the night.

THE BRIDEGROOM OFFICE

These are the early, somber days of Holy Week. The weather itself is wet and gloomy, extra quiet, and almost still as we relive those last days of Jesus before reaching the moment of his sacred passion. The Gospel readings in the liturgy are all significantly telling stories, as if the sacred writers such as St. John are trying to convey what was going on in the Lord's mind as he approached his hour.

In the center of the oratory lies for our veneration the icon of the Bridegroom, the Man of Sorrows, a beautiful, powerful icon recently completed by Olga, our iconographer friend and neighbor. It is truly a spiritual work of art. It is an icon I have deeply loved throughout the years, and it became a source of inspiration and spiritual support during the period of my operations. It is an icon I return to often, regardless which time of year it might presently be.

The icon is sometimes venerated under different designations. The Greeks called it "the Extreme Humility of Christ," others called it "the Kenosis," that is, the self-emptying of Christ. Others simply call this icon "the Bridegroom." All the designations are appropriate and convey something of the total self-abasement of the Lord at the moment of his Incarnation, during all of his earthly life, and especially during its culmination on the cross. These days when we keep memory of his sacred passion, the icon is there in total silence, speaking volumes to the heart that longs for him.

TUESDAY OF HOLY WEEK: THE PASSOVER LAMB

The LORD said to Moses and Aaron in the land of Egypt: this month shall stand at the head of your calendar; you will reckon it the first month of the year. Tell the whole community of Israel, On the tenth of this month every family must procure for itself a lamb, one apiece for each household... and apportion the lamb's cost in proportion to the number of persons, according to what each household consumes.

EXODUS 12:1–4

We are in the middle of Holy Week, deeply immersed in the mystery of the Lord's Passover. Just as we prepared for Holy Thursday, a new tiny lamb appeared in the morning in the monastic sheepfold. He is the last of the season, the smallest of all, with the name Benjamin. Our little Benjamin brings to mind vividly the image of the true Passover Lamb. He reminds us, in the words of an ancient Christian writer, St. Melito of Sardis, that "Christ was led forth like a lamb; he was slaughtered like a sheep. He ransomed Israel from the land of Egypt; he freed us from our slavery to the devil as he freed Israel from the hand of Pharaoh. He sealed our souls with his own Spirit and the members of our body with his own blood....He was sacrificed in the Passover lamb."

WEDNESDAY OF HOLY WEEK: THE REPENTANT HARLOT

Today, as we prepare ourselves to enter into the most sacred of Triduums, the last days of Holy Week, the days we mourn and commemorate the sacred passion and death of the Lord, we are invited to follow closely the events that took place during those poignant last hours. In the Byzantine tradition, Holy Wednesday commemorates a special event: that of the repentant woman coming to Simon's house where Jesus was dining and pouring precious ointment while washing his feet. This ointment washing was a symbol of the one Christ's body was to undergo a few days later, prior to his burial. During the long Matins service of the day, we read:

> The sinful woman hastened to buy precious ointment of myrrh,
> with which to anoint the true Benefactor and Savior of her soul.
> And while buying it, she cried aloud to the merchant:
> "Provide me oil of myrrh that I may anoint Him who has cleansed me from all my sins."
>
> Drowning in her sinfulness, she found in You, O Savior, a haven of salvation.
> And while pouring out on your feet oil of myrrh mixed with her tears, she cried to You:
> "Lo, You are my Savior, He who accepts the repentance of the sinful.
> O Master, in your great mercy, save me from the waves of sin."
>
> Today, Christ comes to the home of the Pharisee,
> and the sinful woman draws near Him, falling at His feet, crying:
> "You behold me, O Savior, sunk in sin, filled with despair by reason of my deeds,
> yet I am not rejected but accepted by your great love.
> Grant me, O Lord, total forgiveness of my many sins and save me."

The repentant harlot spread out her hair before You, O Master,
while Judas stretched out his hands to your enemies:
she, to receive forgiveness; and he, to receive money.
Therefore we cry aloud to You who was sold for money and yet set us free:
O Lover and Savior of mankind, glory to You.

APRIL

APRIL 1

HOLY THURSDAY: THE MYSTICAL SUPPER

Be zealous, then, in the observance of one Eucharist. For there is one flesh of Our Lord, Jesus Christ, and one Chalice that brings union in his Blood.

ST. IGNATIUS OF ANTIOCH

Holy Thursday commemorates the institution of the Eucharist. As we approach our evening celebration, we must remember this is a profound mystery, *mysterium tremendum*, a mystery not to trivialize or take lightly, a mystery that must never become routine or taken for granted. Now that we have been purified by the holy fast and Lenten observances, we can reach the table of the Lord with sincere hearts and minds. All things converge into the Lord's sacred Passover meal, the mystical supper, the heavenly banquet to which all those looking for salvation are invited. Behold, this is truly the time of our salvation, in which the Lord's divine gifts poured lavishly into our lives are at our disposal. In that blessed night of Holy Thursday, the night anticipating his hour, the Lord leaves us the gift of himself as testament of his boundless love. He loves us until the end, as the Gospels tell us, and at the end he had no more to give but himself.

The early Church, the Desert Fathers and Mothers—indeed, St. Benedict himself—didn't know a daily reception of the Eucharist as it has now become the practice in most places in the Western Church. They were faithful to the weekly synaxis, as were the early Christian communities, when on Sundays they all received the Body and Blood of the Lord. It took them all week to prepare themselves for its receptions, and then another in thanksgiving for having partaken of the divine gifts and its assimilation intimately into their lives. These early disciples of the Lord, and I include here our monastic forbearers in the desert, approached the sacred mysteries with such a serious attitude and reverence that it could never become a daily routine in their case. For them, the Lord's mysterious eucharistic presence could never be measured in terms of time, hours, days, or even weeks. They hungered for him all week long, and once they received him in the mystery of Communion, they felt themselves totally possessed by him. This transcended any notion of time. Therefore, nothing in time could separate them from him. St. Mary of Egypt, days before dying, expressed vividly this real hunger for the divine mysteries. This weekly Eucharist is still the practice of the Eastern Church and Eastern monasteries. The reception of the Lord's Body and Blood is usually preceded by the beautiful preparation prayer composed by St. Basil:

> Of your mystic supper, O Son of God, receive me today as a communicant; for I will not speak of the mystery to your enemies; nor will give You a kiss like Judas. But like a thief I confess You: Remember me, O Lord, in your kingdom. Remember me, O Master, in your kingdom. Remember me, O Holy One, in your kingdom.

GOOD FRIDAY: THE CROSS

Glory to Your Passion, O Christ,
Glory to Your long-enduring suffering, O Lord.

BYZANTINE OFFICE

During the year I am writing, Good Friday falls on the day in which we also keep memory of our Mother among the saints, Mary of Egypt. Be it as it may, it is a lovely coincidence, for Mary of Egypt was at all times a lover of the cross of Christ. It was her wish to venerate the true cross in Jerusalem that prompted her conversion. Today, therefore, with Mary of Egypt, with Mary the *Theotokos*, with Mary Magdalene, and with all the other Marys, we keep our eyes fixed on the cross, fixed on the crucified one. As Mary of Egypt, with contrite hearts, with true repentance, we run toward the cross where the mystery of our salvation is accomplished. Like her, it is only in encountering the cross that we begin to fathom something of the immense love that motivated our Savior to endure it for our sake.

In our bare and stripped chapel, a candle flame flickers next to the stand where the crucifixion icon lays. As we pray and venerate the icon, we mournfully, repeatedly sing over and over again the same troparion we have been singing all throughout Lent, but today with such poignancy:

Before Your rugged cross,
We bow down in worship, O Master,
And your Holy Resurrection
We glorify.

As we pray, sing, weep, and lament over the suffering endured by the Lord for our sins, we keep company with our Lady and all those faithful friends who remained with him until the end.

HOLY SATURDAY

Whenever something disagreeable or unpleasant happens to us, let us remember Christ crucified and his deep silence in the tomb.

ANONYMOUS (A CONTEMPORARY DESERT MONK)

Since yesterday we have been in silent and profound mourning. Late last night, we kept vigil with our Lady, the disciples, Mary Magdalene, Nicodemus, and the noble Joseph of Arimathea, as Jesus' body was descended from the cross and deposited in his Mother's arms. Quietly, and with deep sorrow, we followed the preparations for the burial and partook in the funeral procession to the tomb. As we relived these hours, tears came to our eyes, and we could not find consolation anywhere. As we accompany the Lord to his resting place, we reached the garden where the tomb lays. There we quietly sing:

O blessed tomb! You received within yourself the Creator and the Author of life. O strange wonder! He who dwells on high is buried beneath the earth by his own consent.

BYZANTINE TEXT

Today a profound, respectful silence pervades the entire monastic enclave. It is a mournful silence, the silence of Holy Saturday, which speaks volumes, for today is indeed the most blessed Sabbath on which Christ sleeps. Keeping watch by Christ's sepulcher, the Christian experiences a profound feeling of peace. This is not just any burial, and this also is not an ordinary tomb. Deep down we know that from this very tomb, tomorrow, early in the morning, the Lord shall rise. We hold on to that promise as we depart and take leave from the tomb.

EASTER: CHRIST IS RISEN!

Christ is risen! Indeed he is risen!

EASTER GREETING

Today, joy has entered the whole world. One feels it palpably in every aspect of life and hears it proclaimed from every corner of the world and in every language. Easter greetings arrive here through emails in English, French, Spanish, Portuguese, and Italian. They all tell me that "Christ is risen," to which I reply, "Indeed, he is risen!" It is the traditional greeting for Christians of the East and West, which today share the same date for the paschal feast. How much one's heart rejoices that today we are all one, sharing the same Pascha as it was done for 1,000 years during the centuries of the Church undivided.

As I uttered with joy the greeting to those who called today or knocked at our doors, it comes to mind that St. Seraphim of Sarov thus greeted each of his visitors all year. For the saints, they who already dwell at the threshold of heaven, Easter lasts forever. They are blessed to anticipate the eternal feast that lasts forever. It is as if they are already partaking of the eternal now. What would it be like then, I inquire? What would it be like to see the shining presence of the risen Lord as Mary and the disciples saw him, radiant on that first Easter morning? What would it be like to behold his sacred wounds and kiss his feet as Mary intuitively tried to do it early on Easter morn? What would it have been like the first time he showed himself to his Mother, the *Theotokos,* she who stood by him until the end? As I try to meditate on these eternal verities, all beyond my poor understanding, all I can do is glance at the glorious resurrection icon in the lectern accompanied by many candles and then kiss and venerate the icon as I utter: "Glory to your holy resurrection, O Lord!"

BRIGHT WEEK

Today the whole creation is glad and rejoices,
For Christ arose from the grace on the third day.

BYZANTINE EASTERTIDE OFFICES

During the last three or four days, incredible and glorious spring weather has been surprising all of us local folks, just in time for our Pascha, as we here lovingly refer to Easter. The days are full of light, sunshine, and plain transparency. More and more plants are in bloom on the monastic confines, including the ones we keep in the greenhouse. The monastic land seems to be singing of Christ's resurrection with full voice and one accord. Gloriously I contemplate this magnificent sight on this first day of what we call "Bright Week." As I stroll around from one task to another, I continue to repeat the resurrection hymn we chant each morning at Lauds right after a proclamation of a resurrection Gospel account:

Let us behold the Resurrection of Christ,
And worship the holy Lord Jesus,
Who alone is the all sinless one!
We worship your cross, O Christ,
And your Holy Resurrection we praise and glorify,
For You are our God, and we know no other God than You.
We call upon your Name.
Come, all you faithful,
Let us worship Christ's Holy Resurrection,
For behold, through the cross joy has come into the world.
Forever blessing the Lord, we praise his Resurrection,
For he endured the cross for us.
And by his death he destroyed death.
Jesus, having risen from the dead as he foretold,
Has granted us eternal life and great mercy.

THE RESURRECTION AND SPRING REBIRTH

Our Lord has written the promise of the resurrection not in books alone, but in every leaf in springtime.

MARTIN LUTHER

Easter, our paschal celebration, always coincides with the spring rebirth that is taking place in nature in the land. It is obviously visible everywhere. The surrounding countryside makes the point. The grass is getting greener by the day. The trees are flowering. The forsythia, daffodils, narcissus, and hyacinths are in full bloom; the tiny lambs become a graceful sight in our fields, and our hens are providing us with tons of fresh eggs. One of them is already sitting on her eggs in the expectation of hatching them by the end of the month. This is an early phenomenon this season, for they usually don't start sitting on their eggs until May or so. I think our chickens, like people, are bit confused by the weather, by the rare warm temperatures we are enjoying so early in the season. Some local farmers are still concerned about a possible late frost. The changes I see taking place all around remind me that Easter is also a time of spiritual rebirth and inward renewal, a time of palpable hope and new life at all levels. Christ is risen indeed, and by his resurrection he makes all things new, and that includes our own spiritual lives. We can now put aside our dreary old self and embrace the newness of life achieved by the power of the Lord's resurrection. The physical world is full of joy because of the resurrection. Our inner world must be also. For it is there where we are most ourselves.

THE ORATORY

The angels in heaven, O Christ, our Savior,
Sing praises to Your Resurrection.
Deem us also, who are here on earth
Worthy of glorifying You with a pure heart.

BYZANTINE HYMN FOR EASTER

The chapel, the Lord's little house, looks radiant in its exquisite simplicity during these lovely days of Bright Week. After the usual Lenten/winter stark, somber mood in which it was kept—no flowers, no decorations of any sort—suddenly the presence of the risen Lord in the resurrection icon and the paschal candle seems to change it all. There are fresh forsythias, daffodils, narcissuses, and other flowers by the icon, the altar, the crucifix, and of course, by Our Lady of the Resurrection in her cherished corner. Bright candles surround the resurrection candle, and they are all lit during the chanting of the offices. This is a week to relax and enjoy singing God's praises for the same office, psalms, and hymns are repeated all week. I rather enjoy that and find not a moment of monotony in it. Bright Week is a unique period of time. After all, it takes more than one time and constant repetition to try to absorb the mystery contained in our paschal celebration. It is a special treat to bask in the warm presence of the risen Lord, being nurtured and fed by the readings, the Gospel accounts, the Easter music. I try to imagine what the Lord's visits to the disciples must have been like. I spend extra time in the chapel, lingering quietly in his presence, just imagining how our Lady and the disciples must have felt, overwhelmed and overjoyed each time he made himself visible to them. I am sure the angels, the only ones present at the moment of the resurrection, sang their loveliest alleluias!

APRIL 8

EXQUISITE WEATHER

Christ the Lord, by his Resurrection,
has turned all our sunsets into dawns.

ST. CLEMENT OF ALEXANDRIA

We are having exquisite spring weather perfectly consonant with Bright Week. The last of our late winter days are now behind us. At times, it is hard to believe it was only three weeks ago that we had one of the heaviest snowstorms of the season. The local folks, all of us, seem now relieved by the positive changes in the weather. Everyone seems to be talking about their garden projects, such as selecting the best seeds and continuing to clean their yards. Monks, being private beings and lovers of silence, tend to mind their own business and generally keep limited interaction. However, monasteries do attract some visitors, friends, guests, neighbors, students, and volunteers, and they tend to be my sources of information. There are students from Vassar and the Culinary Institute of America, who visit here habitually and volunteer their service in our small farm and gardens. With them, one shares a common interest in local sustainable agriculture. It is a source of profound joy to discover this renewed interest among young people, and it is a point of intersection between us monks and them. Monks are natural lovers of the place, of the land where they spend their days and one day will die. There we sing the Lord's praises daily and work the soil to produce nourishment for the monastic table and those who partake of it. In doing thus, as in all things, the risen Lord is glorified!

FIRST PLANTINGS

To see a world in a grain of sand,
And a heaven in a wildflower,
Hold infinity in the palm of your hand,
And eternity in an hour.

WILLIAM BLAKE, "TO SEE A WORLD..."

Steady gardeners that we are here in the monastery, we have been dreaming about the upcoming seed time and planting season since early in the year. Of course, it was too cold to think of planting in January, but one could at least page through the seed catalogs, keep an inventory of those we saved from last year, and make a list of the ones we need for the upcoming season. During these past two months, whenever the weather permitted, we have been cleaning the debris in the gardens, raking the leaves, adding compost and lime, and preparing the beds and smoothing the ground for early planting. These labor-intensive tasks have kept us extra busy during these early spring days, full of sunshine. The planting really started last week, when the students buried in a certain garden spot some Jerusalem artichokes left over from last fall. Some survived being consumed during the winter months—plenty were eaten and shared with others—and so they are now replanted.

Today, due in part to the early warm weather, we decided to plant and fill the first of the raised beds. The students raked the ground, and soon after—with a fine spade—they started carving lines for the planting. The rows are rather close to each other. Our own monastic planting style is rather intense. We tend to be frugal and save space in everything. Today we planted some salad greens, a variety of lettuce, arugulas, mesclun, and also some Swiss chard and beets. Some of the garlic, of which we have plenty, was transplanted to another spot. All in all, it makes one feels good realizing that our early planting is taking place under the auspices of Bright Week, when new life is given to us by the risen Lord.

THE GLORY OF THE PASCHAL MYSTERY

Life is a larger word than Resurrection, but Resurrection is, so to speak, the crucial quality of life.

WILLIAM TEMPLE

Our spirits were uplifted this past week by the joyful celebration of the *Mysterium Paschale.* It is such a unique week in the entire monastic/liturgical calendar that it is no wonder it is simply called Bright Week. Radiantly bright indeed is the entire week, rich in meaning, for the entire universe partakes of the newness of the Easter life. All of life, in humans and in Mother Nature, is renewed at this time by the power of the resurrection and the grace and strength of the Holy Spirit. Christ has triumphed over death. Therefore, all things are made new. All time and seasons belong to him, as the *Exultet* proclaims in lovely fashion.

In this tiny monastic enclave, dedicated to the mystery of the resurrection, our inner joy seems to have no limit, no boundary. Following in the path of the Lord's disciples and the early Christians, we continue to proclaim with our lives the *Magnalia Dei*, that is, God's wondrous deeds. Filled with the new light we received at Easter, we in turn try to expand the radiance of that light concretely by doing all things, even the smallest tasks, with a Christlike attitude. The full splendor of the resurrection must be translated into the daily, the minutia, and monotony of the daily, so that in all things God may be glorified.

THOMAS SUNDAY

The doubt of Thomas was arranged as positive faith,
O Savior, in accordance with Your will,
In order that no one would ever doubt the Resurrection.
Only to him did you reveal yourself,
Both the print of the nails, and the prick of the spear,
So that he confessed to you, saying:
"Thou art my Lord and my God."

ST. ROMANUS THE MELODIST

Today is the first Sunday after Easter, the Sunday we usually call "Thomas Sunday," for the Gospel reading in church recounts Thomas' story after the resurrection. Not being present when Jesus returned and showed himself to the disciples, Thomas had a hard time believing in the resurrection. Thomas was skeptical by nature, and his doubt simply reflected the type of man he was. Nevertheless, as we hear in the Gospel today, the Lord lovingly rebukes him and confronts Thomas for his lack of faith. Thomas then, seeing the Lord and touching his glorious wounds, can no longer reject the obvious and humbly exclaims the now famous, "My Lord and my God," to which the Lord, God's infinite wisdom, replies, "Thomas, because you have seen me, you have believed. Blessed are those who have not seen and yet believe."

Faith in the resurrection, in the power of God, shall always remain a challenge for believers throughout the ages. And yet we are all called to trust the Lord blindly and grow in faith. Faith in Jesus assures us of his promise that we also shall see and touch him one day.

APRIL 12

LAMBING SEASON

No one has a right to sit down and feel hopeless. There is too much work to do.

DOROTHY DAY

Lambing season is in full swing in the Hudson Valley, and that includes us here in the monastery, where we keep a small flock of sheep. As we emerge from our long winter slumber, it is comforting to witness the arrival of the tiny new lambs. It certainly verifies the fact that spring is truly here.

Lambing season keeps us busy, for it is a high-maintenance activity. For a few weeks, it becomes a full-time job. The lambs and mother ewes are kept separated from the rest of the flock, fed and maintained at regular hours, and one must be on the watch for wild predators who may wish to prey on the little ones. Because it is early in the season, the flock is not put out to pasture yet. They remain in the barn enclosure and are daily fed a certain amount of hay, grains, salt, leftover vegetables, fruits, and some old bread. In a few weeks, as the weather gets warmer, we shall lead the sheep to graze in one of the fields. The extra care we provide for the flock during lambing season always pays off later in the year, for it is a beautiful sight indeed to see the healthy little lambs bouncing joyfully in the fields, following their mothers wherever they go.

THE WAYS OF THE GOSPEL IN CONTRAST TO THE WAYS OF THE WORLD

Peter, priest of Dios, ought to have stood in front when he prayed with others, because he was a priest. Yet, because of his deep humility, he chose to stand behind everyone else.

THE DESERT FATHERS

The stark realism found in the Desert Fathers reminds me of the clear, concrete teachings we read in the Gospels, of the life example of the Lord himself. Unfortunately, in contrast to the faithful example of these Desert Fathers, I also discover how distant we are today from trying to follow our Master closely. Unfortunately, church structures in general—regardless of denomination—are not much help, since they themselves encourage ambition, power, prominence, and clericalism. It is well-known that the poor Desert Fathers stayed away from bishops and church dignitaries, just as they stayed away from the devil. To them, the hierarchical structures reminded them more of the Roman Empire's worldly power from which they tried to escape when they fled into the desert. Their only wish was to follow the humble example of Jesus, their Lord and Master. They also remembered he taught "the disciple is no greater than his Master." How could they justify ascending the ladder of clerical culture, which they saw and knew to be an antithesis to the Gospel, to the life example of the Lord himself? Their obedience, as they understood, was foremost to their Master, Christ the Lord, to his example and teachings.

SPRING IN THE HUDSON VALLEY

Whoever is wise will take note of these things, and ponder the merciful deeds of the LORD.

PSALM 107:43

Those who inhabit New York's Hudson Valley and have lived here for years often mention there is no better place to live the reality of each season. This is particularly true for those who love spring. After the last of the snowstorms is past and much of the ice and snow are melted away, springtime makes its radiant appearance. There is a special magic to spring. The trees in our hills, the lovely lakes and streams, the shrubs and bulb plants suddenly are in full blossom. The grass is green again with that new "tender green," as an Irish friend calls it. Spring's new green and yellow seem to define the season somehow, as the warmer weather and longer days make their full entrance into the valley.

One notices how people enjoy the outdoors more, looking for ways to employ their time wisely, either in the garden or on hikes in the woods for relaxation. And now the Mid-Hudson Bridge has been transformed into a walkway, which many residents use to walk for a bit of adventure and wonder. In a way, it is a form of enjoying the view from the river and catching something of its fresh spring breeze. Here in the monastery, one partakes of the blessings of spring, and like many of the local farmers and gardeners, we plunge deeply into the labor of our farms and gardens. We thank the Lord daily for the beauty of the valley.

THE MONASTIC CHANT

But the wisdom from above is first of all pure, then peaceable, gentle, compliant, full of mercy and good fruits, without inconstancy or insincerity. And the fruit of righteousness is sown in peace for those who cultivate peace.

JAMES 3:17–18

Young people who frequent our monastery often ask me the reason for the monastic chant in our daily offices and liturgy. They seem to be fascinated by its extreme simplicity, repetition, and almost archaic quality. They tell me the chant is not often heard elsewhere except in monasteries, and they wish to know why monastics uphold this tradition.

Without going into long expositions about the origins and history of the chant, I simply tell them that we cultivate and adhere to this tradition because we see it as a true vehicle of prayer, as a means to enhance the daily praise of God. The chant, I tell them, is full of that wisdom, gentleness, and peace of which St. James speaks in the text above. Since the chant, except for the Russian monastic chant, is usually sung in unison, it brings all those who sing it into a unity of sound, unity of spirit, unity at prayer. This is a symbol of the unity we seek with God in the monastic life and also a symbol of the unity that the three divine persons share within the mystery of the Blessed Trinity.

In a monastery, chanting is never a performance but a simple humble tool, a spiritual practice that leads us right into the mystery of God. The chant need not always be done in a foreign language such as Latin, Greek, Russian, or Arabic, as they do in the monasteries of Egypt and the Orient. Yes, one can chant in those languages, but diverse chants adapt themselves easily to English and other languages, and as such they help us to pray better when we can understand the language used in the plainsong. Chant is, above all, a prayer: a prayer constant, fervent, and humble, a prayer filled with wisdom and peace from the Holy Spirit.

RETREATS

Go, sit in your cell, and engrave it in your heart.

ABBA AMMONAS, DESERT FATHER

The arrival of spring and good weather in general increases the number of visitors to the monastery, in particular those searching to make a retreat or seeking a place of spiritual rest. St. Benedict reminds us in the *Rule* that such visitors are never lacking in a monastery and must be as welcome as Christ himself. Visitors sometimes knock at our doors from far away or places one never heard of. It never ceases to amaze me, and respectfully I ask myself, *How do they find us?*" More and more I learn from these transient visitors the deep need for silence and quiet. The world is a vociferous, noisy enterprise today, and one can easily get lost in its turbulent midst. Some of the new arrivals come to a monastic solitude such as ours simply for a change of scenery, others with a deep spiritual hunger, others when traversing a life change and in need of quiet to reflect and make sense of their lives.

Retreating to a monastery has a long and remarkable tradition. Throughout the centuries, sages have sought out desert solitude to retreat, reflect, rest, recuperate, and renew their inner selves. The Lord did this himself during the forty days in the desert, and others today sometimes imitate his example by seeking out shelter in a monastic ambience. Our visitors often tell me how a quiet stay in our midst enhances their minds and spirits and gives a much-needed rest to their physical beings.

STEADY PLANTING

We await the final outcome of events, remembering who it is who plows the earth of our souls.

ST. JOHN CHRYSOSTOM

The soothing warm weather emboldens our spirits to steadily continue the work of early planting. The Vassar students who are working in our good-sized vegetable garden have decided to plant several varieties of sunflowers today. Every year, we plant a few rows of sunflowers by the fence surrounding the garden. In late summer, when the sunflowers are in full bloom, one gets the feeling of being fenced in by their natural display of rare beauty. There is something very attractive about the line of sunflowers encircling the garden. Since they are usually giant, tall, and strong, one gets the feeling that they are the natural guardians of an enclosed garden. Come summer, when the sunflowers show the splendor of their rustic beauty, I shall be able to cut a few and place them in large pottery vases in the chapel. A simple bouquet of sunflowers and large zinnias brighten our otherwise dark and austere oratory. Moreover, their presence in such a sacred place offers humble and subtle homage to the Lord who made them.

APRIL 18

PATIENCE

Patience gains all things.

ST. TERESA OF ÁVILA

The daily monastic routine is good pedagogy at all times. The small struggles of our daily monastic life, be they planting and weeding the garden, feeding and tending to our farm animals, the steady vinegar preparation, or any other daily chore are all occasions to learn to practice patience. All the situations teach me daily how much in need I am of learning the lesson of Christian patience. Christ, our Master, was patient until the very end. He endured his passion with utmost humble patience. In contrast to the rest of us, who are always trying to escape discomfort and pain, Jesus embraced it bluntly and made no fuss about it. The lesson and mystery of being patient as Christ was is encapsulated in the mystery of the cross. Christ practiced and lived patience until the end of his life, even accepting death on the cross. Patience seems to be the normal framework that allows us to imitate and encounter the Lord in life's smallest details, no matter how cumbersome they may be.

PLANTING THE EARLY SALAD GREENS

They sowed fields and planted their vines, brought in an abundant harvest. God blessed them, and they increased greatly.

PSALM 107:37–38

Sustainable agriculture comes naturally to monasteries that carry with them a centuries-old tradition of cultivating the land and living from what their gardens produce. Though many in our times contest this premise, often calling it impractical for the twenty-first century, some of us hold on to this cherished monastic tradition. For this is not only monastic but also a basic human activity based on real human needs. This is perhaps one reason why I feel closer to local farmers, growers, and participants in the local farmers markets. We all share the same goals and aspirations.

A concrete application of sustainable agriculture for us here today is preparing the land with organic soil enrichment and making the necessary rows for the planting. We are salad consumers in the monastery, so our earliest seasonal planting consists of multiple varieties of salad greens: lettuce varieties, mesclun, regular arugula, arugula selvatica, chicories, radishes, mustard greens, crests escaroles, and chervil, which blends so well with the greens. With the Vassar students helping today, we organize the raised beds where the planting takes place. The French intensive method of planting the crops in the raised beds very close together works well there, and so we adhere to that tradition. All in all, there were about fifteen varieties of salad greens planted today. That is quite an accomplishment. Sustainable agriculture is all about eating local, regional produce, developing healthier eating habits, a deep appreciation for the land that produces such wonder, and profound gratitude to the Lord for his continual care for us all. For, indeed, if the Lord does not watch and protect our crops, our work is in vain.

THE LIVING TRADITION

Why do you seek the living one among the dead?
LUKE 24:5

Behold, I make all things new.
REVELATION 21:5

Recently someone sent me an article about a certain new monastery founded by a group of monks from a distant country. Like some new groups that seem to be emerging these days, this one wishes to return to what members call the ancient observance of *The Rule of St. Benedict.* Some of the ideals they pursue perplex me a bit. As a trained psychologist, I am interested in searching out the deeper motivation of some of these new groups, for they in some ways seem to share many principles and ideals among themselves. In most cases, there seems to be a certain rejection of the renewed structures of monastic life, and their intention is to return to something they imagine to be pure and undiluted, especially where it concerns worship. Most of these individuals prefer to celebrate their religious offices in antique styles and languages, often a dead language not even spoken by the Lord or the apostles. And it is not enough that the Eucharist be celebrated in Latin, it must be in the *antiquor* rite, that is, the Tridentine rite. It is pure, solemn, dignified, reverent—or so they claim.

In my view, these groups are more concerned with aesthetics, ritual pageantry, and a certain idea of perfection than they are about the simple, pure worship of God. They often idealize a certain past that was neither perfect nor totally coherent, such as the times of the Middle Ages. Their claim seems to me to be one more consonant with the romanticism of a certain period and culture than one based on the soundness of the Gospels and the reality of today. This is the basic idea and motivation that guides their conception of monastic life and worship. They don't mind at all spending millions of dollars constructing monastic buildings in the so-called classic medieval style, for they say these are meant to be fortresses to last 1,000 years. It doesn't bother them in the least that Christ lived poor, frugally, to the extent that he didn't even possess a stone on which to lay his head. The example of Gospel living doesn't apply to their case; what matters is one's romantic notion of what is beautiful classic, perfect, perennial. The humble realism found in the Gospels is totally absent from their thinking. What matters to them are the external structures that represent this idealized conception of worship and monastic life. The externals count in their case, and about the rest one does not worry.

These attitudes or sort of fantasy are not new. Actually, they were prevalent in all ages, and Jesus faced them again and again during his own earthly days. How often was he criticized for not following the minutia of the law or not adhering to certain rituals? He reminded the Samaritan woman that the days will come when the Lord will not be worshiped on this mountain or that mountain, in this style or that style, in this language or that language. Instead, he said the Father seeks those who shall worship him in spirit and truth. Jesus had no patience with people who were only concerned with trivia, externals, fantasy, or superficiality. He always went to the heart of the matter and reminded his followers that God is not to be found through purely external rituals but only through pure faith.

During these days of Eastertide, the forty days after the resurrection, it is a good practice to pray to the Lord to grant us the gift of simplicity, faith, and realism found throughout the Gospels. They are essential for true Christian living, for we can't go about like the Pharisees, claiming that we worship God simply through merely external practices. We must be concerned primarily with what is interior, hidden, surpassing the judgment of human eyes, and seek the Living One among the living and not among the dead.

The risen Lord, the Living One, is the Lord of all of life. Each generation is called to rediscover him anew, to encounter him in the time we live in. To romanticize the past and to wish to return to old anachronistic forms is to miss the point of the Holy Spirit's action in the times in which we live, act, and move. God is the Lord of the living, and as we turn the page on history, we open to a new one, where new light and new understanding are given to us of the mystery that has been from the beginning and shall be unto ages of ages.

It is true that all of us are enriched by past traditions. One has much to learn from them. But tradition itself is a living thing. It continues, it progresses. It goes on as we speak. Tradition is not stuck at a certain point in history. As it continues to develop under the guidance of the Spirit, it enlightens and inspires renewed forms of worship and monastic living. Tradition doesn't tell us to return to the past. On the contrary, it opens new possibilities as we confront our own time in history. Christ is the Lord of the living, and being alive means moving forward with him courageously, walking the Gospel path with new insights and determination.

St. Anselm of Canterbury and St. Anastasius of Mount Sinai, Monks

PRAYER

When I was a young monk and remained in my cell, I set no limitations to unceasing prayer. The whole night was for me as much the time of prayer as the day.

ABBA ISIDORE, DESERT FATHER

The monastic life is essentially and foremost a school of prayer. In the monastery, the monk or nun slowly learns to stand before God daily. In the quiet of his heart, the monk learns to speak to God, and even more importantly, he learns to listen to God. If we practice silence in our everyday life, it is not for the sake of shutting out speech but for creating a quiet heart inside each of us that is capable of hearing God's voice within. The monk faces the daily reality that he is poor, unstable, limited, and totally empty of any gifts. The wonderful paradox about prayer is that during it, God fills that emptiness to overflowing. No matter what our spiritual state is, what our poverty, attachments, illusions, or human distractions may be, whatever our frailty and failures be, through our prayer intercourse the Lord raises the level of our ordinary lives to another realm. We may not reach the ecstatic state of some of the mystics, but instead become a humble, living prayer candle, whose fire and flame also enkindles others to seek the Lord through continual prayer.

EARTH DAY

The earth is the L*ORD's and all it holds,*
The world and those who dwell in it,
for he founded it on the seas,
established it over the rivers.

PSALM 24:1–2

It is a lovely day in the Hudson Valley. The weather is perfectly glorious. As I drive to do errands in Poughkeepsie, I notice the apple trees are all in bloom. I am totally taken by their gentle beauty and by the fact that they are blossoming rather early this year. After all, it is April and not May when they usually blossom.

The sunny, bright weather seems altogether in synchronicity for Earth Day celebrations. One of the local newspapers makes the claim that Earth Day, now decades old, has become the largest annual civic secular event in the world.

Like all good things, this environmental movement started with a small idea. A certain U.S. senator spent several years raising awareness about the disintegration of our environment. In the fall of 1969, he announced that on April 22, 1970, there would be a large grass-roots demonstration seeking protection and respect for the environment. There was a tremendous response around the country, especially from young people and the media, who gave their support. Thus, Earth Day was born. There is much to celebrate on Earth Day, for many of the U.S. environmental agencies that today look out to safeguard our natural resources were inspired by this mass movement.

Monks are natural ecologists and fierce environmentalists, for foremost with the worship of God lies our stewardship of the monastic land he entrusted to us. In solidarity with people everywhere, we celebrate the earth the Lord has given and entrusted to our care. As we toil it daily, we remember that we are only its present custodians and that we must preserve it carefully for future generations to come.

EARTH TO EARTH

Monastic frugality is an everyday passionate practice in a monastery. Nothing ever gets wasted within the monastic confines. Take, for instance, the leftovers from the kitchen: All the waste, peels, vegetables, and fruits are piled up in a bin and recycled in our good-size compost pile next to the barn.

Composting is essential for our gardens, and throughout the years we are blessed to add new layers of what is described as "black gold" to the gardens. And what a difference it eventually makes! Our gardens are totally organic, thus we refuse to add any sort of chemical fertilizers to the ground. Instead, every year we keep adding the rich compost accumulated from the previous years beside the waste from the kitchen. The leaves collected in the fall, the ashes from the wood stoves, the manure from the sheep and chickens are all unobtrusively saved and added to the compost pile. Time and the winter snow help to decompose all organic matter, and with the arrival of spring the students and I eagerly transport the compressed black gold to wherever it is needed in the vegetable and flower beds. Composting is a good way to remain faithful to our frugal monastic lifestyle and also show respect for the earth and the natural cycles of life.

POTATO PLANTING

We make our way day by day, creeping along, or hurrying or flying, if all comes to the same ultimately, and one day it will all go into insignificance, worked and woven into the present of heaven, wholly.

MOTHER MARIA, HER LIFE IN LETTERS

One of the yearly rites of spring in our monastery is the planting of the potatoes. With the weather being unusually warm this week, I suggested that our five Vassar College interns get their tools and start preparing a certain section of the garden for the planting. No one came to plow this year, so all the labor had to be done by hand. The untidy condition of the garden calls for hard, steady work, and the students were ready for the challenge. They enjoyed knowing that we go through the same delightful ritual year after year: In the spring one group of students does the planting and then in the fall a new group does the harvesting. Moreover, since we save enough potatoes each year for the planting, I let them know that these particular organic potatoes have known and have been cultivated by previous Vassar generations. They enjoy the idea of the continuity of an established tradition. These potatoes, I tell them, bring happy memories to me, as it will do to them eventually. All in all, five varieties of potatoes were planted today; the most common and prolific among them is the well-known red potato. Late April, when the weather is good, is an ideal time for planting them. That means we can start enjoying them at the table as early as July. Thanks be to God.

ROGATION DAYS

How Love burns through the putting in the seed
or through the watching for that early birth
when, just as the soil tarnishes with weed,
the steady seedling with arched body comes
shouldering its ways and shedding the earth crumbs.

ROBERT FROST, "PUTTING IN THE SEED"

I always experience a unique kind of joy on the days we feast an evangelist or an apostle, for they knew the Lord in a close, intimate way, and through their inspired writings they transmitted his message to generations to come. St. Mark the evangelist has always been one of my dear friends, for his Gospel shed abundant light in many dark moments in my life and opened a luminous path to follow.

On St. Mark's day it is customary in monasteries to bless the fields and gardens. Monks keep the ancient tradition of the "Rogation Days," and embark in an intercessory procession throughout the fields and gardens, pleading for God's blessing upon the newly planted seedlings. As the procession marches through the fields, usually the abbot or main celebrant asperges the land with holy water while the monks sing a litany (usually the litany of the saints) begging the Lord for a good and safe harvest in the months to come. Later on in the season, just before the feast of the Ascension, they shall again repeat the rogation ritual and once more pray that the Lord may render fruitful what has been seeded and planted in his name.

GARDEN UTENSILS

A gardener should have a fork, a wide blade, a spade or shovel, a knife...a seed basket for seed-time, a wheelbarrow (more often a little hand-cart), basket, pannier, and trap for sparrow-hawks...a two-edged axe to uproot thorns, brambles, briars, prickles, and unwanted shoots, and stakes or hedging hurdles...timbers, palings, and stakes or hedging hurdles....He should also have a knife from his belt to graft trees and seedlings, mattocks with which to uproot nettles or verch, darnel, thistles, sterile oats, and weeds of this sort, and a hoe for tares.

DE UTENSILIBUS, TWELFTH-CENTURY ENGLISH MANUSCRIPT

Garden books from the past and their all-practical quotes are not necessarily instances of nostalgia for a past that no longer exists. On the contrary, I continue nurturing my spirit with their wise counsels, finding some of the past gardening principles timely and invaluable. This particular quote from a medieval English manuscript seems so consonant with a principle St. Benedict established in the *Rule*: that all garden utensils must be treated and respected as the sacred vessels of the altar. I always find this particular passage of the *Rule* impregnated with that basic common sense that characterized St. Benedict. Monastic horticultural records from subsequent ages never deviated from the wisdom found in the past. They simply added to it the new knowledge accumulated from their most recent experience. The monks learned from the experience of their elders and also continued finding new ways of caring for their land, sometimes inventing newer practical tools that facilitated their work.

DELIGHTING ON A SPRING DAY

Green turf amid silent trees and soft light airs
And a spring of running water in the grass,
They freshen a jaded mind, they give me back to myself
They make me abide in myself.

MEDITATION AMONG THE TREES,
TWELFTH-CENTURY FRENCH MANUSCRIPT

Today's sunshine and the balmy weather make one reflect on spring's particular charm. As I drive the mountain road across the Taconic Parkway, I glance at a glorious tapestry of diverse greens in the trees, in the fields. Everything everywhere has now turned green, a tender, almost mellowed green. That new green in nature is a clear symbol of a renewal of life all around us. After a long, harsh winter, still lingering in our minds and not yet totally forgotten, spring emerges as a new reality, a new beginning built on the memory of the past season. Farmers and gardeners know intuitively the connection between last year's decay and the promise of renewal spring brings. They experience it daily in the fertility of the soil. Out of the dead leaves from the fall, the mulch, and winter debris, spring brings new life to the soil, new life to us humans, new life to all of nature. The deadly decay experienced during winter doesn't possess the last word. The resurrection occurs in spring, and thus our liturgy attests to the ever-changing power of the season, its unique power to renew God's earth and the world around us. The resurrection sanctifies spring as a season, makes it whole and fertile, magical and full of wonder.

One Little Task at a Time

Do one little thing
It is much more efficient
Than doing nothing

HAIKU SAYING

Sometimes, during our early spring days, one gets overwhelmed by the multitude of formidable tasks at hand. They arrive all at once and we must decide which to attend to first. I do not enjoy either the pressure or the "hectic, overwhelming" feeling. It is not monastic, and I often wonder how the Desert Fathers would have reacted under such conditions. As I place my hands on the task in front of me, I reflect on how best to handle in a proper monastic manner the work pressure I presently feel.

From the monastic tradition of work, I learned in the past the most efficient approach to any given task is to concentrate on one thing at a time and avoid what is now called multitasking. I give my full attention to only one thing at a time, concentrate the present moment to it, no matter how small or big the task may be. This helps me put all my energy and efforts on only one thing: the matter at hand. It also helps me avoid a scatter-minded attitude, a terrible enemy of the soul. Choosing only one small task at a time and becoming fully engaged and focused on it alone helps me avoid all forms of compulsion. I do one task at a time, no matter what, and when it gets concluded I move on to the next. The same approach awaits me until it becomes a steady habit and I no longer think about it constantly or feel pressured or overwhelmed. This healthy monastic attitude helps me to achieve mastery over myself, being in control of the tasks instead of being controlled by them.

FARM STEWARDSHIP

Stewardship is the acceptance from God of personal responsibility for all of life and life's affairs.

ROSWELL C. LONG

No trick from the weather ever stops us in the monastery from our daily duties at the farm or in the gardens. As St. Benedict reminds us in the *Rule*, we are stewards of the land the Lord has entrusted to us and all it contains: our buildings, farm animals, gardens, fields, water, trees. Monastic stewardship is all-embracing, and it requires the constant care and sustained nurturing of those precious gifts God placed at our disposal. There is no room for indifference or carelessness in monastic stewardship, but there is plenty of space for creativity and finding new ways of becoming better servants of God.

Today's events in the animal care and husbandry aspect of our lives are a case in point. Our chickens, a bit confused by the early warm weather, began sitting on their eggs about three weeks ago, and today the first of them hatched: six baby chicks, three white and three yellow. This burst of new life in the chicken coop is a special occasion of joy here for all those involved. It is also a reminder of our responsibility and vocation to be loyal stewards of God's creation. Monastic stewardship means cooperation with the Lord to tend and lovingly care for these new arrivals, these precious little animals that in years ahead shall provide us with part of our daily nourishment. Monks, as faithful stewards, treasure and show immense respect for even the smallest of God's gifts.

PLANTING THE BEANS

He who would a gardener be
In this book can hear and see
Every day of the month and year
And what skills he must master.

JON GARDENER, *THE FEATE OF GARDENING*
(ENGLISH, FIFTEENTH CENTURY)

Spring is advancing rapidly this year. There is so much work to be done in the vegetable garden. Even with the help of the Vassar interns three times a week, we can hardly accomplish all the projects we have in mind for a particular day. Today a certain section of the vegetable garden needs to be turned and smoothed, thoroughly cleared for bean planting. This section of the garden is next to the potato patch that was planted last week. I thank the Lord for the good weather, for it motivates us wholly by creating inside of us an irresistible desire to plunge into the task at hand. As we plant the seeds (or beans, as is the case today), one comes to comprehend how much gardening and the spiritual life are intertwined in daily monastic life. The monk gardener respects the fact that the Lord appoints each season for a certain task and each task for its corresponding season. There is a special grace, an extraordinary synergy in working and toiling daily in harmony with the seasons. God is the Author and Creator of the seasons, and who knows better than him when and how we must labor to render the soil fertile, thus bringing fruit from the earth to feed our needs.

MAY

MAY 1

ST. JOSEPH, THE WORKER

Dear St. Joseph,
Humble patron saint of all workers (including gardeners),
We praise and honor you,
For you taught Christ our God
The meaning and joy of human labor.

SALUTATION TO ST. JOSEPH, THE WORKER

After a long, severe winter such as the one we just traversed, the magic month of May arrives with plenty of sunshine all around. Midspring inexorably brings joy to all gardeners, for not only the early flowers and shrubs are in bloom, but now is the time to seriously begin gardening out-of-doors.

We gather our tools from the shed or garage, wherever they are stored. We clean them up and make them ready for the occasion. We continue cleaning and clearing the vegetable patches, the flower beds, and herb gardens, getting them ready for early planting. Gardening tasks at this time are multiple and demand our full engagement.

As I dig some rows in the vegetable garden and enjoy the rays of the sun invigorating my tired back, I think of St. Joseph, the worker and gardener. I am sure that with his carpentry skills he also cultivated a small cottage garden sufficient enough to provide for the needs of the Holy Family. At all times, St. Joseph is a perfect model for all monks, for all Christians. No one outside of Christ himself lived more perfectly the monastic motto, *ora et labora*. With unique tenacity, St. Joseph combined marvelously his complete devotion to God with fidelity to work and to his ordinary daily duties, such as carpentry and gardening.

As I continue dutifully toiling throughout the day, I often address to St. Joseph the following supplication:

> Our father St. Joseph,
> humble man of God,
> diligent guardian of Jesus and Mary.
> Remain always
> the faithful guardian of our souls.

MAY 2 · St. Athanasius, Bishop and Church Father

NEW GARDENING TRENDS

Things only have the value that we give them.

MOLIÈRE

Here in the Northeast, there is a new trend of sound ecological farming and simpler landscape design. It is a form of gardening and arranging landscapes that integrate the natural setting, the beauty of the garden's location, and the function for which it is designed. This new type of gardening applies especially to flower or all green gardens and to vegetable and herb gardens. The concept is there for all of us to rethink and improve on our more traditional approaches to gardening. I immensely support a concept that puts greater emphasis on simplicity and the functional aspects of a particular garden. All true gardeners should be mindful of these principles and put them into daily practice. It will make life easier for them and certainly simplify their tasks.

TWO CHERISHED APOSTLES

The act of putting into your mouth what the earth has grown is perhaps the most direct interaction with the earth.

FRANCES MOORE LAPPÉ, 1976

Today the liturgy marks the feast of two apostles of the Lord: Philip and James. Not much is known about this particular James, but Philip is better known to us, for he seems more present in the Gospels. He is particularly known for his request to Jesus: "Lord, show us the Father," to which Jesus wisely responded, "Whoever has seen me has seen the Father." Jesus' response reveals to us something of the mystery of the triune God, of his intimate relationship with his Father. His response sustains and nurtures our prayer. It strengthens our faith; it restores our hope.

Yesterday afternoon, before the rain arrived, I transplanted several basil plants and the two types of parsley we grow in the greenhouse into the outdoor raised beds in the vegetable gardens. They have thus joined all the seedlings previously planted during these past two weeks: salad greens of all varieties, beets, carrots, leeks, turnips, arugulas, and garlic. To many people, these gardens seem like time-consuming chores: all pointless, impractical, a waste of our time. To those of us who daily work the land and try to live from a sustainable form of agriculture, we know that one day these tiny seedlings will be transformed into full-grown vegetables and herbs that time and again shall nurture and sustain our particular quality of life, the type of path we have chosen, in conformity with our faith and the human Gospel values we cherish.

PRAISE TO OUR LADY

Hail, from whom alone there springs
 the unfading Rose;
Hail, for thou hast born the
 sweetly smelling Apple.
Hail, Maiden unwedded, nosegay of the only King
 and preservation of the world.
Hail, Lady, treasure-house of purity, raising us
 from our fall;
Hail, Lily whose sweet scent is known to
 all the faithful;
Hail, fragrant incense and precious oil of myrrh.

ACATHIST HYMN TO THE *THEOTOKOS*

THE DAZZLING UNCERTAINTY OF THE WEATHER

Spring shows
What God can do
With a drab and dirty world.
REV. VIRGIL A. KRAFT

One of the brightest insights into our New York-New England weather, according to Mark Twain in a speech he gave in 1876, "is the dazzling uncertainty of it." We dwellers of this immense space called the Northeast know full well that Mark Twain's comments are timely; they still apply today. For instance, it can be clear and sunny in New York City and New Jersey, and here on the Dutchess County-Connecticut border it could be raining or snowing heavily, as it has the last couple of days and as the weathercasters seem to predict for the remainder of the week until Sunday, when the sun is expected to reappear for Mother's Day. My work in the garden under such conditions is limited to the in-between moments, when the rain decides to take a rest.

Frankly speaking, I can't complain too much about the inconveniences brought by the rain, for, in fact, after the intense work of the last two weeks, we need the rain to help the tiny, recently planted seeds germinate and sprout. As Hugh Johnson points out in his 1996 book *Hugh Johnson's Gardening Companion,* "Rain never falls when we want it, but it falls in the end, and if it did not there would be no gardens, no plants, no life at all."

THE LILACS ARE IN BLOOM

The gift of perfume to a flower is a special grace like genius or like beauty, and it never becomes common or cheap.

JOHN BURROUGHS (1837–1921)

In the monastery land and throughout the surrounding countryside, the lilacs are coming into full blossom, enticing all of us with their glorious colors and pure, intoxicating perfume. On a clear day like today, or even on a rainy day like yesterday, it is a joy to work in the garden in close proximity to the lilacs. They have grown so tall through the years. I still remember them as small bushes when I first planted them. And Dolores, our French friend from New York City who loved lilacs, would always visit the monastery the week they were in bloom. She would take a bouquet of them back to her apartment.

The delightful scent from the lilacs can be sensed, smelled all throughout the property, even from the chicken coop. Today I'll enjoy placing some lilacs on the monastery dining table and some others in the chapel, by the paschal candle and the resurrection icon. As we enter the chapel for prayer, we shall inhale their sweet fragrance as pure incense, breathing a canticle of praise to their Creator. Like all good things in the garden, God created the lilacs for our pleasure and joy. What better thing can we do than offer them back to the Lord in a simple act of praise?

PLANTING AND FARMING FOR THE SOUL

A humane, sustainable agriculture has always been an integral component of the Christian monastic tradition. From St. Antony, the father of monks, who cultivated his garden in the middle of the desert, to St. Benedict following the same path in Subiaco and Monte Cassino, to the Cistercian monks and nuns in the Middle Ages cultivating large parcels of land, monks have been concerned with the way food is raised and how it gets from the monastic farm, or grange as it was called in the Middle Ages, to the kitchen table. Some monks were even inspired to write recipes for the vegetables and herbs grown in their gardens!

In our day, many people, especially the young, are rediscovering the connection between the way food is grown and the environment. Here in our small monastery, we have a positive experience with the Vassar students who are part of an environmental studies program at the college. They apply for an internship with us to learn from the monastic tradition its age-old, faith-based environmental approach to sustainable agriculture. Not only do the students learn and partake of the agriculture methods inspired by our tradition, they get credit from their school for it.

Today a group of students, myself, and a volunteer continued with some of our early planting tasks in the vegetable garden: a variety of beans and Swiss chard were planted in neat rows. Another student, with the help of her visiting mother, worked in the herb garden cleaning, weeding, planting thyme, oregano, and dill, and then planting a variety of mints. This collaboration between the college environmental community and the monastery brings to mind Van Jones' speech to the 2009 Green Jobs Conference: "In an environmental movement, you don't just count what you make, you count what you save. And when you invest in connecting the people who need work most....With the work that most needs doing, you save the soul of this country. That's what you save."

TENDING CREATION: THE LAND, THE GARDEN

The fourth-century father, St. Ephrem the Syrian, says in his *Hymns on Paradise*:

The fool, who is unwilling to realize his honorable state,
Prefers to become just an animal, rather than a man,
So that, without incurring judgment, he may serve naught but his lusts.
But had there been sown in animals just a little
Of the sense of discernment, then long ago would the wild asses have lamented
And wept at their not having been human.

St. Ephrem does not condone an ecologically destructive anthropocentrism. He does not say that human beings are masters over creation with the right to use it solely for their own selfish purposes or comfort. Rather, he reminds us that everything comes from God and that without God's constant nurture, nothing would be and nothing could grow. "Neither the one who plants nor the one who waters is anything," writes St. Paul, "but only God, who causes the growth." Indeed, we are not only "co-workers" in God's great garden; we ourselves are God's garden (1 Corinthians 3:7–9). This is the ground and reason for a noble type of humility on our part, as simple mere creatures among all other creatures loved by God.

THE INNER LIFE

In the beginning there are a great many trials and much suffering for those who are advancing toward God and afterwards, ineffable joy arrives. It is like those who wish to light a fire; at first they are choked by the smoke and cry, and by this means obtain what they are after (as it is said: "Our God is a consuming fire" (Hebrews 12: 29): So we also must kindle the divine fire in ourselves through tears of repentance and hard work.

AMMA SYNCLETICA

For the desert monks, as it should be for all of us, all true inner life consists in making real in our lives St. Paul's words: "For me, to live is Christ." All interior life is about Christ being present in our lives, truly living in us. St. Benedict never ceased to repeat to his disciples the same teaching: "Prefer nothing to the love of Christ." And of course, we know Christ is a concrete person, not an abstraction, an idea, or something subjective.

All true inner life demands this continual personal rapport with him who is both the Son of God and the beloved of our hearts. At all times we keep close to him, as Abba Paul counsels us, and in all life's circumstances we keep our eyes fixed on him, Christ, our Master. Eventually our spirituality is reduced to this simple, continual rapport/dialogue with him who is both our Savior and our Beloved. As the *Book of Canticles* describes it: "My Beloved to me and I to him."

PLANTING FROM SEEDS

Do not damage the land or the sea or the trees....

REVELATION 7:3

It is a command from the revealed word of God not to hurt the environment and to care for the land, the water, and for all living things, God's own creation. And among these living things we include not only all human beings but also the kingdoms of animals and vegetation.

Planting continues in earnest in our gardens during these early May days: We divide and transplant certain herbs and perennials, and ceaselessly we continue planting seeds in the vegetable garden: carrots, beets, turnips, radishes. There is a perennial mystery in the propagation of plants from tiny, almost microscopic, seeds. Again the Lord provides human beings with this wonderful gift, this unique reality called a seed. And from the seeds, all our food in the vegetation kingdom is raised weekly, monthly, yearly. As a Chinese proverb tells us: "All the flowers (and all the vegetables) of all the tomorrows are in the seeds of today."

MAY 11

THE HOLY ABBOTS OF CLUNY

If we truly and humbly seek God, he will show himself to us, and if we keep him, he will remain close to us at all times.

ABBA ARSENIUS

Today the monastic family keeps the memorial of the Holy Abbots of Cluny, a monastery famous in the Middle Ages and whose millennium was recently celebrated. I remember once reading their conception of a monastery, something that moved me deeply. They saw a monastery not as a series of monastic buildings but primarily as God's house, as the place where the Lord dwells and manifests himself to others. In a monastery, poor and simple as it may be, God's glory shines forth, and those who visit it (St. Benedict says guests are never lacking in a monastery) feel the rays of his glory shining through the warm welcome offered to the visitor. Monastic hospitality becomes God's epiphany to the guests and to those who welcome them into the monastery, a continual reminder of the Lord's presence in our midst.

MAY 12

Sts. Epiphanius of Palestine, Monk; and Germain of Constantinople, Bishop

EEDS

I ask not for a larger garden,
But for finer seeds.

RUSSELL HERMAN CONWELL

A short piece of wisdom from the 1854 *Farmer's Almanac*:

Scatter ye seeds each passing year,
Sow amid winds and storms of rain,
Hope give the courage,
Faith cast our fear,
God will requite thee
With infinite grain.

The simple act of sowing and planting seeds in due season is a powerful and most rewarding one both for gardeners and farmers. The power comes from the fact that in cooperating with the Creator, we build up our own food security and that of those who partake of our table. We basically garden to feed ourselves naturally, inexpensively, and in a healthy manner, and there is always the added joy when the fruit of our work is shared with others.

Ascension Day

O Lord, life-giving Christ,
When the apostles saw you ascending upon the clouds
A great sadness filled them.
They shed burning tears and exclaimed:
O dear Master, do not leave us orphans!
We are your servants whom you love so tenderly,
Send your Holy Spirit, as you promised, to enlighten our souls.

BYZANTINE VESPERS OF THE FEAST

The feast of the Ascension is always a glorious feast, for it is Christ's final glorification on earth before he departs to the Father. It is a beautiful feast but also one full of nostalgia. From Easter plus forty days, we have truly enjoyed the presence of the risen Lord in our midst, and suddenly—like the apostles—we are seemingly left as orphans. The Lord is taken from us. Through faith, we know he's ascending to the Father and from there, in a mysterious way, he will be closer to us than ever. But he will no longer be visible. Humans that we are, we crave his physical presence, just as the apostles once did.

Today the Lord ascends to the Father with the same body that once was born in a humble stable in Bethlehem and later underwent the pain of being crucified in Calvary. Today the Father bestows upon him the glory that was his from all eternity, and from where he shall come one day to judge the world. While it may seem we will be left orphans until he comes again, he promises to all his followers the consoling presence of the Holy Spirit. The Spirit reminds us daily of all the Master taught and lived, and Christ shall signal to us the ways to follow him steadily during our earthly pilgrimage until the day we also ascend and share in his glory.

A GARDENER'S PRAYER

The thirteenth-century Cistercians were known for their love of agriculture and steady gardening. One of them, Guerric d'Igny, expressed it beautifully in his own gardener's prayer. This is my own translation from the French:

Lord Jesus,
You are the true gardener of our souls;
You are their creator and cultivator,
And the fierce guardian of your garden.
You plant the seeds by your words,
You water them by your Spirit,
And you make them grow by your power.
Lord, whoever is invited into your garden
Becomes himself a well-watered garden
That keeps growing and blossoms,
And whose fruits are ever multiplied.

A FATHER OF CENOBITES

Our monastic calendar marks today the memorial of a cherished father of early monasticism, our father, Pachomius. In our modest chapel, his icon stands close to that of our father, St. Antony, thus showing them as pioneers in the monastic movement. One of the lesser-known *Apophthegmata Patrum* (sayings or quotes from the Desert Fathers) describes him best:

> Abba Psenthisios, Abba Souros, and Abba Psoios used to agree in saying this: "Whenever we listened to the words of our father, Abba Pachomius, we were greatly helped and spurred on with the zeal for good works; we saw how, even when he kept silence, he taught us by his example. We were amazed by him and we used to say to each other, 'We thought that all the saints were created as saints by God and never changed from their mother's womb, not like other men. We thought that sinners could not live devoutly, justly, because they have been so created.' But now we see the goodness and mercy of God manifested in our father, Pachomius, for see, he was of pagan origin and he has become devout; he has kept all of God's commandments. Thus even we also can follow him and become equal to the saints whom he himself has followed. Truly as it is written: 'Come to me, all you who are weary and are carrying heavy burdens and I will give you rest' (Matthew 11:28). Let us die to ourselves then, and let us live with him, because he has brought us to God in the right and correct way."

STEADY GARDENING

All the days of the earth, seed time and harvest....

GENESIS 8:22

Gardening is a very wholesome employment.

SHAKER SAYING

After the last few days of steady rain, the weather has broken, and the trees throughout the monastic enclave are in full blossom. As I drive by, I see many stores and roadside vendors are showing the best of their gardening selections outside. Everywhere in the locality, we see signs to entice avid gardeners to get to work. In one of the stores I visited today, they were displaying colorful perennials and annuals just arrived from the south, where they were first grown in huge greenhouses. Next to the flowers, one could see rows and rows of early vegetable seedlings, some herbs, both perennial and annual, all ready to be planted outdoors. It is mid-May, just past Mother's Day, and one feels an intensity in the air to rush to our gardens and do the necessary planting. In our monastic gardens, with the help of Vassar students and other friends, we have been working steadily since early April. We are not totally behind in our work, but of course we are well aware that we don't have a minute to waste. We toil steadily each day, counting always on the Lord to bless the work of our hands.

THE GLORY OF THE ASCENSION

O Christ, splendor and glory of the Father,
as we behold your Ascension on the holy mountain,
we sing a hymn to the beauty of your countenance.
We bow down to your Sacred Passion,
We venerate your Resurrection
And glorify your noble Ascension.
O Lord, ascended into glory, have mercy on us.

BYZANTINE VESPERS OF THE ASCENSION

We are truly blessed and enriched spiritually here in this small monastery by being able to be nourished daily by the liturgical traditions of both the East and the West. In the Eastern Church, the Ascension feast is described by a Greek word that translates as "the taking up." This expression signifies that by ascending into his glory Jesus completed his work on earth, that is, the work of our redemption. In contrast, the expression used in the Western Church is that of the ascension, which implies the Lord was raised up to the glory of the Father by his own power. Both expressions complement each other perfectly and enrich our understanding of the mystery. It is a feast of great antiquity; like most feasts, it originated in the East, where the living memory of the ascension became a permanent tradition among the disciples of the Lord. The Church fathers, both of the East and the West, testified through their beautiful homilies as to the prominence of the mystery of the ascension. At the conclusion of second Vespers today, the paschal candle in our chapel shall be extinguished. This is a reminder to us that Christ, our true light and the Light of the World, has departed from the earth.

A PRAYER FROM THE MOZARABIC LITURGY

Most loving God and Father,
You know how weak I am,
Do not leave me to myself,
But take me under your protection
And give me the grace
To act upon my holy resolutions.
Enlighten my understanding
With a lively faith,
Raise up my will to a firm hope,
And inflame it with active charity.
Give me strength in my weakness,
And pour your light
Into the darkness of my heart.
Grant that I may make good use of your grace,
And persevere in faithfulness.
Heavenly Father,
Grant me the guidance of your most Holy Spirit
That I may discern your holy will,
And by the grace of the same Spirit
I may also accomplish it,
Gladly and with my whole heart,
For the glory of your Son, Jesus.
Let me, O Lord,
Spend the days ahead in gladness and peace,
Without stumbling and without stain of sin.
I praise you Eternal God,
Who are in all and above all things,
World without end. Amen.

THE MONTH OF MARY

O Mary, tranquil sea,
Distributor of peace,
Mary, fruitful earth.
You are the new tree
Which carried forth the Word, the perfumed
And only Son of God.
In you, fruitful earth, was seeded the Word.
You are both at the same time:
The earth and the tree!

ST. CATHERINE OF SIENA

The beautiful month of May is, in a special way, dedicated to our Lady, the *Theotokos.* Though the month is filled with countless activities because of the demands of the season, nevertheless one is filled with a particular joy in thinking often about the Mother of God and her unfailing protection over this small monastery dedicated to her: Our Lady of the Resurrection. At noontime, after the office and the *Regina Coeli*, her litany or some of the Akathist verses are sung in her honor. These beautiful salutations to Mary Most Holy mark the noonday hours with quiet serenity and a sense of profound peace. "Holy Mother of God, pray for us, intercede for us. Be always our refuge and come to our help."

REALISM IN MONASTIC LIFE

It was said of Abba Theodore and Abba Lucius of Enaton that they spent fifty years mocking their temptation to leave the desert by saying, "After this winter is past, we shall leave here." And when the summer came, they said, "After this summer is past, we shall go away from here." They passed all their lives doing this, these Fathers whose memory we should always preserve. And they remained at their place until the end.

ABBA THEODORE OF ENATON, *SAYINGS OF THE DESERT FATHERS*

Today while working in the garden quietly, I kept reflecting on the nature of our simple monastic life. From the beginning—from the time of the Desert Fathers; to our father, St. Benedict; to St. Bernard; up to our times—monastic life has never been static or conceived to be so. One of the principles enunciated by St. Benedict in the *Rule* remains of timeless importance. With that particular wisdom of his, he mentions that if the abbot and the monks find a better way of arranging the daily offices, different from the one he elaborated in the *Rule*, to go ahead and simply change it. St. Benedict, truly a man blessed by God, was utterly practical, filled with wisdom and common sense.

As I consider the wisdom of his teachings, I become more and more aware that a sort of monastic life based on the romantic monastic revivalism that issued from nineteenth-century France, Germany, Italy, Belgium, and Spain will eventually run out of steam, as is already happening in many monasteries that are rapidly closing their doors. Nineteenth-century notions and principles were probably good in their day, but are terribly dated and old-fashioned for the upcoming centuries. Life—of any sort and fashion—is never static but in constant motion, steadily evolving. We need a renewed vision of monastic life as evolving and moving with the times toward our ultimate destination: the consummation of all things in Christ.

And yet, monastic life, as it moves forward trusting in God, must also remain always faithful, guided by the principles of the Gospel as St. Benedict points out in the prologue of the *Rule*—principles which, in my humble view, remain timeless. I am not one who thinks that because we do not see notable growth in monasteries that monastic life itself is in danger of dying, disappearing. I know many people do. I think things will change and new forms will emerge—all in God's own time—that shall reconnect us all with the original ideals of the early monastic fathers and mothers. Monks and nuns will continue to live and seek God alone, not as people from past ages, but as people of the times and culture in which the Lord has planted them. To everything there is a time and season.

MAY 21

THE GARDEN

Around this time last year, during a busy planting season, a fellow gardener sent me this through the mail:

> Once upon a time, a man (or monk!) cultivated a garden with meticulous care. He tended it, carefully weeding so it would not be overcome with weeds. Each morning a rather "pious" man walked by, looked over the garden, and would say to the gardener: "You know, you really should be very thankful to God for this beautiful garden." After many weeks of this comment, the gardener replied: "You may be right, but you should have seen this garden when only God was taking care of it."
>
> AUTHOR UNKNOWN

MAY 22 · *St. Romanus of Auxerre, Abbot; and St. Rita of Cascia, Nun*

ECOLOGICAL WISDOM

> *All things in nature work silently. They come into being and possess nothing. They fulfill their function and make no claim. All things alike do their work, and then we see them subside. When they have reached their bloom, each returns to their origin....This reversion is an eternal law. To know that law is wisdom.*
>
> LAO-TZU, SIXTH CENTURY

So much in our daily monastic life consists in tuning ourselves again and again to the quiet, silent rhythm of Mother Nature, for Mother Nature herself is but the mirror of the Creator. There are never contradictions between the two.

Pentecost

Veni, Sancte Spiritus!

I remember a few years ago someone asked me what Pentecost meant to me. I thought for a few minutes, and then I responded by simple words:

> *Fire, Light, Mystery, Life, Promise, Fullness, Fulfillment, Plenitude, Gift, Exuberance, Heat, Radiance, Breath, Intensity, Sweetness, Consolation, Completion.*

Fire: The burning bush on Sinai was a symbol of the Holy Spirit, of the fire that cannot be extinguished, the incandescent fire of God's love, limitless, boundless.

Light is the light of God, divine light itself, that most blessed light that shines intimately in our inner heart, illuminating our darkness.

Mystery: Of the three divine persons, he is the most mysterious of all, and yet he is the one with us now, communicating God's life to our souls, until the end of time. When he wishes and to whom he wishes, he may open a bit the door to give a glimpse into his inscrutable mystery.

Life, the Holy Spirit, fountain and source of life. St. Seraphim affirms the whole purpose of our Christian life consists in the acquisition of the Holy Spirit. There is no life without him, and all spiritual life is in the Holy Spirit, fed and nurtured by him. We live, exist, and have our being in the Holy Spirit.

Promise: Jesus promised to his disciples, to each one of us, the Holy Spirit. He is the fulfillment of that promise.

Fullness: The Holy Spirit communicates to the soul mysteriously, intimately, quietly, the fullness of divine life.

For us, there is no life in Christ, except in the Holy Spirit. Our lives are fully in Christ when possessed by the Holy Spirit.

A CONTINUATION OF PENTECOST

Fulfillment: All of the ancient prophecies come into full fruition today. The spirit of the God that moved in the waters at the beginning of time appears today as living flames, as tongues of fire over the heads of the disciples. The Holy Spirit is the realization that the fullness of time has arrived.

Plenitude: The Holy Spirit is equal to the Father and to the Son, and when he is given to us at Pentecost, he brings with him the presence of the Father and the Son, for the three are inseparable. The plenitude of the Trinitarian life, the supreme divine gift, is given to us in the Holy Spirit.

Gift to the believer,
To those who hope and put their trust in Christ,
The Holy Spirit grants his gifts in abundance.
He's a treasury of blessings!

Exuberance: The Holy Spirit is the exuberance of God's goodness, God's love, God's mercy. There is no equal to the sweetness, tenderness, and delicacy his presence exudes.

Heat: The Holy Spirit is the kindling fire that with its heat keeps alive our spiritual lives. This divine heat transforms our inertness into a living, longing, and craving for God!

Radiance: The Holy Spirit is the living mirror of the Father, and the bright, luminous radiance of the Son. When we look at him, we also see the Father and the Son.

Breath: Jesus breathed the Holy Spirit over the disciples. He is the breath of God and the giver of life.

Intensity: With the presence of the Holy Spirit in our daily lives, we can feel in our activities a certain intensity. He incites us to complete surrender to the God who loves us.

Sweetness: The Holy Spirit is the best of comforters. He is the soul's sweetest guest. He is pure refreshment here below.

Consolation: The Holy Spirit, in our labor, a welcome rest, tempering heat with coolness sweet, solace, and consolation in time of trial.

Completion: Pentecost is a time of plenitude and fullness. When we experience the descent of the Holy Spirit into our lives, into our innermost, we are reminded of everything taught and said by Jesus, and the same Spirit gives us the proper understanding of those teachings. He completes our happiness today.

To love eternal life.

THE RULE OF ST. BENEDICT

I trouble not myself about the manner of future existence. I content myself with believing, even to positive conviction, that the Power that gave me existence is able to continue it, in any form and manner he pleases, with or without this body; and it appears more probable to me that I shall continue to exist hereafter than I should have had existence, as I now have, before existence began.

THOMAS PAINE, 1794

If we have but once seen any child of Adam, we have seen an immortal soul. It has not passed away, as a breeze or sunshine, but it lives; it lives at this moment in one of those many places, whether in bliss or in misery, in which all souls are reserved until the end.

JOHN HENRY CARDINAL NEWMAN, 1843

The seed of immortality has been planted in us at our inception into this world and regenerated at our baptism. It continues to unfold daily, even when we lose the awareness of it, until the day when we arrive to the lasting vision of God.

FARMERS MARKET

To fulfill God's commandments in one's activities.

THE RULE OF ST. BENEDICT: INSTRUMENTS OF GOOD WORKS

With the weekend including Memorial Day quickly approaching, I remember that the local farmers market opens on the same weekend. After finishing feeding our farm animals this morning and performing other duties around the monastery, I become fully engaged in preparing food to sell at the market. I prepare several varieties of vegetarian dips that are always popular with our regular customers: tapenade, pesto, poivronnade, salsas, and eggplant: poor man's caviar. Our dedication to farming, to our organic gardens, and to participating in the local market are visible signs of our firm commitment to sustainable agriculture, the type of agriculture that is fully human, monastic, and protects the ecological health of our fragile environment. It also provides for some of the economic needs of the monastery, and it contributes to the well-being of our neighbors and customers. Our stewardship of the monastic land and the sharing of its products are done primarily for spiritual reasons, seeking first that God be glorified in all things.

COUNSEL FROM ABBA MACARIUS

We read in the *Apophthegmata Patrum* (the *Sayings of the Desert Fathers*) that on a particular occasion Abba Macarius was asked, "How should we pray?" The old monk responded, "There is no need to use a lot of words; just stretch out your arms and say, 'Lord, do with me as you will, and know best, always have mercy upon me.' And if the conflict continues or grows fiercer, then say, 'Lord, help!' He knows very well what we need and is always ready to bestow his mercy upon us."

There is one lesson I wish we could all learn from the Desert Fathers, and that is their secret addiction to constant uninterrupted prayer. We must hear the Lord's admonition to pray without ceasing and daily aim at only one thing: to pray without putting a stop, to pray some more and continue praying, and ultimately, to never cease praying. And while doing this, we can beseech the Lord to grant us the gift of this "holy addiction" to prayer. We can simply ask him, in the apostles' words: "Lord, teach us to pray."

THE GIFT OF QUIET

To this day, I am drawn joyfully to cathedrals in every land, mosques and temples too. The stone, the light, the naves, the murmuring and mystery and quiet.

PETER MATTHIESSEN,
CIRCLE OF LIFE: RITUALS FROM THE HUMAN FAMILY ALBUM

For the past week, a California couple and their young son have been staying in our small guesthouse named after St. Scholastica. Today before leaving, they decided they wanted to plant a fruit tree on the property. They chose a nectarine, in the hope that it might survive our harsh winters. As I was leaning over the tree to examine it closely, I thanked them for their kind gesture. They told me they decided to find a way of thanking the monastery for the service of hospitality, and in particular for its quiet. The woman said, "It is so quiet here, and that is really a gift the monastery offers to and shares with us outsiders. Except for the sounds of nature, the wind or the animals, everything here remains still, quiet, silent. Here I discovered," she continued, "that I can be comfortable with quiet, with a world without noise, with the unknown. Monastic quiet is in itself a unique gift."

A FARMER'S WISDOM

Resplendent and unfading is Wisdom, and she is readily perceived by those who love her, and found by those who seek her.

WISDOM 6:12

A few times a year, I visit a farmer across the Hudson River in the Catskills. He is a professional grower, and in spite of his years he cultivates two large parcels of land, one in the Catskills and the other a bit north from us in Columbia County. With the help of migrant workers and other paid workers, he grows every type of vegetable known to us, and multiple varieties of each, from salad greens to tomatoes, acorn squash to leeks, and everything in between. His two gardens are strictly organic and they produce fantastic results. He tills the land with a certain reverence, with utmost care, as he has done for years. He personally tends to every plant, even the smallest, in his gardens. Watching over crops, weeding with his helpers, picking up every dry branch along the rows, and watering when needed. It is no wonder that his devotion to the land and his gardens renders such exquisite produce at harvest time.

Each year, it is a delight to pay a special visit to his large vegetable stand on the roadside and admire the fruit of his labors. Occasionally, I may purchase a particular vegetable or two that we don't grow in our own garden. Or some of the fruits from nearby orchards. The farmer takes pride that all he sells is grown "right in my own back yard," as he puts it. The roadside stand usually remains open until Thanksgiving, and no matter what time of day one visits him, he is always surrounded by his faithful clients who year after year depend on him for their daily food. He has earned their deepest respect, so much so that they have put the honor system into practice. At nighttime, when a client stops by the stand to fetch a needed item and the farmer is not there, they simply leave the money in a box.

GOD IS LOVE—TRINITY SUNDAY

Through the Holy Spirit, "who proceeds from the Father and reposes in the Son," we know the Son in his divinity and in the nature of man he assumed. And it is by and in the Holy Spirit that we live in the Father.

ST. SILOUAN OF MOUNT ATHOS

Dorothy Day wrote, "We cannot love God unless we love each other, and to love we must know each other. We know God in the breaking of the bread, and we know each other in the breaking of the bread, and we are not alone any more."

Dorothy Day lived the reality of love in her daily life. She put into practice the Gospel teachings about love. She loved the Lord personally and spent time with him daily in intimate conversation, and she also loved each person God sent into her life. She was gifted by the Holy Spirit to see in everyone she encountered the presence of Christ himself. Throughout the years I knew her, I was always moved by how real Christ was to her. She acted like he was there with her at all times. It was this closeness to him that allowed her to see him present in other human beings, especially the poor, the despised ones, and the oppressed. And she loved each one, for again and again she discovered his face present in each of them.

Today is Trinity Sunday, the pinnacle among our liturgical celebrations. On our own, we cannot uncover the mystery that is hidden in the intimate life of the Trinity. We poor mortals are invited to enter into that mysterious divine life and partake of its blessedness, but we could never understand or try to explain it to others. In faith and with the help of the Holy Spirit we accept our human limitations, and we simply bow in love and awe at what the mysterious life of the three divine persons represent: an eternal communion of love where, in the words of the fathers, "The Son is in the Father, the Spirit is in the Son, and the Father is in one and the other."

THE VISITATION OF MARY

During those days Mary set out and traveled to the hill country in haste to a town of Judah, where she entered the house of Zechariah and greeted Elizabeth. When Elizabeth heard Mary's greeting, the child leaped in her womb, and Elizabeth, filled with the holy Spirit, cried out in a loud voice and said, "Most blessed are you among women, and blessed is the fruit of your womb."

LUKE 1:39–42

Today, the last day of May, we conclude the month fittingly with the feast of the Visitation of Mary to her cousin Elizabeth. During the liturgy we heard once more the beautiful account from St. Luke describing in detail this lovely encounter between Mary and Elizabeth, between Jesus the Savior and John, his precursor, both still inside their mothers' wombs but already so aware of each other. Mary, having departed her home in Nazareth right after receiving the visit from the Archangel Gabriel and conceiving the Son of God in her womb, was still pondering with deep emotions, almost speechless at the mystery that was just accomplished in her. When she knocks at the door of Elizabeth's house and enters, both Elizabeth and the child in her womb leap for joy at the sight of Mary. Elizabeth, filled with the Holy Spirit, bursts into a deep exclamation: "Most blessed are you among women, and blessed is the fruit of your womb. And why does this happens to me, that the mother of my Lord should come to me? ...Blessed are you, indeed, who believed that what was spoken to you by the Lord would be fulfilled" (Luke 1:42–43, 45). And our Lady, otherwise always calm and reserved, upon hearing Elizabeth's salutation can no longer contain herself and in turn bursts into a song of praise: "My soul proclaims the greatness of the Lord; and my spirit rejoices in God my savior" (Luke 1:46). Today, as we celebrate the feast of the Visitation, we recall once more God's wonders accomplished "in the fullness of time" in both in Mary and Elizabeth.

JUNE

JUNE 1 · *St. Justin, Martyr*

EARTHLY LEGALISM

The grace of the Holy Spirit is not bound to any law.
ST. GREGORY THE GREAT

One of the great lessons of the Gospel is to see how Jesus was not bound by the laws of his time; in fact, he often rejected them. At one point, when the Pharisees criticized Jesus' disciples for eating some otherwise forbidden food not in accordance with Jewish law or custom, Jesus rebuked them by saying it is not what goes into the mouth that really matters but what comes out from inside the person, out from his heart, his mind, his mouth. Another time when the Lord was criticized by the same people for healing someone on a Saturday, and therefore not adhering to the law, Jesus responded by saying that the law is made for man and not man for the law.

Societies, including ecclesiastical ones, often abuse authority and place extra burdens on human beings, especially the poor and the most vulnerable, and justify their actions claiming their authority comes from God. Jesus was adamant in rebuking this attitude then as I am sure he is also adamant in rebuking it now. I have sometimes noticed that this type of legalistic attitude often breeds contempt and intolerance of others, of those who are different from us and don't fit the norm. There are enough Gospel stories showing us how Jesus detested this sort of attitude. It was so contrary to the example of his own behavior. Those who have ears to hear must remind themselves that "the Spirit breathes where he wills" (John 3:8) and is not bound by the excessive laws of people.

EVENING IN THE GARDEN

Bid the refreshing north wind wake
Say to the south wind blow
Let ev'ry plant the pow'r partake
And all the garden grow.

AMISH HYMN

Quietly, after Vespers, I enjoy taking a last stroll through the gardens to quickly inspect them and wish them good night. This daily practice becomes routine and makes me experience the magic of the evening at this precious hour. There is a great deal of peace and tranquility in our gardens, especially during the evening hours. I always find a favorite spot where I tend to linger a bit longer, as I gaze at St. Fiacre in the center of the vegetable patch and utter a short prayer for a good crop. He is the guardian of our gardens, a solid monk gardener whose only aim was to please God by cultivating the earth and collaborating with the Creator. This daily garden walk often reminds me of the one told in the Scriptures, where at the end of the creation story the Lord walked through the garden and found pleasure that all was in good order.

CHRISTIAN MONASTIC SOLITUDE

At once the Spirit drove him out into the desert.

MARK 1:12

This morning, during the period assigned to *lectio*, I was reading—really savoring—a Gospel passage often read at the beginning of Lent, when Jesus withdraws for forty days to the innermost of the wasteland: the desert. It reminded me of the clear and humble place assigned to solitude in monastic life. Furthermore, it brought back to mind a quote from Thomas Merton that someone once sent me in the mail: "There is something about being alone that is at the core of Christian life. A person cannot truly come to know the Father by constant activity; rather, real Christian action, real love for others, springs from hearing the voice of God in times of rest and quietness, in the desert. The example of Jesus himself bears this out."

MINDFULNESS

Today is added to our time
Yet while we pause it glides away
How soon shall we be past our prime
For where, alas, is yesterday.

AMISH HYMN

In the Buddhist tradition, monks cultivate what they call a state of mindfulness. The Christian monks call it recollection. In truth, both are one and the same reality expressed under different names. Mindfulness or recollection keeps us aware of the grace of the present moment and of that ultimate and eternal reality, which is God. By concentrating mindfully on the present, our breathing becomes freer and our inner faculties are restored to one of calm, quiet, and peace. Interiorly, we become freer, and we indeed feel free. We rejoice and savor the actual present moment, with its joys and sometimes its sorrows. All present events somehow seem to reflect that eternal reality, and life itself becomes simpler, more real.

THE MONASTERY BELLS

O happy is the man who hears
The warning voice
And whose celestial wisdom makes
His early only choice.

MENNONITE SONG

Several times a day the monastery bells, the *Vox Dei*, ring, calling the monks and our guests to prayer. At nighttime, at the end of Compline, they ring once more, preparing us to enter into the quiet of the night—what the monks call "the great silence." When the bells ring, all speech stops, all work is concluded, the telephone is no longer answered. The clear sound of our bells is a call to mindfulness. When we hear that mysterious, wordless sound, we end all conversations, we stop the activities around us, and we retire into the sacred silence, the silence necessary to hear God's voice. The Buddhist monks attribute a lovely saying to the bells that is also totally applicable here to our similar circumstances:

Listen, listen,
This wonderful sound brings me back to
My true home.

The pure sound emanating from our bells not only releases us from the tensions of the day by calling us to the quiet of prayer and silence, they go further and do more by simply returning us to a clear and peaceful state of being.

CORPUS CHRISTI

Here is the school of Christ—the upper room—
Where men shall learn to know the bud and bloom
Of saintly lives; where Christ himself shall teach.

W.M. LIVINGSTON

This is my body, which will be given for you.

LUKE 22:19

Today's feast is in honor of the Body and Blood of the Lord. During the institution of the first Eucharist, the evangelists relate how Jesus broke the bread and distributed it to his disciples. He did the same with the wine as partaking of his blood. There is a great deal of rich symbolism in the breaking of the bread and in the sharing of the cup. The Lord said: "Take and eat," and also, "Take and drink." The two go together, and as the Lord instructed us, they must never be separated. A loaf of bread is usually broken so that it may more freely be shared with others. By sharing the gift of broken bread and the cup of wine with his disciples, and doing it on the very eve of undertaking his sacred passion, Jesus is, in effect, announcing to all the mystery of his body's forthcoming brokenness, his own suffering and death, the very fact that he is willing to lay down his own life so that one day all of us may obtain life everlasting. The mystery of the Eucharist can only be understood in the light of the cross. "Do this in memory of me" (Luke 22:19).

RECOLLECTION, MINDFULNESS, PEACE

It is a wonderful, luminous, warm June day! Everything is lush, green, neat, almost spotless throughout the countryside. I luxuriate in early June's pleasant temperatures while I have them. I know that eventually, as the season grows older, I will have to confront the hot summer weather, something not always agreeable to me physically or otherwise. But we are not there yet, and I must not rush ahead of God.

This morning I found among old papers a quote I saved. It is by Robert J. Kreyche and, in my humble view, always timely:

> Recollection...peace...joyful contemplation. Don't trade these goods for all the oil of Arabia. Whenever you find yourself at loose ends, at odds with yourself and the world, distracted, "emptied," drifting from God, call a halt to everything. Get recollected first, and then start over again—(this time) in peace.

THE SEQUELA CHRISTI

If anyone wishes to come after me, he must deny himself and take up his cross daily and follow me.

LUKE 9:23

For St. Benedict and all the early Desert Fathers and Mothers, what distinguished the monk and nun from other Christians was the simple fact that he and she took seriously this Gospel invitation to follow the Lord, much like the martyrs did in the early Church. The monk never thinks of himself better than others; on the contrary, he sees himself as the least among all and therefore always chooses the last place in all situations. But having heard the invitation from the Master, he knows he has no other choice but to walk in the steps of Christ for the rest of his life. This he does willingly, and his only goal becomes the humble imitation of the Master. The Christian monastic life is essentially a walking pilgrimage, one that the monk undertakes with his eyes fixed on Christ alone.

A MONASTIC HARP AND POET

Today we feast a humble monk and a great Church father. The *Martyrology* reminds us that St. Ephrem died in Edessa, Syria, in the year 373, where he was also a deacon, a theologian, and a gifted and most unusual poet. Being divinely inspired, he composed heaps of hymns and poems to honor Christ, our Savior, his mysteries, and his holy Mother. Many of the hymns were entirely liturgical. It was thus that he became known, and was called commonly by all, the "Harp of the Holy Spirit."

> Even today on this earth of thorns
> we can see in the field
> the spikes of wheat which God,
> despite those curses, has given:
> cradled with them, the grains receive their birth,
> thanks to the wind;
> at the will of the Most High,
> who can perform all things,
> does the breeze suckle them,
> like a mother's breast it nurtures them,
> so that herein may be depicted a type
> of how spiritual beings are nourished.
>
> ST. EPHREM, *HYMNS ON PARADISE*

SACRED READING

Listen readily to holy reading and devote yourself often to prayer.

THE RULE OF ST. BENEDICT, CHAPTER 4

Daily reading of the Scriptures, especially the Gospels, the fathers, the Desert Fathers and Mothers, and all subsequent monastic literature, is what nourishes the soul of the monk deep down. To sit down on an early morning in the solitude of one's cell and to slowly begin to digest the wisdom handed down to us by our ancestors in monastic life is simply an act of faith, an act of reverence for those who preceded us. I often get completely absorbed by them, by their example, by their profound faith, and by their wisdom. Reading them slowly digesting them, meditating and tasting every word in the sacred text then becomes pure delight for the soul. As far as I am concerned, it can go on for hours unending, but I know time is limited in our day and that there are other chores in the monastery that demand my time and attention. However, since we live in quiet silence throughout the day, our memory and recollection can continue ruminating the sacred texts throughout the day, ever exploring the wise lessons and spiritual incentives provided by those unique authors. I thank the Lord for those daily periods of stillness and quiet reading. They nurture our prayer; they provide food for the soul.

MODERATION IN ALL THINGS

During these early June days, I find myself working early and hard during the morning hours, using my hands and brains in the tasks at hand, always trying to keep the monastic balance indicated by St. Benedict and not going into excess in either way. "Moderation in all things" remains the ideal, the rule. There is joy in keeping things in order, in proper balance, in equilibrium....It is an ideal not always easy to achieve, but it is what we aim for. Sometimes I get completely absorbed in one task or another, be it gardening or cooking, reading or minding the farm, cutting the grass or fetching the mail, and when I catch myself in that moment, I then realize it is time to return to the center, to my innermost, where God is waiting for me.

JUNE 12

A LOVING PROVIDENCE

I am, in God's hands, my own master.

JACQUES-BÉNIGNE BOSSUET, BISHOP

Deep down I realize that the basic feeling of contentment, trust, and peace often found in the hearts of monastic people (or any Christian) is simply due to the fact that they know their lives to be in the hands of a loving Father who knows all their needs, spiritual and temporal. Moreover, this loving Father, as Jesus assures us in the Gospel, finds divine joy in comforting his children and providing for their needs. "Our Father, who art in heaven," we pray, "give us this day our daily bread."

THE CHARM OF A PLACE: HUDSON VALLEY

Praised be Thou, my Lord, for our mother the Earth,
Which does sustain us and keep us. And bringeth forth divers fruits, and flowers of many colors and grass.

ST. FRANCIS OF ASSISI, "THE CANTICLE OF THE CREATURES"

Early June is paradise on earth in the Hudson Valley. The splendor of Mother Nature becomes visible in every corner of the valley: in the fields and gardens, in the mountains and hills, in the river and lakes, in the woods, vineyards, and orchards. We are particularly blessed in having this region as our home. It is rich in history, agriculture, art, and education, and we can enjoy each of the four seasons to the fullest. In my mind, I run thought after thought over special valley places where I find distinctive joy and inspiration. The long vistas from the Catskill Mountains come to mind, where I'm always moved to pray (from Psalm 121): "I raise my eyes to the mountains. From whence shall come my help? My help comes from the LORD, the maker of heaven and earth."

Some of the vistas over the Hudson River are particularly striking, especially on clear days when they have the lovely Catskills as background. As one drives through the rolling fields and hills of Dutchess and Columbia counties, passing through working farms still fully functioning, one discovers the charm and serenity that emanates from such places. Life is there, life aplenty. I love those quiet scenes that combine simple beauty and the impression of rugged human work. The Lord gave us the gift of earth to work and cultivate it but also to command and care for it, nurture it, and treat it with utmost respect. The earth is a gift from the Lord and it belongs to him alone. "Praise the LORD, for he is good...who spread[s] the earth upon the waters, for his mercy endures forever" (Psalm 136:1, 6).

REFLECTIONS ON A JUNE DAY

A cheerful glance brings joy to the heart;
good news invigorates the bones.

PROVERBS 15:30

Daily writing and reading feed our minds and souls almost as much as prayer does. I find all these activities to be closely associated with one another, almost intertwined. Since we are mindful of the shortness of our time in this world, it is imperative that we use time wisely and always focus on things that nurture the spiritual part of us. Why waste time on things that are superfluous, ephemeral, that don't really matter or count for eternal life? At the end, we must let go of all of it! Amidst pondering these reticent thoughts in my mind, and as I take a brisk walk to the mailbox, I am interiorly fed by the tranquility and natural beauty of the landscape. Mother Nature is particularly striking and enjoyable during June: The sky is so clear, the air pure, and the new tender green in the trees and the fields looks restful to the eye. We are now at that moment when we are hastily transitioning from spring into summer. As I continue my walk, I reflect slowly, very slowly indeed, on the words of "Madly Singing in the Mountains," a Chinese poem written by Po Chu-I more than 1,000 years ago:

Each time that I look at a fine landscape:
Each time that I meet a loved friend,
I raise my voice and recite a stanza of poetry
And am glad as though God had crossed my path.

SIGNS OF THE SEASON

To receive grace we need only to love its Donor.

MATTHIAS JOSEPH SCHEEBEN, 1886

Today we honor the memory of a simple young shepherdess, St. Germaine of Pibrac. She was from a region near Toulouse, France, where she is still honored and revered by the country folks of her village. Many others come from all regions of France in pilgrimage to her tomb to beseech spiritual favors through her intercession. She was always as humble as she was loving and totally devoted in the service of the Lord. As a young shepherdess, she loved all sheep and lambs and in particular the flock assigned to her care. It has been part of our monastic tradition here for many years to honor her memory by shearing the wool from our sheep on her feast day. The shearing is done quietly today, usually in the morning, before the summer heat arrives. The wool is then stored in large plastic bags and given to several people—weavers, knitters, students, and others—who manage to bring the best out of the clean, rustic treasure from our flock by spinning and weaving. There is always an extra demand from someone who appreciates picking the wool from our flock. This annual ritual usually marks the end of our spring days, as we now slowly but surely transition into full summer weather, summer activities, and all that the new season has in store for us. One of the things I am hoping and praying for is abundant rain for our crops. It has been dry now for almost too long. Rain and dew, bless the Lord!

REST IN THE LORD

Abba John the Dwarf gave this advice to a disciple: "Keeping watch means to sit in one's cell, always keeping the remembrance of God. This is what is meant by the words: 'I was on the watch, and God came to me'" (Matthew 25:36).

THE DESERT FATHERS, *APOPHTHEGMATA PATRUM*

There are times after a long and heavy day's work that one simply feels physically tired, worn out. This is a human reality for many, and I am not different. Often when this occurs, I stop my present activity for a while, go to the chapel, and sit in front of Christ's large icon. I gaze at him for a long time and he, in turn, looks at me. My eyes rest in his presence, in that momentary glimpse at him. We don't say too much to each other, we are simply mindful of each other. There I find both physical and mental rest. I hold on to the words from the Psalm (62:2): "My soul rests in God alone," and I repeat them slowly over and over again. While doing it, I am reminded of the Lord's own words, his own promise: "Come to me, all you who labor and are burdened, and I will give you rest" (Matthew 11:28).

DESERT WISDOM

Abba Bessarion was considered an outstanding personality and teacher among the Desert Fathers. His teachings, or "sayings," were mostly recorded by one of his disciples named Doulas. Here are two extracted from the wisdom of Abba Bessarion:

> A monk who shared a lodging with other monks asked Abba Bessarion, "What should I do?" The old man replied, "Keep silence and do not compare yourself with others."
>
> A monk who had sinned was turned out of the church by a priest-monk. Abba Bessarion got up and went to him, saying, "I, too, am a sinner."

APPRECIATION OF SACRED SCRIPTURES

Everything in the Sacred Books shines and glistens, even in its outer shell: but the marrow of it is sweeter if you want the kernel, you must break the shell.

ST. JEROME

Throughout the history of the Western world, the Scriptures have been the great instigators of revolt against the worst forms of clerical and political despotism. The Bible has been the Magna Carta of the poor and the oppressed.

THOMAS HENRY HUXLEY, *CONTROVERTED QUESTIONS,* 1892

St. Benedict, in his wisdom, teaches the monk to grow in appreciation and love of the living word of God. By requiring the monk to take out time daily for *lectio divina,* that is, the reading and study of the Scriptures, he thus encourages the monk to remain faithful to this holy occupation. Since the monastery is a school in the Lord's service, a place for special training, St. Benedict uses the time assigned to sacred reading as an occasion to train the monk to discover the treasures contained in the Scriptures. During those quiet hours of personal intimate contact with the word of God, the monk slowly learns to assimilate quietly the truth and wisdom contained there. Primarily and above all, through repeatedly reading and ruminating over the Gospel lessons, assimilating them freshly during these hours of daily contact with them, he learns to discover the person of Jesus Christ, God's revelation to the world, the mystery hidden from all ages. Suddenly, it all becomes alive in the pages of the Scriptures.

A MONASTIC MEMORIAL

They keep the Rule *with a very devout observance,*
That Rule *that long ago Benedict gave to his followers,*
St. Romuald passed it on later to others
In founding his order.
All should be craving this solitary retirement,
Disdaining all the goods of this fleeting world,
Would that many might choose to please God, and him only,
Here in the monastic desert.

FROM *"EREMITICAE VITAE DESCRIPTIO,"* MEDIEVAL HYMN

The monastic calendar marks today the memorial of St. Romuald, abbot and founder of the Camaldolese Monks and Nuns. The Camaldolese monastic ideal consists basically in following St. Benedict's *Rule*, as other monks do, with a particular application to the eremitical life. St. Benedict, of course, conceived his *Rule* primarily for cenobites, but he also held in high esteem the monastic eremitical or solitary life. In fact, he suggests in the *Rule* that certain monks, after a time of probation in the cenobitic life, may be called by the Lord to a more solitary life in a hermitage. St. Romuald's experiment made it possible for certain monks to combine the blessings of both the cenobitic and semi-hermit life. The monastery he founded, the Sacro Eremo, located in Tuscany, consists to this day of a community of hermits living the monastic ideal together. Like the ancient desert monks, the Camaldolese are zealous in safeguarding the gift of monastic solitude.

JUNE 20 · St. Adalbert, Monk

A TASTE FOR GOD

Your mind dwells in the deep,
beyond our reach,
and your thoughts are a mystery
no man has explored.

ISAAC THE SYRIAN, MONK AND WRITER, CIRCA 460

One of the unique gifts from the Holy Spirit is the one he places in the center of our souls: a taste for God, a taste of God. This, of course, is impossible to receive without faith. It all begins with the gift of faith. Through faith, and in deep prayer, little by little, ever so slowly, the Holy Spirit develops in our innermost a special taste for God, for his mystery, for his presence. The taste for God and the desire for his presence is such that one loses the desire for anything else. Nothing else really matters, except to satiate this deep hunger, to taste again and again this plenitude of life, this life of constant union where the taste of God is continuous. This special gift from the Holy Spirit is precisely the "life in abundance" that Jesus spoke of and promised to his disciples.

JUNE 21

SUMMER

Summer made its official entrance today. The days are beginning to feel hot and dry.

I start early and rise at dawn to pray and work, *ora et labora*, safe from the heat and from interruptions later in the day. While at prayer, in quiet silence, I ponder God's glory reflected on the earth and concretely in the monastic land here at hand. Our fields, green meadows, woods, and hills, near and far, all proclaim God's glory. Our enclosed vegetable garden is filled with his presence. What more can I ask or demand from the Lord? It is enough to know and to feel his divine presence permeating every inch of the monastic property, every inch on the monastic day, every inch of our poor beings. All that is left is for us to offer him continual praise. *Laus Tibi Domine!*

THE PURPOSE OF THE MONASTIC RULE

The concern must be whether the novice truly seeks God and whether he eagerly shows keen interest for the Work of God, for obedience and for trials....If he promises perseverance in his stability, then after several months have passed let this Rule *be read in its entirety to him and let him be told: "This is the law under which you are choosing to serve. If you can keep it, come in. If not, feel free to leave."*

THE RULE OF ST. BENEDICT, CHAPTER 58

Mother Maria, who as an Orthodox nun lived for many years under *The Rule of St. Benedict* in an Anglican monastery, wrote the following commentary, very appropriate for a solid understanding of the monastic *Rule*:

> When St. Benedict says that he wrote a little *Rule* for beginners he does not mean that a *Rule* for the advanced should follow. His purpose is to prepare the soul for that moment when it catches fire of itself. *Rule*, hardships, sacrifice all remain, but they have now become part of the monk's own natural being. They are both the framework and the expression of that life which he bears within himself. The obedience to the *Rule* is but an outward sign of the total surrender to truth, which sovereignly reigns in the soul, its beatitude and deep inward delight. This kindling of the fire, this rebirth of the soul to the blissful awareness of God, is a mystery which is not at our command. Master and disciple together can do but one thing to hasten its advent: with a single mind to submit to the continual practice of the renunciation of the self in every sphere of life. The master is the more truly the master, if, by his example, he makes the disciple love, in the expectation of God, the hardships of the ascent.

JUNE 23

THE MONASTIC DESERT

The desert is a place for asceticism, not for worldly affairs.

ABBA JOHN THE EUNUCH

For the early monks, retiring into the desert was not an escape. It meant, primarily, moving into the realms of freedom: freedom from exploitation, freedom from preconceived ideas of holiness, freedom from worldly conformity, and especially freedom from being possessed by possessions. The desert was a place to confront one's own bareness, one's insecurities, one's sinfulness; and on the other hand, the total gratuity and transcendence of God's infinite love. In the desert, the monk finds delight in occupying the last place in all instances, in keeping his head bent in humility and deep prayer, asserting only: I am a worm.

THE BIRTH OF ST. JOHN THE BAPTIST

The Master proclaimed you to be a prophet,
Higher than all the prophets
And greater than any man born of a woman.
For the One whom the prophets and the Law foretold,
You beheld him in your very flesh,
He, who is truly the Christ,
And you were more honored than all,
For you were chosen to baptize him.

FEAST OF THE SYNAXIS OF JOHN THE BAPTIST

Today we celebrate a beautiful feast, a totally monastic feast, a feast of joy and good tidings. It is the solemn commemoration of the birth of the Lord's forerunner, John the Baptist.

From ancient times, John the Baptist, a true desert dweller, has been the monastic prototype. God sent John, his messenger, into our world to highlight and call attention to the prophet Isaiah's announcement: "All the ends of the earth [shall] see the salvation of our God." John the Baptist heralded the good tidings that a Savior, the Messiah, shall come among us and inhabit our world. He was chosen to be Christ's precursor and also was to become the "friend of the Bridegroom." Throughout the year, the liturgy provides us several occasions to honor John the Baptist and meditate on his special role on the plan of salvation. For instance, today we celebrate his birth, and toward the end of August we shall render homage to his martyrdom, and, of course, during Advent, the figure and message of John the Baptist is with us almost daily.

Today, as throughout our Advent days and through the whole year, we must heed his message of conversion and humble repentance and follow his example of exceeding joy at the nearness of the Savior, the Messiah. If we do this, we also shall experience that unique joy granted to him while leaping in his mother's womb at the closeness of Jesus present in the womb of Mary, his Mother. O holy precursor of Christ, intercede for our salvation.

ON THE KENOSIS OF GOD

Christian wisdom from Gustave Thibon, a twentieth-century French writer:

From the start, God was for me Power and the Law, later he became Light and Love, and finally, Absence and Night. It is perhaps there, in the latter, that he resembles himself the most. Each day he becomes to me more and more the Stranger and the totally Unknown, therefore, I have become a sort of agnostic worshiper. It is not virtue that God demands from us, but rather that we discover him poor and powerless. I don't aspire to enlighten humanity with a flashlight, says he, my only ambition is to help them better understand/contemplate the Son after having secretly followed him in a messy manner, from ruble to ruble, through all the successive images and ideas we make ourselves of him. It is essential to convey and show all human beings the face of the true God, the God who, in his utter humility and abasement, becomes for us an infant and also the crucified One, who being all love becomes weak and powerless for our sake, the God who waits for us in silence and for whom we become responsible here on earth....I love our present times, for they give us the rare chance to choose between the power of men and the weakness of God. While religion seems to dwell on waiting and counting for a miracle, profound faith leads us simply to the worship of the Mystery.

CHRIST, OUR ONLY HOPE

We are born into this world with a deep passion for objective truth. We seek it everywhere we go and in every way possible. The scientist releases his mind in search of knowledge and yet undiscovered truth, the poet and the artist seek ultimate truth through creative freedom and inspiring beauty. The Christian monk, however, knows only one humble truth: He is sinful and lonesome, he is poor and deprived, and thus he has nothing or no one to lean on except Christ, his Savior. Christ is his only hope and thus, together with St. Paul, he repeats to himself day and night: "Christ Jesus our hope" (1 Timothy 1:1).

Le Christ, notre seule esperance. Christus, spes mea.

A HUMBLE SERVANT IN GOD'S PLAN

Preserve and save your servants, O Theotokos, *from every danger. For after God Himself, all of us fly unto you for refuge and steady help, you are our sure rampart, offering your children unfailing protection.*

"THE GREAT CANON TO THE MOST HOLY *THEOTOKOS*"

In the Eastern Church, the beloved icon of Our Lady of Perpetual Help is often called the icon of Our Lady of the Passion. In the center of the icon lies the image of the *Theotokos*, as if she was sheltering the Child Jesus from the view of the two angels at the top, carrying the instruments of the passion. Our Lady's presence in the icon, as always, radiates a serene beauty through her silence and quiet demeanor. Who but a mother to whom it was once prophesied that one day a sword would pierce her heart could understand the excruciating, immense suffering awaiting her beloved son? Ultimately, even if reluctantly, our Lady submits herself to God's plans for his Son and her Son. Like our Lady, we also are invited to live our own submissions to the Lord with complete trust in his plans for each of us.

THE VISION OF GOD

For this is why the Word became man, and the Son of God became the Son of man: so that man, by entering into communion with the Word and thus receiving divine sonship, might become a son of God.

ST. IRENAEUS

The feast of an apostle, apostolic father, or early Church father such as Irenaeus always brings a unique type of joy to this small monastic enclave. They are our fathers in the faith, living instruments of the Holy Spirit, and without them the apostolic faith would not have been transmitted to us. St. Irenaeus was a disciple of St. Polycarp, who was a disciple of John, the beloved disciple. Thus the continuity and living tradition was established, and thus St. Irenaeus, who was born in Smyrna and later moved on to Lyons, France, and became its bishop, directly transmitted the apostolic faith to the Church of God in Gaules. Throughout the year we have the occasion to read St. Irenaeus' luminous teachings, always clear and concise, during the Office of Vigils. Here is a small sample of his unction and wisdom:

> The glory of God gives life; those who see God receive life....Men will therefore see God if they are to live; through the vision of God they become immortal and attain to God himself....God is the source of all activity through creation. He cannot be seen or described in his own nature and in all this greatness by any of his creatures. Yet he is certainly not unknown. Through his Word the whole creation learns that there is one God the Father, who holds all things together and gives them their being. As it is written in John 1:18, "No one has ever seen God. The only Son, God, who is at the Father's side, has revealed him." From the beginning the Son is the one who teaches us about the Father; he is with the Father from the beginning. The Word revealed God to men and presented men to God. Life in man is the glory of God; the life of man is the vision of God.

AGAINST THE HERESIES

STS. PETER AND PAUL, APOSTLES

Rejoice, O Peter, the Apostle and special friend of the Master, Christ, our God.
Rejoice, O truly beloved Paul, preacher of the faith and teacher of the universe.
Because of your unique privilege, O sanctified Pair,
Beseech Christ, our God, to save our souls!

FROM THE *FESTA MENAION* FOR JUNE 29

It is not easy to write about the Apostles Peter and Paul. So much is attributed to them, so much has been handed down by tradition as coming down from them, and yet the tradition began to be elaborated only long after their deaths. What seems to be concrete, true, are the passages in the Scriptures that refer to them and their own letters to various of God's churches. This is particularly true of Paul, who was a gifted and avid writer. Christ taught the work of love, lived the reality of love, and demanded love from his disciples as the one sign that they were truly his followers. The work of love was to be the authentic recognition that they were his and that he was truly in their midst. By abiding in love, with friends and enemies and every one they ever met or came across in their lives, they remained faithful and totally centered in that main, crucial message from their Master. Peter and Paul, as well the other disciples, learned to direct every inch of their beings toward Christ. Their only boast was in him, and it was part of the work of love they were called to accomplish. They may not have triumphed successfully in earthly ways, and they might have surrendered themselves to human failure. But as followers of the Master, they simply went on, leaving all earthly realities behind, shaking off the dust from their sandals, whether they felt victorious or simply lost the battle in human terms.

Peter and Paul, pillars of the early Christian community, taught us that, in order to live the Master's commandment of love, we must live with our own weaknesses. It is not for the disciple to excel over the Master, they would say. We fail and fall daily, and yet his yoke is easy, light, made to fit each of us, no matter what our size or dysfunctions are. The apostles learned to die to themselves, carried their own crosses, so that they could conform to Christ alone. For Peter and Paul, as well as for the other apostles, to die unto Christ was to be born again, to renounce slavery and become free, to be released from all worldly attributes, seeking to resemble the Master alone. During his earthly life, Peter was challenged by the Master about the truth of his pure love for him. Peter, not doubting for a second, replied three times, "Lord,...you know that I love you" (John 21:17). Paul, heavily persecuted at the end of his earthly pilgrimage, would comment to his disciples, "What will separate us from the love of Christ?" Romans 8:35). Both disciples knew and were mindful of the supremacy of love as Christ's primordial teaching. They totally agreed with their fellow apostle, John, who never ceased repeating to his disciples, "Beloved, if God so loved us, we also must love one another" (1 John 4:11). At life's end, for the Master as for the disciples, only one reality counted: the work of love.

THE GOSPEL MESSAGE

Behold, I am coming soon. I bring with me the recompense I will give to each according to his deeds. I am the Alpha and the Omega, the first and the last, the beginning and the end.

REVELATION 22:12–13

Christ is with those of humble mind, not with those who exalt themselves over his flock.

ST. CLEMENT OF ROME

As I quietly perform my daily garden duties, I reflect upon certain realities that come often to my mind; for instance, how much our present American socioeconomic system, our policies, our politics, our materialistic values are in total contradiction with some of the teachings of Jesus. Many of the things we extol and uphold daily are totally opposite to the living example and the testament the Lord left to his followers. "No disciple is superior to the teacher," he said in Luke 6:40, meaning we are not free to act differently from Jesus if we claim to be his disciples.

Someone asked me recently what I thought of undocumented immigrants (of which there are plenty in our area). I replied that for me the only answer rested in Christ's words, that whosoever welcomes a stranger welcomes Christ himself. The Lord rejected a value system that enhances materialism, greed, egocentrism, violence, discrimination of any type and sort. For instance, when we engage in the violence of war or continue to exalt the so-called privilege to bear arms and for whatever reason kill other human beings made in God's image and likeness, we do it in complete opposition to him who taught us in Matthew 26:52, "All who take the sword will perish by the sword." When I hear our politicians speak of prosperity for some instead of everyone's general well-being, often protecting only the very wealthy, I hear a message that reminds me precisely of that which the Lord criticized in some of his contemporaries. It is a fact, our politicians often preach only about material prosperity, never about prosperity for the soul or true spiritual prosperity, a type of prosperity that renders fruit unto eternal life.

A wise and sensible American writer, Professor George Santayana, wrote and counseled: "To be poor in order to be simple, to produce less in order that the product may be more of a choice and beautiful, and may leave us less burdened with unnecessary duties and useless possessions—that is an idea not often articulated in the American mind." And, I may add, it is not often articulated in American Christian minds, despite Sunday after Sunday hearing the Gospel message in church. It is well overdue for all of us to learn anew the Gospel lessons and to acquire a Christlike mind, one that allows us to see all things as Christ saw them and lived them in truth. Lord Jesus Christ, have pity on us, sinners.

JULY

JULY 1 · *St. Simeon the Simple, Monk in the Dead Sea Desert*

July's Personality

Providence is the care God takes of all existing things.

ST. JOHN DAMASCENE (675–749)

With July's arrival, we reach the period that becomes the heyday of summer. Everything in nature shows its full potential: incredible growth, a sense of fullness permeates every aspect of life. The almost perfect weather makes us appreciate why July is sometimes called "the middle age of the year." Our gardens, ripe with fruits, odorant herbs, and lovely flowers, bestow on us a feeling of contentment and peace. They become truly a colorful, aromatic paradise, a symbol of the true paradise, our eternal home, where we shall dwell forever with God and the saints. My thoughts cannot go any further, I get lost when I reach that point. July somehow, mysteriously, contains the promise of the Lord's endless day, when God shall be all in all!

JULY 2

Lessons to Learn

Let us learn humility from Christ, humiliation from David, and from Peter to shed tears over our past offenses; but lets us also learn to avoid the despair of Samson, Judas, and the wisest of men, Solomon.

ABBOT HESYCHIOS OF SINAI

The monastic fathers never cease to remind us of the absolute need for humility, repentance, and the prayer of tears in one's effort to lead a candid and totally honest spiritual life. One does not hear much about the prayer of tears these days, it seems so countercultural; yet it is a coveted gift from the Holy Spirit. Blessed are they who mourn; doubly blessed are they, indeed, upon whom the gift is bestowed!

A DOUBTING APOSTLE

Then he said to Thomas, "Put your finger here and see my hands, and bring your hand and put it into my side, and do not be unbelieving, but believe." Thomas answered and said to him, "My Lord and my God!" Jesus said to him, "Have you come to believe because you have seen me? Blessed are those who have not seen and have believed."

JOHN 20:27–29

When Jesus chose his closest cooperators, the disciples, he made the choice of ordinary men and women, people who were unlikely leaders in the community. These people knew more about fishing and mending nets than how to preach the good news of the Gospel. Yet the Lord chose precisely people of that caliber and converted them into "fishers of men." The band of the twelve, Thomas among them, was commanded to go into the four corners of the world and preach God's message of salvation to all his children. This message was to be conveyed to everyone, Jews and Gentiles alike, to people of every race, social strata, and nation. The apostles, with Mary of Magdala and other disciples, witnessed the unique event of Christ's resurrection. They had seen, and some—like Thomas—touched the risen Lord. Now it was their turn to reveal and share this truth with others, to travel to the ends of the world and let this be known. The unique call of all the disciples and their followers was to spread the good news of God's loving redemption for his people, through the death and resurrection of his only begotten Son. The disciples, filled with the zeal imparted to them by the Holy Spirit, spread the new faith everywhere they went and willingly sacrificed their own lives as witness to the truth of their words. Almost all of them, except perhaps John, were martyred for the faith of confessing Jesus as Lord and Savior. Christians today of all confessions are also called to follow the example of the apostles and the disciples and witness through the example of their own lives to the truth of the resurrection. *Surrexit Dominus vere!* Christ is risen! Indeed he is risen!

INDEPENDENCE DAY

I tremble for my country when I reflect that God is just."

THOMAS JEFFERSON,
CHIEF WRITER OF THE DECLARATION OF INDEPENDENCE

Had the doctrines of Jesus been preached always as pure as they came from his lips, the whole civilized world would now have been Christian.

THOMAS JEFFERSON

As proud Americans, and as we celebrate today our country's Independence Day, it may be wise to reflect upon some of the teachings of our nation's Founding Fathers. These two quotes from Thomas Jefferson distill much wisdom and are as applicable today as when they were first uttered. They sharpen our understanding of the true, original American ideals.

JULY 5 · *St. Athanasius the Athonite*

A SEASONAL PRAYER

Lord God, You who give both
the sunlight and the rain
that our earth may be fertile
and our grain and produce may grow,
we bless You for the
changing seasons of our souls.
You give us alike the warm brightness
of joyful days, and the clouded skies of disappointment.
May we receive them both with trustful gratitude
desiring most of all
that the seed of your rich purpose
may take root is us and grow.
We ask you this our Lord Jesus Christ, your Son,
also our Redeemer and Risen Savior. Amen.

MONASTIC GARDEN DESIGN AS AN IMAGE OF PARADISE

In antiquity, the early monks conceived of their gardens as sacred places, as living images of the Garden of Eden where the Lord delighted himself, walking with and enjoying the company of man. Those early monks were very protective of that sacred space. For them that space was truly holy ground that they found filled immensely with a divine presence. From the earliest Desert Fathers—who took up solitary, quiet lives of prayer in the Syrian, Palestinian, and Egyptian deserts—monks of all times sought to reproduce in their gardens a sanctuary of harmony, symmetry, peace, and beauty. During the Middle Ages, they designed different types of gardens to fit diverse purposes: the cloister garden, often a perfect quadrangle with several even paths leading to a fountain in the center, was often the garden used for reading and meditation. The kitchen and herb garden had their own intrinsic structures. Their purpose was to provide medicinal herbs to the monastic healer and some special produce for kitchen usage. The large orchards and vegetable gardens were also designed harmoniously so that when the monks worked or walked them habitually they would keep at all times the image of paradise somehow present in their midst.

Monastic gardens, originally and historically conceived as sacred spaces, as places of holiness and pure spiritual delight, provide to us the idea of their critical and vital role in the conception of gardens today. Today's gardeners, through their contact with the tradition of monastic gardens and their perennial organic principles, learn to develop for our times a sensitive approach to redesigning natural landscapes that, if respected and admired as such, can continue to sing God's praises unto the next generation. An early twelfth-century description of a monastery garden arrangement in England is described thus: "Where the orchard leaves off, the garden begins, divided into several beds, or cut up by little canals, although standing water, do flow more or less...this water fulfills the double purpose of nourishing the fish and watering the vegetables."

JULY 7

THE QUIET MONASTIC WITNESS

To be a witness does not consist in engaging in propaganda, nor even in stirring people up, but in being a living mystery. It means to live in such a way that one's life would not make sense if God did not exist.

EMMANUEL CARDINAL CÉLESTIN SUHARD

The prophet Isaiah (55:6) invites people to "seek the LORD while he may be found, call upon him while he is near." There lies the mystery of the monastic vocation, the continual search for God. St. Benedict, a loving father to his monks, never ceased to remind them the only purpose for embracing monastic life is to seek God alone. Nothing else matters. The monk, like the prophets of old and the Desert Fathers, is called to live consciously in God's presence day and night, watching constantly in prayer. In doing so, in living humbly and without any pretensions, the life of the monk becomes a witness to the mystery of the invisible God. The monk need not teach or say anything to those around him. By the fact that his life is hidden with Christ in God, his utter silence speaks volumes to the world.

JULY 8

THE DIVINE PRESENCE

To pray is to make the effort to enter into the realm of an ineffable presence that is unique and eternal. This presence is the one of an invisible reality, the one that existed before time and shall still be there after time ends. This great, infinite, and eternal reality—hidden to our physical eyes—is the mystery of God being totally present in a loving communion of three divine persons: Father, Son, and Holy Spirit. It is an eternal presence, ever more real than we are to ourselves. It is the only reality that endures and transcends all time and understanding. It is only through prayer, and a gratuitous gift from the Holy Spirit, that this grace of coming near and touching the divine presence is made possible to us. In the intimacy of deep prayer, the divine energies, transform the soul into the image and likeness of the God we seek.

JULY 9

QUIET SUMMER DAYS

The longest journey is the journey inward.

DAG HAMMARSKJÖLD

These are the long, almost interminable, quiet days of summer. Many of our friends are on vacation elsewhere, and the younger ones seem to be heading toward the beaches and the mountains where the air is cooler and somehow more bearable. Here in the monastery, we are preparing for our annual vinegar festival, which brings many people to the monastery. The festival is always held the weekend following St. Benedict's Solemnity on July 11. From mid-July to mid-August is the beginning time to harvest the fruit of our labors, a time when I see the local farmers engaged in their second hay cutting, a sunny time when the berries and early vegetables begin to arrive in tons, a time of fulfillment for mother earth. When I have a few extra minutes, especially during the heat of the early afternoon hours, I try to find some time for reading and writing. It is soothing rest for a weary soul.

JULY 10

STILLNESS

I remember vividly being told a medieval legend where a monk once asked himself how heaven could exist without boredom since eternity went on and on and on....Bemused by his speculations on the matter, he wandered into a wood where a nightingale was singing. He stood there to listen, enchanted. After listening a while, he returned to his monastery. But when he reached it, no one recognized him. He gave his name to the monks and the father abbot. But even the abbot did not recognize his name. Finally, they looked at the chronicles and annals of the abbey, and there they recognized what had happened. A thousand years had passed since the monk had left the monastery. And while he was listening, time stood still.

SOLEMNITY OF ST. BENEDICT

Listen carefully, my son, to the Master's instructions, and attend to them with the ear of your heart. This is advice from a father who loves you, welcome it, and faithfully put it into practice.

PROLOGUE TO *THE RULE OF ST. BENEDICT*

Today the Roman calendar marks the celebration of our father among the saints, St. Benedict of Norcia. The man of God, Benedict, blessed in name and by grace, is one of those rare saints whose life and work influenced the eventual course of history.

St. Benedict was born in a small town north of Rome called Norcia. During his teenage years, his parents sent him to study in Rome. During his stay in the great metropolis, Benedict encountered among his peers a lifestyle directed to selfish pleasures, and he felt repelled by it. "Wishing to please God alone," as his biographer pointed out, he decided to leave Rome and the worldly concerns encountered there, and he withdrew to the wilderness of the Subiaco mountains. Once there, he embraced a quiet monastic life of deep silence, charity, continual prayer, and profound solitude. After several years, a few disciples began to congregate around him. He then organized the monastic life of his monks based on the *Rule* for monasteries he wrote especially for them, as well as the monastic tradition received from the ancient Desert Fathers and St. Basil the Great. St. Benedict died around the year 547, leaving his *Rule* to his sons and daughters, as well as the countless generations that would follow, as a testament of true Gospel living. He counseled the monks to take the Gospel as their only guide and thus walk the path that Christ cleared for us. He directed his monks to climb the ladder of humility, every degree and step of it, seeking God alone and preferring nothing to the love of Christ. The Lord Christ was to be the monk's only Master, and the imitation of the Lord's life and teachings his only task.

MONASTIC WORK

I must believe no type of work is beneath me, since Jesus was a carpenter for thirty years, and St. Joseph all his life.

BLESSED CHARLES DE FOUCAULD

Humble, vigorous, manual work is an integral reality in monastic life, part of its daily routine. St. Benedict, whom we feasted yesterday, reminds monastics that "they are truly monks when they live from the work of their hands." Monks are not mendicants, and St. Benedict would have been shocked by the idea of begging for gifts, for material support, or endowments. That was never part of the monastic ideal, not with the Desert Fathers, St. Basil, or St. Benedict. I sometimes conjecture how this frightful practice was introduced into certain monasteries. Even today one notices certain monasteries having no embarrassment in sending begging letters for some of their large projects. The one clear exception is the Cistercians, who seem to work for everything they need and often build, and maintain themselves, their own monasteries. I see no problem with accepting an occasional gift, an unrequested one, from a friendly benefactor who wishes to bequest something to a community. Where I see contradictions with monastic principles is when monks or nuns implicate themselves with huge, costly projects well above the income earned from their own work, thus placing themselves in the precarious situation of having to beg or get involved in fundraising. No matter how one may justify it, this is neither evangelical nor monastic. Throughout the centuries, there has always been a tension, a distinction between institutional monasticism and the charismatic one. Institutional monasticism, due in part to their large holdings, enterprises, and huge buildings, tends to be more materialistic and acquisitive in scope. Charismatic monasticism, by its essence, tends to be poorer, simpler, more dependent on the Gospel promise of God providing for his children, especially those who humbly work to earn their own living and live within the confines of their limited income. Can anyone imagine the Lord, who had not even a stone where he could lay down his head, or St. Benedict approving of the wealth and largesse some monasteries possess today? And monks who are called to imitate the Lord in their own lives know the Gospel dictum that "no disciple is superior to the teacher." St. Teresa of Ávila, in her wisdom, taught her nuns to choose poor, simple, small dwellings as their monasteries, just the basics, for, she said, she didn't wish those buildings to make much noise when they fell down on Judgment Day.

These days, when we are witnessing the closing and selling off of so many huge monasteries and religious buildings, I can't help but ask myself if the communities that inhabited them might not have otherwise survived had their lifestyle been totally different. Paradoxically, a poorer and simpler form of monastic life has lasted in the Egyptian desert, in Mount Athos, in smaller monasteries and hermitages across the world, for long centuries to this day. We know for a fact that monks there continue to live within their means, by the labor of their hands, and keeping the traditional Gospel frugality they inherited from the early fathers.

JULY 13

Confidence in God's Goodness

Never lose trust in God's mercy.

THE RULE OF ST. BENEDICT, CHAPTER 4

God is all goodness. Sometimes I look gratefully at our Christian life, our monastic life, for simply giving us the chance to bask daily, continually in the light and reality of God's goodness. There are days when the entire day seems submerged in this unique feeling, perception, experience of God's goodness. It is a vivid sentiment, something totally unexplainable, which one perceives deep within oneself. One senses being totally surrounded, and therefore protected, by God's immeasurable goodness. It is not a usual feeling that one can bring about on one's own. It is simply there. It is a bottomless perception, a strong affirmation, of the mystery of God's goodness. I realize then that God himself is infinite goodness. Wrapped in the mystery of God, I find that one can't separate him from his own goodness. My total trust and confidence in God is not based on who I am or in anything I have done or accomplished. None of us have any merit of our own in any way or form. And I know God is not looking for any of it either. My trust and confidence in him is based on knowing—and, yes, experiencing—the fact that God loves to give freely of himself to us, his creatures. By sometimes experiencing personally the reality of God's goodness for long periods, something which I don't have words to describe, I find that it naturally grounds my trust and confidence in the reality of God's tender love for us and the mystery of his mercy. With complete serenity and trust I place myself into his hands as I pray with the words of Psalm 131:

> *LORD, my heart is not proud; nor are my eyes haughty.*
> *I do not busy myself with great matters, with things too sublime for me. Rather, I have stilled my soul, like a weaned child to its mother, weaned is my soul. Israel, hope in the LORD, now and forever.*

JULY OBSERVATIONS

Upon the small, soft, sweet grass,
That was with flowers sweet embroidered all,
Of such sweetness and such odour overall....

GEOFFREY CHAUCER

Monastic life, all of life, is often encircled by the seasons of the year and the wise rhythm of Mother Nature. Author John Donne once described it: "We cannot awake the July flowers in January! Nor retard the flowers of the spring to autumn. We cannot bid the fruits come in May, not the leaves to stay on until December."

As we pace though the routine of our July days, they seem to me rather endless and tedious, totally mind-numbing. In part this is due to the wearisome hot temperatures. I try to overcome these fatigued feelings with the help of prayer and the Scriptures. I occasionally look at the sunflowers and the hollyhocks in the gardens, growing taller by the day, and the tomatoes beginning their transition from pale green to semi-reddish colors, indicating possible ripeness and maturity. All of that is a help to stimulate my mind and bring me comfort, in spite of the otherwise uncomfortable, heavy, humid weather. The Hudson Valley is known for its high humidity, and there are those of us who do not fare well during such weather. It is all a question of the "patient endurance" mentioned by St. Paul. At the end, I adjust myself to whatever is there. I even find that I like it all. The Lord is present in everything, in every event, at every hour of day or night throughout July and the successive months and seasons to come. Our tired bodies and weary souls can find strength and rest in that conviction. Ever mindful of his loving presence I, who otherwise immeasurably abhor the heaviness of July's heat and humidity, find enough support to go on. With the words of Psalm 37 I pray: "The valiant one whose steps are guided by the LORD, who will delight in his way, may stumble, but he will never fall, for the LORD holds his hand."

FROM A MEDIEVAL ORTHODOX MYSTIC

My Christ,
you are the Kingdom of heaven,
you are the land promised to the meek,
you are the meadows of paradise,
the hall of the celestial banquet,
the ineffable bridal chamber,
the table open for all comers.
You are the bread of life,
the wonderful new drink,
the cool jar of water,
the water of life.
You are the lamp
that never goes out for all your saints,
the new garment, the diadem,
the one who distributes diadems.
You are our joy and repose,
our delight and glory.
You are gladness and laughter, my God.
Your grace, the grace of the all-holy Spirit,
shines in the saints like a blazing sun.

SYMEON THE NEW THEOLOGIAN

QUEEN AND BEAUTY OF CARMEL

Regina Décor Carmeli,
Ora pro nobis!

Today the community of the faithful honors the memorial of Our Lady of Mount Carmel. It is a memorial that comes from antiquity and is the only one honoring our Lady during the month of July. It is a cherished feast for the Carmelite family at large and one of great joy in places such as Italy and Spain, where Our Lady of Carmel is much loved. For many Christians in the East, it is the moment to start preparing for the great feast of the Dormition/Assumption a month from now. As usual in the Eastern tradition, there is a customary fasting period in preparation for the Dormition/Assumption celebration. Here in the monastery, we salute the Mother of God with the words recited during the Byzantine Small Compline Office and plead for her unfailing protection:

It is truly proper and right to call you blest, O *Theotokos*,
For you are the ever-blessed and all-immaculate
  Mother of our God.
You are more honorable than the Cherubim,
And beyond compare more glorious than the Seraphim.
For You humbly gave birth to God the Word,
Therefore, O *Theotokos*, we magnify you!

THE HOLY SPIRIT

The Holy Spirit is not something that stands by itself, something that we can pray for and have as a thing in itself, it is born from Love and is of Love, all its treasures are of Love, and if we are to believe the Gospels it is received by Love and Love only.

FLORENCE ALLSHORN (1887–1950)

No generation can claim to have plumbed to the depths the unfathomable riches of Christ. The Holy Spirit has promised to lead us, step by step, into the fullness of truth.

LEO JOZEF CARDINAL SUENENS (1904–1996)

The Holy Spirit is with us at all times. There is no real spiritual life apart from the Holy Spirit. St. Seraphim of Sarov constantly repeated this teaching to his disciples and all visitors who approached him: "The true goal of our Christian life consists in the acquisition of the Holy Spirit." The Holy Spirit came at Pentecost over everyone, and he filled the world with himself. *Et replevit orbis terrarum.* No one can manipulate or control the Holy Spirit, no earthly power or ecclesiastical authority, no one at all: For as the Scriptures remind us, he "breathes where he wills" (John 3:8). And he doesn't accept being stifled! There is only one thing we can do positively, and that is to submit and surrender to him at all times, to allow him to possess us, as St. Seraphim loved it to say. *Veni, Sancte Spiritus.*

JULY 18 · *St. Pambon, Desert Monk*

LANGUAGE

Mystical language expresses the gratuitousness of God's love; Prophetic language expresses the demands this love makes.

GUSTAVO GUTIÉRREZ

Language should always be simple, true, genuine, clear, transparent, practical, precise, and totally understandable. It must mean exactly what it intends to say. And when we speak, we must learn the usage or art of language frugality. Often, if not always, fewer words are better, and they usually suffice. That was our Lord's method. He taught us to reply to others with simple yes or no answers. It was also the method followed by the Desert Fathers who, with their short and to-the-point sayings, conveyed timeless wisdom.

JULY 19 · *St. Macrina the Younger*

A GARDENER'S PLAINT

I have grafted all the trees in my garden with the fairest grafts that I have seen for a long while, and they are beginning to put forth green; also I have dug another garden and I have carefully planted cabbages, porray, parsley and sage and other goodly herbs. And furthermore I have pulled up and cleared from it the nettles, brambles and wicked weeds, and I have sown it full with many good seeds; and in it I have likewise many fair trees bearing diverse fruits, such apples, pears, plums, cherries and nuts, and everywhere have I very well looked after them, yet all I have earned this week is 3d. and my expenses.

A GARDENER AT BURY ST. EDMUNDS,
FROM A FOURTEENTH-CENTURY MANUSCRIPT

JULY 20 · St. Elijah, Prophet

FEAR OF THE LORD

The fear of the Lord *leads to life; one eats and sleeps free from any harm.*

PROVERBS 19:23

Today it is often forgotten that the fear of the Lord is a gift of the Holy Spirit, and therefore it is not often cultivated by many Christians. Fear of the Lord, in the biblical tradition, implied an honest and sincere respect for God, for his holy will, for his holy name, and for all his commandments. The Desert Fathers taught this daily to their disciples: "As the breath which comes out of our nostrils, so do we need humility and the fear of God" (Abba Poemen the Shepherd). And Proverbs 9:10 reminds us that "the beginning of wisdom is fear of the Lord." Blessed are those who walk in the fear of the Lord, in the ways of wisdom!

JULY 21

GOD'S GLORY

That in all things God may be glorified.

THE RULE OF ST. BENEDICT, CHAPTER 57

St. Irenaeus of Lyons used to say that the glory of God consisted in man being alive. *"Gloria Dei, homo vivens."* I often wondered what he meant by that. It sounded nice, but I must confess that for a long time I really didn't understand the meaning of it until I correlated it with St. Benedict's statement in the *Rule.* If I understand St. Benedict correctly, we monks—all human beings, really—must live justly, must be alive in such a way that our lives glorify God. We need not wait until we get to heaven to start singing the eternal Sanctus: We must begin here on earth, on the place where God has placed us. And we do this as the saying goes, by "blooming where we are planted." *Gloria a Patri, et Filio, et Spiritui Sancto.*

AN APOSTLE TO THE APOSTLES

When You spoke to Mary,
the ointment-bearing woman with joy,
You ended the wailing of Eve, the first mother,
by Your Resurrection,
commanding Mary and the disciples to proclaim that the Savior is indeed risen from the tomb.

MATINS, SUNDAY OF THE OINTMENT-BEARERS

The *Roman Martyrology* for today reads: "Memorial of St. Mary Magdalene. She was delivered of demons by Christ, and placed herself at the service of the Lord, following him until the end in Calvary. She was chosen to be the first to recognize the risen Lord, and she announced the good tidings of the resurrection to the Apostles. Devotion to St. Mary Magdalene was spread from the abbey of Vezelay dedicated to her and from La Sainte-Baume in Provence, where the tradition says she lived a penitential life in a nearby grotto."

THE INTERIOR CLOISTER

A garden enclosed, my sister, my bride,
a garden enclosed, a fountain sealed!
SONG OF SONGS 4:12

During the Middle Ages, it was popular among monks to describe monastic life as an interior cloister, an enclosed garden. The idea that this was interior, enclosed, reassured them that it was protected on every side by God's presence. In a classical monastery of the period, the quadrangle cloister was built in the interior of the monastery, and it was usually surrounded by four heavy stone walls on every side. The beautifully built cloisters, where monks made their processions and often used as a place for prayer or reading, opened into an open space, an interior harmonious garden with a fountain placed in the center. The cloister area and the enclosed garden were always considered places of strict silence and recollection. If one passed another monk in the cloister corridor, one never uttered a word but simply bowed one's head slightly as acknowledgment and a sign of respect.

The concept of the "interior cloister" came from this concrete and regular practice in medieval monastic life. Thus, the attractive imagery of an "interior cloister" and an "enclosed garden" became the symbols for the heart, that innermost center of ourselves, where the Lord's presence is felt more profoundly, one that always must be safeguarded in secret and protected from the intrusions of distraction and evil. These concepts and imagery may seem a bit outdated to some of our contemporaries, but the fact remains that they carry with them deep biblical roots. For the concept of the heart as the center and symbol of the whole person is one that we find referred to again and again in all biblical literature. In the traditional Semitic languages, the heart always symbolized the whole person. Hence the first commandment is that one must love God with one's whole heart. Likewise, the Gospel sentence: "The kingdom of God is [within] you" (Luke 17:21). All our intimate dealings with God occur always in our innermost, within the confines of our own hearts.

GOD'S PRESENCE IN THE DAILY

LORD, you have probed me, you know me:
you know when I sit and stand;
you understand my thoughts from afar.
You sift through my travels and my rest;
with all my ways you are familiar.

PSALM 139:1–3

We live in such a materialistic and greedy world today, where little is given or offered free. The ever-consuming society seems always self-centered in itself and the pursuit of endless ephemeral pleasures. Yet there is also the pain of loneliness and alienation that readily comes with this attitude. I often notice that deep down people are basically lonely. How blind we humans often are, for much is freely offered to us at a higher realm, and we either dismiss it or take it for granted. God's presence is all around us. We are surrounded by him, and I am reminded by St. Paul that in God we are, move, and have our being. God's presence in our daily is a gift from above, and it's gratuitous. We simply need to open the eyes of our hearts and look for him. Those who have faith and sincerely seek his face find him everywhere. God's presence is like an immense river, bearing us up and propelling us constantly toward him, toward his mystery. God knows we need his presence in our otherwise empty lives, and he doesn't hesitate to give it to us, making us partakers of his divine life at all times. It is his grace, therefore, that gives meaning to our lives and sustains our day.

THE APOSTLES

Blessing in the highest
to the One who proceeds from the Father,
to the Holy Spirit
through whom the apostles
drank the immortal cup
and invited the earth to heaven.

"HYMN TO THE HOLY SPIRIT," ARMENIAN LITURGY

The feast of every single apostle or evangelist is an occasion of joy in this monastery. We are deeply attached to them, to each one of them in particular. Each was deeply loved by the Master. And it's thanks to them, to their precious recollections and memories, to their tireless preaching to the four corners of the world, that the Master's words and teachings were transmitted from generation to generation up to our times. The small college of apostles and disciples that Jesus formed around himself was part of a divine plan, and, as usual, the Holy Spirit was its executor. One can sense how each apostle was totally possessed by the Holy Spirit. They were his chosen instruments. At Pentecost, the Spirit poured himself upon them in a way that could never be described or measured. It was all part of God's plan, of God mystery. I think about the apostles often, I treasure their memory, and rejoice at their presence in their icons in the chapel. They are our friends. They plead for us. In our daily, when we ring the bells that call us to office, we peal them twelve times as a simple reminder of each of these, the Lord's servants.

THE HOLY ANCESTORS OF GOD

By giving birth to you, O Mother of God,
Joachim and Anna were delivered from the reproach of barrenness;
Adam and Eve were delivered from the corruption of death;
And we, the people, having been saved from the stain of iniquity,
cry unto you:
The barren one gives birth to the Theotokos,
who nourishes our life.

KONTAKION FOR THE NATIVITY OF MARY

Today the *Roman Martyrology* reads: "The memorial of Sts. Joachim and Anna, inheritors of the Alliance and Promise made to the people of Israel, from whom emerged the blessed Virgin Mary, Mother of God. The devotion to St. Anna was particularly developed in Brittany, France, especially after the apparitions that took place at Auray in 1623."

A beautiful icon of Sts. Joachim and Anna boost their presence in our small chapel. The icon is there to remind us daily of God's human family: They are the loving parents of Mary, the *Theotokos*, and the grandparents of Jesus. I am sure the Lord loved and honored his grandparents with that particular affection all grandchildren feel toward their grandparents. As for us, poor humans, we pray to them and count daily on their powerful intercession.

JULY 27

AN ORDINARY JULY DAY

The daylight hours are the longest during July, and just as well, as there is plenty to do during the day. After today's Morning Office at sunrise and a small breakfast, I went out into the garden for a quick inspection. The sunlight was just beginning to touch the fields and the treetops, and soon it was reflected in the all-surrounding Mother Nature. *It is a fine, quiet, typical July morning,* I said to myself. Later in the day, I shall return once more or several times more to the garden, not only to inspect our crops, but this time with an old basket to pick some of the sweetest tomatoes ripening at this time. They are the first to arrive, and one can already sense the faint, sweet smell from their plants. As I pay this early-morning visit to the garden, I become more and more aware of the endless blessings received in this place. The Lord's presence is truly among us. What else can one wish for? All that is left for us to do is to let his presence invade us totally and enjoy it thoroughly. *Benedicamus Domino.*

JULY 28

THE LORD'S GAZE

Be aware that God's gaze is upon you, wherever you may be.

THE RULE OF ST. BENEDICT, CHAPTER 4

As I till the soil during these last July days, I am aware that the Lord's gaze is nowhere more focused upon us than when we labor in the garden. Scripture tells us that from the beginning the Lord walked with humankind in the Garden of Eden. Our lives have been intertwined with the Garden saga ever since. Metaphorically, our lives are "like watered gardens," (Jeremiah 31:12). And by the Divine Gardener's infinite and tender care, they shall never again be "neglected." It was in a garden, after all, that the Lord languished and prayed before going to his death, and also it was from a tomb set in a garden that he rose triumphant from the dead.

THE GIFT OF FRIENDSHIP

Mary has chosen the better part and
it will not be taken away from her.
LUKE 10:42

Master, the one you love [Lazarus] is ill.
JOHN 11:3

Now Jesus loved Martha and her sister and Lazarus.
JOHN 11:5

Behold, today's memorial feast allows us to dwell on a topic not often reflected upon enough: the friendships of Jesus. Anyone who reads the four Gospel accounts can certainly verify the revered role the Lord assigned in his life to friendship, to human emotion, to intimacy, to human closeness, and to loving others. He started with the love he had for his parents, Mary and Joseph, and continued on with the trusting human intimacy he shared with the disciples, his friends, and close followers. Jesus, the Word of God, became totally human in everything except sin, tells St. Paul. In embracing our lowly humanity, he embraced all the feelings and emotions human beings are capable of. He embraced human love in its totality, first as fulfillment of the commandment to love God above all things and our neighbors as ourselves. And secondly, he embraced it by raising all human love to a most noble and high level, by telling us that there was no greater proof of love than to give one's life for a friend.

In today's Gospel episode, we see how comfortable Jesus was in the company of his dear friends Mary, Martha, and Lazarus, and how comfortable they were with him. Real friendship is always a two-way street. They could demand anything of him, and he could respond to each and every one of their needs. It is always touching to read that, just before undergoing his passion, one of the lasts visits he paid was to Bethany, to the home of Mary, Martha, and Lazarus. This time the purpose of the visit was to console these dear friends at the painful loss of their brother, Lazarus. Jesus felt the pain so deeply that he cried when he heard that his beloved friend, Lazarus, had died. And lo and behold, he goes one step further, doing what only a man who is also God can do: He prays for Lazarus and calls him from the tomb. Can anyone ever doubt the extent and power of Jesus' love? In all instances, he is pure, boundless, infinite love. The example of his life, totally motivated and guided by love, should be for us sufficient reason to pursue the work of love at all cost. Love for one another was his message and the only authentic proof of true discipleship. "This is how all will know that you are my disciples, if you have love for one another" (John 13:35).

THE UNCREATED DIVINE LIGHT

For with you is the fountain of life; and in your light we see light.

PSALM 36:10

July is waning, and we are fast approaching the feast of the Transfiguration, a monastic feast par excellence. The intensity of the light at this time of the year reminds me of the inner light the early monastic fathers gravitated toward, ultimately more effective and more deeply felt than physical light, at the center of oneself. This divine light provides us, human and limited as we are, with the all-powerful sensation of the presence of the living God. The inner spiritual light is totally different from physical light, though there are also some similarities: When the Lord bestows it as a gift upon our souls, that light somehow spiritually assimilates us. This divine light, the resplendent light that surrounded Jesus during his transfiguration, lights up the entire spiritual world and makes visible that which cannot otherwise be perceived. Without this light, we are totally incapable of apprehending or contemplating something of the mystery of God. This divine light provides us poor humans with a glimpse into eternity.

THE IMITATION OF CHRIST

A few days ago, a kind person handed me a simple piece of paper with a prayer printed on it. It is a prayer adapted from a little book I used to read when I was young: *The Imitation of Christ* by Thomas à Kempis. It is a beautiful, simple, down-to-earth prayer. As I read it for the first time, I said to myself, *I shall use this prayer again and again.* It is a prayer that at the moment resonates within me:

Most gracious God and Father,
You are the glory of my soul
And the joy of my heart.
You are my hope in time of need
And my refuge in the day of trouble.
Keep me free
From all unhealthy attachments
And heal my heart of all unholy desires.
Help me to persevere in the work of love,
Give with generosity,
Act with courage,
And remain strong in faith.
Let me love You
And others
More than myself,
So that one day I may be brought safely
To Your eternal home. Amen.

AUGUST

AUGUST 1 · St. Alphonsus Liguori

THE POOR IN SPIRIT

Power is made perfect in weakness.
2 CORINTHIANS 12:9

Mother Thekla—a true Desert Mother of our times who inspired many during her lifetime and died in 2011—wrote in her book *Orthodox Potential:* "Poverty of spirit is our joy and our weapon against every ill. The poor in spirit ever repent, never cease to look toward God, the One God. Where the world is wise, they are foolish, and this wealth no one can take away from them. When we deny achievement of reason, our work need never end, and there can be no disappointment. To deny achievement of reason is to welcome every effort of mind. To deny the proof of faith is never to cease from prayer. To deny the ties of love is ever to be open to all. Man is not the rival of God."

AUGUST 2 · St. Eusebius of Vercelli

A WORD OF WISDOM

Thus says the Lord God: Look! I am coming against these shepherds. I will take my sheep out of their hand and put a stop to their shepherding my flock.
EZEKIEL 34:10

A holy old monk in France, who throughout the years many sought for advice and spiritual direction, once said to me: "Many of our spiritual leaders, abbots and bishops alike, lack the evangelical qualities of true shepherds. They are more ecclesiastical managers, administrators, business-type people. While they may sometimes be good at managing the temporal affairs of their flock, they lack the wisdom that comes from profound humility and deep union with God in prayer."

AUGUST 3

HUNGER FOR GOD

O God, you are my God—it is you I seek! For you my body yearns; for you my soul thirsts.

PSALM 63:2

There is a profound paradox in the intimate life of prayer. The deeper and closer one is united with God, the more one hungers and pines for him. This hunger is sometimes felt, both spiritually and physically, and it has all the symptoms of real hunger. It can even be painful as it is also delightful at the same time. The only relief one sometimes feels comes from being totally possessed by the divine presence in a state of deep silence and tranquility. There is nowhere else to go. One finds oneself in God, absorbed by God.

AUGUST 4

THE POWER OF LOVE

There is one common factor: All love is in God, all love is to God, all love comes from God.

MOTHER THEKLA

I once asked an elderly monk in France, someone I revered deeply, if he could summarize in a short manner the essentials of the Gospel for a monk. He responded, "Jesus said love one another, pray always, and do not judge." And he continued, "The 'do-not-judge' part is the most difficult of the three, for we often do it automatically, instantly, almost without realizing it. This implies the need for constant vigilance and a continual struggle with our nature."

AUGUST 5

THE PROPHETIC WORD AND THE LAW FIND FULFILLMENT

Be attentive to me, my people;
my nation give ear to me.
For teaching shall go forth from me,
And my judgment, as light to the peoples.
I will make my victory come swiftly.

ISAIAH 51:4–5

Tomorrow is Transfiguration Day, one of the most beautiful feasts of the entire summer.

Every year I eagerly await its arrival, my eyes long to see our Savior resplendent in his white-as-snow garment, giving us a glimpse of his divinity. As I read the Gospel passage of this unique event, I am particularly struck by the presence of two giants from the Old Testament: Moses and Elijah. Their lives and their teaching prepared the way for the arrival of the Savior. Now they are here to witness the fulfillment of the prophetic word pronounced by them long ago, here to see with their very eyes he whom they announced from the beginning of the ages. Tomorrow's great vision shall take place in an isolated place, high up in a mountain, somewhere out of the ordinary course of daily life in the Palestine of the times. Only these two personages and three of the apostles—Peter, James, and John—are chosen to witness the vision, a vision that glows with the light of eternity and penetrates into the mystery of God himself.

TRANSFIGURATION DAY

You were transfigured on the mountain, O Christ our God, revealing as much of your glory to your disciples and they could behold. Through the prayers of the Mother of God, let your everlasting light also shine upon us sinners. O Giver of Light, glory be to you.

TROPARION OF THE FEAST

For those who love heavenly things, the Lord's great feast arrived today. I recall that since yesterday evening the monks of Mount Athos have kept an all-night vigil on the mountain's highest point, praying and singing in preparation for the feast. At dawn, when the first rays from the sun manifested themselves, they commenced the divine liturgy, the summit of their celebration. Every year I unite myself to them in spirit and to all monks and nuns around the world as they delight themselves in the presence of the transfigured Lord. It is truly a monastic feast, one of the most loved feasts in the entire monastic calendar. As one listens to the Gospel account, one is reminded that after beholding Jesus' glory the disciples are forewarned by the Lord about his upcoming passion and resurrection, and they are asked not to mention the mountain vision to anyone until after his resurrection. In listening to the Gospel words, one notices that the Father's voice is clearly heard: "This is my beloved Son. Listen to him."

As I listen to the lector doing the reading, I am reminded of another glorious event, the Theophany of the Lord in the River Jordan, another glorious divine manifestation. Both the theophany and the transfiguration mysteries remind us humans that Christ, the Son of God, never left the Father's side when he descended from heaven to become one of us. In both, in his divine transfiguration and in his glorious theophany, he makes a point of uniting heaven and earth, the divine and the human. Both divine interventions—as well as the Incarnation and birth of the Son of God, the Lord's death on Good Friday, and his glorious resurrection on Easter Sunday—are truly transcendental cosmic events. They changed the world and the course of history forever.

AUGUST 7

LIVING AND GARDENING WITH MYSTERY

By the Lord's *knowledge they are kept distinct; and he designates the seasons and feasts. Some he exalts and sanctifies, and others he lists as ordinary days.*

SIRACH 33:8

When we plant a seed in the garden or in the greenhouse, we commit ourselves to encountering the unknown, to embracing mystery. We know for certain that some seeds will develop and grow, and others for whatever reason will never germinate. This happens often enough, as it did this year with the pole beans, which I had to replant several times before some of them finally germinated and developed. It can be rather frustrating, since it takes a week or more before the signs of germination appear, and when we repeat the process and still get futile results, we must have recourse to prayer and beg the Lord for the gift of patience. The garden teaches us to live daily with unpredictable events, with uncertainty, with mystery. Deep down, I know that we are only the sowers and caretakers, and it is the Lord who is the reliable gardener who chooses when and how to bring fruit from our humble efforts. I find peace in relying completely upon him.

MIDSUMMER

The one who made the earth by his power, established the world by his wisdom.

JEREMIAH 10:12

As we traverse through these early August days, I am perfectly mindful that we are living the heights of our singular midsummer period. The pleasant summer weather brings us often outdoors not just for our daily garden and farm tasks, but also in the evening for the delight of a meal eaten *al fresco.*

During the day, while working and weeding in the garden, I enjoy the intensity of the light while also feeling the vitality of the sun on my back. I usually do my garden chores early in the morning or in the late afternoon, when the rays from the sun are easier to bear. No matter what time of day it may be, these midsummer days make me keenly aware of the vitality of life all around me. Our vegetable, herb, and flower gardens—simple and creative as they are—portray their own unique type of monastic landscape. Before the singing of Vespers, I like to take a last look at the environment around the monastery, and somehow I am always nurtured by all the colorful beauty. Our humble monastic gardens may not be masterpieces—and they certainly cannot compare to those renowned gardens one visits in New York, Connecticut, or nearby Massachusetts—and yet they sparkle with their own simple beauty. They are monastic, they are there to praise God in their tranquil serene beauty, and they are there to provide food for the table, and flowers for the worship of God in our small chapel. During the Hours of the Office, I gaze at the gorgeous bouquet of zinnias, daisies, and sunflowers, and instinctively I understand that this is why they were made: to praise God. Silently, in unison with the monks, they utter the *"Canticum Novum,"* the new song of praise unto the Lord.

A DAILY GARDEN TASK: WATERING

They themselves shall be like watered gardens, never again neglected.

JEREMIAH 31:12

During these hot August days, one of the most important tasks in the garden is daily watering. The Hudson Valley is known for its heat and humidity during the summer months. The ever-vigilant gardener must make sure his vegetable and flower beds are replenished with water, especially in the areas that receive little or no rainfall. Often, when we have been deprived of rain in our region, I use the evening hours to give the plants a good, slow soaking in order to reach the entire root system. In seasons of extreme drought, which occur occasionally, watering twice a day becomes necessary. Each gardener knows his gardens, his plants, and their individual needs. And the gardener also knows the essential role water plays in replenishing and cultivating the soil. Irrigation brings gladness to the garden. It comforts the plants and gives them joy to continue growing and producing new fruits. Thoughtful watering refreshes not only the dried plants in the garden, it refreshes the soul of the gardener.

PRAYING WHILE LABORING

One does not live by bread alone, but by every word that comes forth from the mouth of God.

MATTHEW 4:4

When someone asks how we pray during the day while doing our ordinary tasks such as gardening or cooking, I simply respond that prayer is plain, uncomplicated conversation with God. I listen to him and he listens to me. It is a mutual exchange. In the garden, one of God's favorite spots from the beginning of creation, the Lord speaks to us in many forms and fashions: through the soil we till, the plants we cultivate and touch, the breeze we feel, the heat of the sun, the gentle refreshment from the rain, and the sweet scent from the herbs and flowers. Oh, indeed he speaks to us in unimaginable ways! All we need to do is remain quiet and listen to his voice attentively. An interior disposition is necessary, otherwise we are so full of noise ourselves that his words can't be heard. Stillness, inner quiet, a sound intuition, simplicity of heart, and a deep love for God's word in the Scriptures are the best dispositions for prayer, for hearing and responding to God's voice in the depths of our hearts.

AUGUST 11 · St. Clare

MID-AUGUST

What your hands provide you will enjoy; you will be blessed and prosper...within your home...around your table.

PSALM 128:2–3

It's almost mid-August, and while staring at the newly turned red tomatoes in the garden, I keep wondering if the large salad bowl in my hands is big enough to carry the ripe ones into the kitchen. The tomato harvest in mid-August, when the year stands firm, is truly a yearly miracle. Any gardener who has ever raised vegetables knows this. After being deprived during the long winter months of the freshness and taste of home-raised tomatoes such as our garden is producing now, I am overwhelmed by our present seasonal bounty and by God's blessing upon our humble garden work. As I ponder the endless ways one can prepare and serve tomatoes at the monastic table, I quietly keep repeating, *Te Deum laudamus.* Yes, we give you praise and thanks, O Lord, for the wonders you do daily for us. *In Te, Domine, speravi, non confundar in aeternum.*

THE MYSTERY OF TIME

Draw near to God, and he will draw near to you.

JAMES 4:8

In the garden, we experience intimately the mysterious presence of what we call time: the days, weeks, months, and seasons succeed each other almost mathematically, one by one, without ever missing a second or a minute. The inescapable reality of time, as experienced subtly in our gardens, makes me turn inexorably to him who is the author and Lord of time. The Lord gave us time, or what the Greeks call *chronos,* so that through the ordinary calendar days we may reach what the New Testament calls *kairos,* salvation time.

"Behold, now is a very acceptable time; behold, now is the day of salvation," says St. Paul in 2 Corinthians 6:2. In proclaiming this truth, the apostle is telling us to make heed and use time wisely. For this is indeed the right time, the ripe time, the appointed time, for us to accept the Lord's gracious invitation to enter into a communion of fullness with him.

COMMON SENSE VERSUS WISDOM

So there is meaning in our journey. We in search of God, and God in search of us.

BASIL HUME, *TO BE A PILGRIM: A SPIRITUAL NOTEBOOK,* 1984

Gardening, though simple and basic, is a deeply spiritual activity. True gardeners find it to be a source of infinite joy and satisfaction. For them, gardening is a daily school they attend. In that school they learn those secret lessons that enhance and enrich the soul.

The place where one gardens becomes our spiritual home. Those cultivated green acres are priceless. From there we learn the true meaning of work in progress, we watch the succession and changes of the seasons, the pleasure of touching the soil with our own hands, and ultimately the reward of tasting its results. Not much is required of us, except that we learn to toil under God's protective eyes, and that we do our work in peace and with joy.

Today, while laboring in the garden, I kept thinking about how essential common sense is in daily life, throughout all our activities. Common sense, a gift from God, is distinct from wisdom. There is a subtle difference between the two, and in contrast to wisdom, common sense is something we can cultivate and somehow acquire the practice by acting thus in our everyday living. Common sense always comes in handy, no matter what, and it helps prepare the way for when the Holy Spirit bestows the gift of wisdom upon the soul. Wisdom is an altogether different matter. It is a form of infused knowledge, a pure gift from above, and the Lord grants it sometimes to someone imbued with profound humility. Furthermore, he grants it only when he pleases. When wisdom descends upon the soul, one begins to see things by pure intuition, even the most complex of matters, in the split of a second, all at once, in all their depth and complexity. It seems to me as if the process of reasoning is shortened or dispensed with, and one simply sees and understands all reality in the light of God. Wisdom is truly a mysterious thing, and one never arrives to it by oneself. As all gifts from the Holy Spirit, one simply discovers one day that the gift is there. Suddenly our usual outlook and understanding deepens, we begin to see all reality in a new way, in a new light, and we can't explain it. This is particularly true when reading the sacred Scriptures, when wisdom sometimes provides a total new intuition upon passages or words read and heard many times before. Now, suddenly, the same words or passages are perceived in fresh new light, for a new and deeper insight is then provided. The ways of God are indeed mysterious, and who can really understand them?

GOD'S GLORY

They sow fields and planted vineyards, brought in an abundant harvest.

PSALM 107:37

It is a time of fullness in the local Hudson Valley orchards and gardens. I recently went to the Arlington farmers market in Poughkeepsie, where a friend sells local products from our monastery: plants, eggs, vinegars, jams, chutneys, tapenade, and salsa, among other things. I was overwhelmed by the beauty and quality of the products I saw: peaches and plums of all sizes and colors, the newly arrived sweet corn, endless varieties of heirloom tomatoes, sweet and hot peppers, and most marvelous and delicious small eggplants, sometimes called Japanese eggplants. It is such a treat to cook and prepare them in endless forms. They are not only easy to cook, but because they are so fresh and tender they require little time for cooking. Their flavor, no matter how they are prepared, seems just perfect at this time of year. Before cooking them, I always slice them in halves, place them in cold water with just a pinch of sea salt, and leave them for an hour or two "to sweat" a bit, as we call this process in French. It always works for me.

I tend to enjoy all things, especially fruits and vegetables, in their own season. Therefore, I don't mind the tedious, hard work in our garden. One must have the willingness to use his own back and know to till and work the soil, but if we daily keep in step with the garden's own rhythm, we shall in due season be the grand beneficiary of its unparalleled magnanimity. And as we delight in the products from the garden, the labor and work of our hands, we realize how much God's glory shines through on earth.

THE DORMITION AND ASSUMPTION OF OUR LADY

Come, let us rejoice in Zion,
the divine and fertile hill of the living God,
beholding the *Theotokos.*
For Christ, her Son, transported her to the most worthy
and divine abode,
In the Holy of Holies; for she indeed is his Mother.
Come, you believers, let us approach the tomb of the *Theotokos,*
kissing it with our lips, hearts, eyes, and brow,
touching it meekly, receiving from its ever-flowing fountain
precious gifts of healing.
O Mother of the living God,
accept from us our farewell praise,
and protect us with your light-giving divine grace.
Grant victory and peace to your Christian people;
and for us who sing to you,
obtain forgiveness and redemption for our souls.

ST. JOHN OF DAMASCUS,
"THE NINTH ODE OF THE DORMITION CANON"

AUGUST 16

How varied are your works, Lord!
In wisdom you have made them all;
the earth is full of your creatures.
PSALM 104:24

The humble, often tedious garden labor is repeated day in and day out. It is an experience of faith. In the garden, I am reminded daily that this soil, this earth we walk and work upon, is indeed God's creation. The Lord created the world and allowed it to evolve at its own pace, and in doing so he continues to reveal many hidden aspects of himself in his handiwork. We are all the work of his hands, and if garden work does anything, it inspires gratitude and thanksgiving to God for having made us in his image and likeness. It encourages us daily to look forward to sharing one day in the blessedness of his divine life.

AN UNUSUAL PILGRIMAGE: GARDENING

Let us concern ourselves with things divine, and as pilgrims sight for and desire our homeland, for the end of the road is ever the object of the traveler's hopes and desires, and thus, since we are travelers and pilgrims in the world, let us ever ponder on the end of the road, that is our life, for the end of our roadway is our home.

ST. COLUMBANUS, SANCTI COLUMBANI OPERA

We are pilgrims in this world. We are all indeed in via, traveling toward the eternal city of God. The pilgrimage we undertake often has its ups and downs, its moments of groaning and grief, and also its occasional joys. As long as this life pilgrimage endures, we are assured of those long periods of dullness, darkness, doubt, and boredom. To help and cheer us on our way, God provides a place of rest: our gardens. The garden then becomes to each of us a secret place of repose and delight, a place where the pilgrim can be refreshed, restored, and find inspiration to continue the journey.

AN UNPREDICTABLE FRIEND: TIME

That I may proclaim your might to all generations yet to come. Your power and justice, God, to the highest heaven. You have done great things; O God, who is your equal?

PSALM 71:18–19

Toiling daily in our gardens, I notice the many changes upon the plants as time passes by. From the perspective of time, nothing ever stays the same. Indeed, the flux of time measures and rules over all our garden activities and over the garden itself. It is a good thing, therefore, to choose time as a friend and companion and not fight its many inconsistencies, especially in the weather. Again and again, I remind myself that time, an element created by God, is there to help and enhance the work undertaken in our gardens. If time dictates and measures most of our garden activities, it is because the Lord himself assigned to time such a task. It is wise, therefore, for the gardener to cooperate and create a partnership with that most unpredictable of partners, time.

THE GARDEN AS HEALER

Nature has a purpose. Each and every person, creature, plant, and thing has a mission to help further the realization of heaven and earth.

MEISHUSAMA

While working in one of our several humble gardens, I'm often penetrated by a deep feeling that this is the place where heaven and earth connect and converge. Plants, be they flowers, herbs, vegetables, shrubs, or trees, all contain a higher purpose intended by the Creator. Humble creatures that they are, all plants possess healing qualities, often a mystery to us, and their secret is only known by God. They heal the very spot where they are planted and deeply rooted. It is no wonder that our spirits expand and feel elated in the garden at the mere contact with these humble creatures called plants. All plants and vegetation of the earth, bless the Lord.

A MELLIFLUOUS MONASTIC VOICE

We learn much more from the trees of the forest than from books. The trees and the rocks often teach us things that cannot be learned elsewhere...you will see for yourselves, that one can extract honey and oil from the hardest of stones....

ST. BERNARD

It is indeed a unique gift and admirable grace from God that allows the monk (and all those other "monastics" by extension) to live in the peace and desert of the cloister.... There, we silently cultivate our gardens, nurture our trees and shrubs, smell the sweet scents that emanate from our herbs, and all along, learn from the nature of their being, discovering that ineffable "something" that God left imprinted in each of them....

ST. BERNARD

I enjoy reading the writing of St. Bernard, whose memory we honor today. He uses nature's everyday images to teach us profound lessons about the inner workings of the human spirit. His words and powerful insights, full of that early medieval mellifluous unction, are like sweet dew in the midst of our ordinary daily labors. He imparts wisdom and encouragement to the weary.

THE NATURE OF GOD

What is God? He is everything at once: length, height, width, and depth. These four divine attributes are the object of so much of our contemplation....

ST. BERNARD

It is interesting that St. Bernard uses these four attributes to conceptualize the nature of God, whom we know no one can define. I smoothly make a transition from the divine to created things and rejoice in finding the same attributes in the plants in our garden. Each one is endowed with a certain length, height, width, and depth. And all of them, together become a symbol and image of paradise, the place where God dwells.

It is no coincidence that both the Bible and the fathers often make reference to the image and symbol of the garden as that of paradise, the blessed place where eternal life flourishes.

THE QUEEN OF HEAVEN

The wall (la muraille) *is the flesh, and the Bridegroom approaches it, thus the Word becomes incarnate.*

ST. BERNARD

Monastic gardens often have walls or enclosures, a reminder and vivid symbol of a monastery as an enclosed garden. The monastic enclosure is not a physical barrier to keep others out but rather a protective fence to encourage exclusively the cultivation of the inner life. One comes to a monastery for a specific purpose according to St. Benedict: to seek God and God alone. That is what the inner life is all about.

Today is the octave of the feast of the Dormition and the memorial of Our Lady, Queen of heaven and earth. When St. Bernard speaks of the wall (*la muraille*) as the flesh, he is for sure referring to Mary, from whom the Word became flesh.... A wall (I much prefer the French term *muraille*, with all its connotations) is both weak (it can fall or be demolished) and strong (a symbol of stability). Faith tells us, and St. Bernard wishes to remind us, that our Lord, the Word-Bridegroom, took flesh from Mary, the *Theotokos*, the stable, well-cemented wall, to save all of us, weak and sinful.

HARMONY AND BEAUTY

"...This beautiful flower over which the Spirit of the Lord finds its rest."

ST. BERNARD

The Spirit of God finds its delight where harmony and perfect beauty are found. A beautiful flower is none but the image of our souls, or what our souls ought to become for the Lord to descend and find rest in them. Inner beauty and harmony of spirit are strong, sweet scents that attract the Lord into our inner dwelling. It is said that St. Rose lived in a hermitage built in a quiet corner of her parents' garden. At that time, it was a wise thing to do, for young women couldn't live alone and unprotected as they do today. It is not farfetched, therefore, to think that young Rose often prayed and labored in the garden, as did the ancient monastic mothers in the deserts of Egypt and Palestine. St. Rose, whose very name evokes the beauty of a flower, blossomed in holiness, and her inner beauty attracted the eyes of the Lord.

AN EXPECTED ARRIVAL: THE HARVEST

It is therefore you who inhabit gardens, you who meditate day and night on the law of the Lord. All the books you read are as many gardens where you stroll and find delight in.

GUERRIC D'IGNY

The medieval Cistercian father, Guerric d'Igny, is quite right in implying that many of us literally "inhabit" our gardens. This insight of his is true in the case of many gardeners, monks and non-monks alike. We may not spend the night in the garden as we do in our monastic cells, but we do spend as many hours toiling in the garden as we do night hours resting in our cells. This is particularly true at certain times of the year and of the gardening seasons: planting time, weeding time, and the time of the harvest. And the harvest time has arrived with all its intensity, eagerness, and demands. Now is the "appointed time" as St. Paul calls it, for the tomato harvest: tomatoes of all colors and sizes, of all textures and tastes. As I quietly go about gathering those fully ripe, carefully placing them into a well-worn old basket, I am reminded of words uttered by Solon Robinson (1803–1880). He wrote with timely wisdom a book called *Facts for Farmers.* In it he said: "Everyone who is happy to live in the country and can gather vegetables daily from his own garden knows the difference between them when gathered thus and properly cooked, and those which have been picked and kept for market even only for one night."

SUNFLOWERS

Shout joyfully to God, all the earth; sing of his glorious name.

PSALM 66:2

What a marvelous sight we behold these days in our rather compact vegetable garden! On the west side there are rows of standing sunflowers in full bloom: tall, radiant, with a pure blue sky as background. Every year this amazing miracle gets repeated, and one never tires of contemplating it. I actually anticipate the flowers' future arrival on the occasion when we place in the ground the first seeds in early spring. I treasure those rustic flowers in the garden, or elsewhere as when arranged in clay vases in a floral bouquet for the chapel. When they are finally placed in our otherwise dark chapel, the sunflowers look so tall and majestic—like a blaze of yellow, orange, and brown—yet always with their own quiet demeanor. Needless to say, they are an incentive to prayer and praise.

Today we keep the memorial of a saintly king of France, the great and humble St. Louis. Thus, I bring out of a small mental box of treasured memories the recollection of many lovely vistas of sunflower fields by the roadways of rural France, either in la France *profonde* or the region of the Midi. I recall them to be more than simply eye-catching; they were really spectacular. It is not mere coincidence that many of the great painters found inspiration in the rare beauty of the humble *tournesol,* translated literally as "turned to the sun." Sunflowers, somehow, not only resemble the sun disk, but are actually intended to gaze toward the sun. And the sun, of course, remains for us the symbol of the Son of God, the true "Sun of Justice" who enlightens all those sitting in darkness.

INSEPARABLE COMPANIONS: TOILING AND PATIENCE

In this strange life we grow through adversity rather than through success. The greatest lessons we have to learn are those concerned with loss, not gain.

MARTIN ISRAEL, ANGLICAN PRIEST

Sometimes, perhaps more often than we think, one encounters a certain frustration in the garden, such as when our cultivated plants are overwhelmed by weeds, or when there is a persistent drought, or the local deer or other animals penetrate the sacred space and bestow destruction upon the hard labor of our hands. On days as such, I pray for the type of patience that St. Teresa says gains all things: "*La paciencia todo lo alcanza.*"

Bearing this sort of conflict with patience allows one to return in time to that priceless serenity the Lord grants those who labor and toil the land under his watch. It would be unrealistic to try to think that it is possible to work the land without certain disappointments, frustrations, and trials. The main thing is to go on toiling, trusting in the Lord and Master of the harvest for an eventual bountiful outcome.

A GARDENER'S PERSONALITY

Solitude is essentially the discovery and acceptance of our uniqueness.

FR. LAWRENCE FREEMAN

We do not need anything, except a watchful, vigilant spirit.

ABBA POEMEN, DESERT FATHER

As I paced through the vegetable patch early this morning, breathing that pure, almost intoxicating early fall air (a bit ahead in this year of rather unusual weather), I reflected on the fact that gardens in general are truly secret reflections of each gardener's personality. When I walk and discover someone else's garden, it is almost as if I am entering into the secret dream world of the gardener. Somehow, each garden carries within itself the subtlest of imprints, the ever-indefinable trait of the person who cultivates it, who cares for it. The garden allows the gardener to flourish and expand his or her personality, helps him or her avoid those life aspects that tend to be negative or pernicious; instead it encourages all that is positive and beautiful in the reality that surrounds us—one seldom meets a gardener with a negative or ugly personality.

PRAYING AND GARDENING

There is another interior kind of prayer without ceasing, namely, the desire of the heart. Whatever else you may be doing, if you fix your desire on God's Sabbath rest, your prayer will be ceaseless. Therefore, if you wish to pray without ceasing, do not cease in your desire.

ST. AUGUSTINE

Today is the memorial day of the well-known St. Augustine of Hippo, who influenced so many throughout the centuries. I deeply enjoy his treatises on the psalms and the role he gives to desire in the unfolding of our prayer. In several other ways, he is controversial in the manner that he, as a Westerner, departed considerably from the theological expositions of the Greek Fathers, particularly on his concept of original sin.

The garden is a good place for one to think about St. Augustine and some of his teachings. The garden refreshes my mind daily and in new ways; therefore it allows me to put aside my own prejudices about certain aspects and teachings of St. Augustine, reflecting instead on what I find positive about him. The reality of prayer—its primacy in our daily lives—is probably the closest point where Augustine and I converge.

While toiling in the garden, tilling, planting, weeding, watering, or otherwise, I often think, *What should the gardener's attitude toward God be?* I know God, in his infinite love for us, watches over the work of our hands and its most pressing needs. He also answers our prayers when we pray for a particular need. In other words, God is always there for us....And his immediate presence is somehow mysteriously felt in the garden. How, therefore, must we, his creatures, respond to such paternal/maternal solicitude and remain attentive to his loving presence? The only answer lies in prayer: constant, unceasing prayer.

In the garden, or even elsewhere, prayer becomes so simple. It is like quietly picking or harvesting the vegetables for our evening meal. Quietly, one surely relishes these precious moments in the presence of the living God. There, in the garden stillness, we ruminate on his words, the psalms, and in silence listen to his voice. We may be moved to utter a petition, or a word of praise, or simply continue listening to his voice. No matter what the weather or temperature, one feels like the Desert Mothers and Fathers must have felt in their tiny gardens. We sense a presence that invites us to dialogue, that is, to uninterrupted prayer.

EARLY FALL PLANTING

Now withers the rose, and the lily is spent,
And both once bore the sweetest scent,
In summer, that sweet time.

ANONYMOUS, THIRTEENTH CENTURY

As I write, our monastery kitchen garden seems to be at its peak, production wise. Yesterday I spent several hours in two of our gardens gathering the culinary herbs for our winter consumption and for the sale at our Christmas Craft Fair. Every day, just before or after Vespers are sung, I keep picking the newly arrived tomatoes (in all sizes and colors), the beans, zucchinis, Swiss chard, potatoes, and, of course, some salad greens for our evening meal. While picking the vegetables, I can't help but thank the Lord for providing us with a good growing season.

The end of summer doesn't mean in the monastery it is the cycle's end for our kitchen gardens. On the contrary, now is the time for planting late-season crops. Planting a late-season vegetable garden provides us with extra crops and with some winter vegetables all the way to Thanksgiving and Christmas. From the middle to late August I usually plant new beets, turnips, leaf lettuces, mustard greens, arugula, string beans (just in case they survive the early frost!), and spinach. These vegetables usually stand more or less equally the hot August weather and the early autumn chill. They also taste sweet and crispy when we harvest them after the touch of a mild frost. By prolonging, as far as possible, the productivity of our gardens, they remain a sign of real life within the monastic enclosure. The garden itself affirms life. It fills us with the goodness of God. It reminds us daily of his loving care for each of us.

A PATRON SAINT FOR GARDENERS

A single green sprouting thing
Would restore me...
Then think of the tall delphinium,
Swaying, or the bee when it comes
To the tongue of the burgundy lily.

JANE KENYON, "THINKING OF FLOWERS"

As I glance at the calendar, I am reminded that today we celebrate the feast of St. Fiacre, a monk-gardener, a patron saint of gardens and gardeners. St. Fiacre was a wandering hermit monk who migrated from Ireland to northern France where he cultivated an extensive fruitful garden. His garden abilities were highly admired in the surrounding vicinity, as were his humility and eminent virtues. His love of God was often translated into the good works he performed for others, including miracles that were attributed to him. The saintliness of the monk-gardener was never in doubt. Here in our vegetable patch, his presence stands out tall, at the center of the garden. From there he watches over and protects his territory. Throughout the growing season many tasks, needs, and results are entrusted to St. Fiacre, for I know he faithfully watches over his humble domain. Here in the monastery, the work of gardening and the spiritual life are very much intertwined, for the care and cultivation of the land certainly is a great assistance to the care and cultivation of the soul. By a gift from God's grace, those two tasks are never separated.

ST. BENEDICT'S GIFT

A young monk asked Abba Poemen, "Is it better to speak or to be silent?" The old monk responded to him, "The man who speaks for God's sake does well, but he who is silent for God's sake also does well."

ABBA POEMEN, CALLED THE SHEPHERD, DESERT FATHER

August days are over after today. It was a full, fruitful month in many more ways than one. A time of much labor, but also of plenitude. The gigantic zinnias and the sunflowers are now in full bloom in the vegetable garden, and they provide enough flowers to create simple arrangements for the chapel. While our chapel is rather dark, even the presence of a single, humble bouquet makes it brighter, radiant, inviting all of us to prayer and praise. We have worked hard, intensely, all throughout last month, and now as August starts its departure I am looking forward to a blessed moment of rest. There is a feeling of deep stillness in the monastery and all around the surrounding area. I am very fond of it, and I am particularly pleased when some of the local people return here because, as they tell me, they find the place very peaceful. Sometimes some of the same people show up unexpectedly several times a month, bringing along someone new. I always welcome them to the peace of St. Benedict and often invite them to a moment of quiet prayer in the chapel. I know when they depart they carry back to their homes a feeling of tranquility and peace. That peace, *pax*, is St. Benedict's gift to them.

SEPTEMBER

SEPTEMBER 1

LABOR DAY WEEKEND AND PROPER REST

Give me this crown, Lord, you know how I long for it, for I have loved you with all my heart and all my being. When I see you I shall be filled with joy and you will give me rest.

SIMEON BAR SABBA'E, FOURTH-CENTURY PERSIAN MARTYR

After work, a rest is welcome.

PETER OF CELLE, MEDIEVAL CISTERCIAN MONK

Labor Day weekend reminds us that rest, holy rest, is as much a law of life as labor. How often we forget this lesson and succumb to the tyranny of endless work, work at odd hours, work without a fixed schedule for rest, overtime work sometimes based on real need and other times based on a desire to conquest, to succeed.

The monk is asked daily to get his hands dirty into the soil, but he is also asked to take time away from it, to spend time in prayer and holy reading, to allocate time for meals and time for rest. St. Benedict reminds us daily in the *Rule*: "in all things, moderation." It is only through this healthy monastic rhythm of prayer, work, and rest that we can achieve a state of serenity, a type of serenity that makes God's presence palpable in our lives.

SEPTEMBER 2

PROVENCE

When God comes to doubt the world, he remembers that he has created Provence.

FREDERIC MISTRAL

Early this morning, after feeding and watering the animals in the barn, I proceeded to the vegetable garden to engage in some much-needed weeding labor. The growing season is at its peak and there is still plenty of work to accomplish in the gardens. While weeding, as I often do, I couldn't help but think of some previous Septembers spent in the lovely French region of Provence. So many past memories make my mind return occasionally to the dear region of Provence, especially to those sites connected with a cherished monastic past: Senanque, le Thoronet, and others. Memory lane takes me back today to the lovely Provençal countryside, its rich agricultural land, the dispersed, small villages built in hills of pine and scrub often filled with wild herbs. There is no doubt the landscape of Provence is one of the loveliest in all of France. I am not surprised monks and nuns of early times decided to settle their monastic homes in the calm, solitude, and peace of that enchanted land. In many ways, I am sure, because of its Mediterranean climate and charm, it reminded them of the deserts of Egypt and Palestine, a place apart to seek God alone.

Here in our own little monastery we keep many contacts with Provence and its people. We also keep alive some of its timeless customs and traditions such as promoting the Provençal *crèches* at Christmastime, with their lovely figurines and *santons*. Our monastery is also known for cultivating and providing the well-known *herbes de Provence* for cooking. We delight in cultivating them in our small but prolific monastic herb garden. And of course, the Provençal-style tapenade, poivronnade, and the pistou made here are everybody's favorite. The demand is such that we can never make enough to satisfy everyone. Provence may seem millions of miles away, but it always remains close in our memory and in our hearts.

Work

What your hands provide you will enjoy; you will be blessed and prosper.

PSALM 128:2

We have been experiencing those typical hotter days that often begin here in the Northeast toward the end of summer. One feels the parching winds arriving from the south, and our gardens are dry and hot. Each evening, I spend several hours watering our crops. And while garden work seems demanding because of the drought, I am also concentrating on our vinegars. We continue to bottle them and take some almost daily to the tiny St. Joseph Atelier/shop, where it is available to a public that continues to come for them, especially on weekends. The vinegar this year, after a long period of fermentation, is excellent in quality, and yet we produced a smaller quantity than last year. Hopefully our supply shall be enough to last until the time of our Christmas Craft Fair at the beginning of Advent. I am not going to worry about it, for there is much to do around here otherwise with our daily tasks. I must also give my full attention to other matters, such as watering the garden, sometimes twice a day, and of course the labor of our incoming harvest. This evening, while engaged in my regular watering duty, I am moved to praise the Lord with the words of St. Francis of Assisi: "Praised be my Lord for our sister water, who is very serviceable unto us and humble and precious and clean."

HARVEST WORK CONTINUES

Creation isn't a commodity to exploit, but a gift to care for.

POPE FRANCIS

While several farmer friends in the Catskill region of New York State are this week picking the sweet corn, here in the monastery we are picking the new potatoes. Thanks to the Lord, our provider, we shall have enough potatoes to last us throughout the long winter months.

One knows true farmers and gardeners by that certain rugged attitude they are usually endowed with, such as their willingness to kneel for hours picking potatoes or root vegetables. Farmers and gardeners almost always show willing knees and strong backs made for the task. They enjoy the earthly feel and smell of the soil, the often tedious weeding jobs, the quick stepping around the diverse field and garden paths, the work of irrigating when the hot sun is crippling the veggies. Above all, they love all things in season: sweet strawberries in June; all sorts of berries in July; bright and tasty red tomatoes in August; new corn and potatoes, tender cabbage, and Swiss chard in September. Thus the glorious work of the harvest goes on and on, it continues until late November, when the last fruits from our fields and gardens are gathered just in time for Thanksgiving. *Deo gratias.*

SEPTEMBER 5

A BIT OF MONASTIC WISDOM: IN GOD'S IMAGE AND LIKENESS

Individuals have no particular identity. It is our destiny to be molded by God, so at the time of our death we have come, by degrees, closer to the likeness of Christ.

THOMAS MERTON

I sometimes reflect on and get overwhelmed by a certain awareness we Christians carry with us. If it is true that we are indeed created in God's image and likeness, what an awesome responsibility we have to live and act in a way that we show him to the world. Our lives must shine in such a way, with such transparency, that only the radiance from the divine presence can be perceived.

SEPTEMBER 6

THE MARVEL OF A VISION

Fly away from the love of the multitude, of the masses, lest the enemy question your spirit and disturb your inner peace.

ABBA DOULAS, DESERT FATHER

There is a particular anecdote in St. Silouan's life that I always like to tell others when I introduce them to him for the first time. It is something that touches the depths of our being, whoever we are. It is said that the saintly monk had the custom of spending the entire night watching in prayer in one of the chapels of the holy mountain. On one of those nights, while keeping his usual vigil, he was gently gazing with tears in his eyes at the large icon of Christ in the iconostasis. Suddenly, as it were, he saw the Lord coming out from the icon and advancing toward him. The Lord's physical appearance, a most intimate personal visitation to the monk in the infinite stillness of the night transformed Silouan forever. He eagerly placed his whole life into the hands of Christ, his Savior. From then on, Christ was always with Silouan and Silouan always with Christ.

THE EVENING OF LIFE

Do not cast me aside in my old age;
As my strength fails, do not forsake me.
PSALM 71:9

Just as a lamp lights up the darkness in a room, so the fear of God, when it penetrates the heart of a person illuminates her, teaching her all the virtues and commandments of God.
DESERT FATHERS, ABBA JAMES

Often, while working silently in the fields, in the woods, or in the gardens, I get a sense, a feeling, of how limited our days on earth are. Eternity is not far away; in fact, it has already started. The psalms refer to this reality that some may reach the age of seventy or eighty or more, but afterward it all ends.

I sometimes feel there is still much to read, to write, and to learn, to see, to hear and touch; so much to explore and discover, yet deep down we know our days are counted. They become fewer and fewer with each passing day. Indeed, time is getting short. Eternity is already opening its doors....And when the end of our days arrives, St. John of the Cross gently reminds us, all we can carry with us is that which was accomplished with love, for indeed, "in the evening of life, we will be judged on love."

THE NATIVITY OF THE THEOTOKOS

Your Nativity, O Mother of God,
has filled the universe with joy!
For from you has shone forth the Sun of Justice,
Christ our God.
He has delivered us from the curse of evil and blessed us,
he has destroyed death to grant us eternal life.

TROPARION OF THE FEAST

"Today, all creation rejoices in you, O Theotokos."

BYZANTINE OFFICE

Our summer liturgical celebrations are winding down and coming quickly to an end. Our next and last seasonal feast before officially reaching autumn shall be "The Glorious Cross" on September 14. That particular day shall bring our summer monastic celebrations to a sober conclusion.

Today's feast is especially cherished in the Eastern Church, for it marks in the Byzantine tradition the beginning of the liturgical calendar. It is appropriately so, for Mary's arrival into the world heralds that other and most important arrival, the one of our Savior, Jesus Christ. Without the *Theotokos* there would have been no Savior. I often think about a particular episode that was told of a certain abba in the Egyptian desert. He was a venerable elder, saintly and wise, and many came to him for advice. One day, a disciple was questioning him about several spiritual subjects and asked: "What about the Mother of God?" The elder remained silent for a long time and then replied: "Ah, my son, there lies a great, great mystery, something no one can describe, something no words can explain."

LIVING DAILY LIFE TO THE FULLEST

Boundless is thy love for me,
Boundless then my trust shall be.
ROBERT BRIDGES, BRITISH POET (1844–1930)

I sometimes get the impression that many people choose to live mechanical lives. They get up in the morning and go to their jobs, they put themselves through the same routine day in and day out, they never much consider the deeper realities inside or outside themselves, and they usually end their day preparing for the same routine the following day. Somehow, one notices a lack of a sense of purpose in this form of existence. Occasionally people approach me, especially the young, inquiring and trying to verbalize the reason for this reality in their lives. It is as if they were caught in a meaningless existence, riding the same train daily, one that never stops. I sometimes remind those who have approached the subject that life may sometimes seem full of uncertainties and dreariness, and that the daily routine, though at times boring, could be transformed into something creative and meaningful. We must start by trying to redesign our day in the light of faith and with the help of prayer. Fear, uncertainty, and boredom are often the result of a life not totally centered on the mystery of God. Faith and prayer strengthen us in our innermost, they provide us a comfort zone from which we can emerge luminous, positive, inspired to face life's new territories with a certain creativity and trust. Deep down, we know the Lord is by our side at all times, throughout all of life's trepidations and the fears and joys of our earthly life journey.

SEPTEMBER 10

THE WORK OF LOVE

Now in the middle of my days I glean
This truth that has a flower's freshness:
Life is the gold and sweetness of wheat;
Hate is brief and love immense.

GABRIELA MISTRAL, CHILEAN POET

Among the desert monks and nuns, our father among the saints, Antony, saw the work of love as the primordial work of the Christian, of the monk. He taught this to his disciples, saying, "I no longer fear God, but I love him. For love casts out fear." And in regard to the commandment to love our neighbor he said, "Our life and our death is with our neighbor. If we gain our brother, we have gained God, but if we scandalize our brother, we have sinned against Christ." He knew well the work of love could never be kindled by fear. Only the experience of love without demands or expectations can lead us to discover that ultimate reality in life, that "God is love and he who abides in love abides in God and God in him." We live and we die daily, and maybe we make small strides as we put all our poor efforts into the one thing necessary: the work of love. Love is not difficult or impossible with God's help. We simply begin by living it, by giving it.

SEPTEMBER 11

GOD'S LOVING CARE

Do not look forward to the changes and chances of this life in fear; rather look at them with hope that, as they arise, God, whose children you are, will deliver you out of them....The same eternal God who cares for you today will take care of you tomorrow and every day, either by shielding you from suffering or by giving you the strength to bear it. Remain at peace, then, and put aside all anxiety.

ST. FRANCIS DE SALES

How true is St. Francis de Sales' intuition. If we truly live in a spirit of faith and trust in God, we must let go of all anxieties, all fears, all earthly concerns daily. Simply know that our daily is in God's hands (in *manus Dei sumus*).

SEPTEMBER 12 · The Holy Name of Mary

OUR LADY'S LOVELY LOWLINESS

We all like to accomplish great things. Mary, however, was satisfied to let God do them in her.

LOUIS EVELY, BELGIAN PRIEST

In the *Magnificat* (Luke 1:46–55), which we sing daily at Vespers, Mary recalls her own personal history, her own dealings with the Almighty from whom she had received everything. And with that attitude of lowliness, her extreme humility, the humility that caught God's eyes and totally enchanted him, she acknowledges again and again God's lavish favors bestowed upon her: "The Mighty One has done great things for me, and holy is his name."

THE CALIBER OF THE GREEK FATHERS

Although we praise our Lord for all kinds of reasons, we praise and glorify him above all for the cross. It fills us with awe to see him dying like one accursed. It is his death for people like ourselves that St. Paul constantly regards as the sign of Christ's love for us. He passes over everything else that Christ did for our advantage and consolation and dwells unceasingly on the mystery of the cross. He says: "It is indeed the proof of God's love for us that Christ died for us while we were still sinners."

ST. JOHN CHRYSOSTOM, "TREATISE ON PROVIDENCE"

There is no way to remain faithful to the Gospel without learning how the fathers defended it, and without sharing in their struggle to make it accessible.

FR. JOHN MEYENDORFF, *CATHOLICITY AND THE CHURCH*

We joyfully celebrate today our father among the saints, St. John Chrysostom. All Christendom owes much to this great Church father. He contributed to the building of the local church with his teachings, his preaching (hence the title given to him, "the golden-mouthed"), and the courageous example of his own life. His heart was inflamed with the fire of charity and always mindful of the poor he assisted and helped. Having become patriarch of Constantinople, one of the most ancient apostolic sees, he was persecuted by his enemies and sent into exile in Armenia, where he spent the last three years of his life. Under the inspiration of the Holy Spirit, he continued to write hundreds of letters and homilies from exile, thus extending until the end of his days a humble ministry of teaching and preaching. His homily for Easter Sunday, the one read every year during the Eastern Church's paschal vigil, is one of the jewels of early Christian preaching. I wish the contemporary churches could have pastors and Christian leaders of the caliber of John Chrysostom and that of other early fathers. Instead we have career ecclesiastics only looking for their own promotion, their own advancement, and for high places in the ecclesiastical ladder. No wonder the Church today is in such a predicament, in such a decadent, moribund state. *O tempora, O mores*!

THE HOLY AND GLORIOUS CROSS

Before your cross we bow down and worship, O Master,
And your Holy Resurrection we glorify.

BYZANTINE CHANT DURING LENT

Today we pay homage to Christ's glorious cross on which the Savior acted out the mystery of our salvation. On the day of our baptism, the cross of Christ was traced over our heads, the seal and mark that from that day on our lives belong forever to Christ, our only Master. As we proceed with our lives forward, making the Sign of the Cross often and carrying our own little crosses daily, we are reminded that we are disciples of Christ, and as such, when we embrace the cross in our lives, we embrace him who in it gave his own life for us. On the third Sunday of Lent, the Eastern Church honors the mystery of the cross with these verses, indeed appropriate for today:

O Lord, who willingly ascended the cross,
Enable us to venerate it with true compunction of heart.
And enlighten us, by the disciplines of prayer, fasting,
abstinence, and good works.
For You are good and love mankind.
O Lord, cleanse me from my many sins by the grace
of your great mercy,
And enable me to see and kiss Your cross,
On this present week of the great Fast (third week of Lent)
For You are the Lover of humankind.
O greatest of wonders!
The wood on which Christ was voluntarily crucified in the flesh
Is today exalted!
The entire world bows down and sings:
"O marvelous might of the cross, I exalt you.
O most precious wood, I honor you and bow down
in reverence and fear,
And I glorify God, who through you, grants me life eternal."

SEPTEMBER 15 · *Our Lady of Sorrows*

A DESERT FATHER'S WISE COMMENT

Abba Joseph related that Abba Isaac said, "I was sitting with Abba Poemen one day and I saw him in ecstasy and as I was in on terms of great freedom of speech with him, I prostrated myself before him and begged him, saying, 'Tell me where you were.' He was forced to, and he said, 'My thoughts were with our Lady, the Theotokos, as she wept by the cross of the Savior. I wish I could always weep like that.'"

ABBA POEMEN, DESERT FATHER

SEPTEMBER 16

A SEPTEMBER REFLECTION

With God, nothing is empty of meaning, nothing without symbolism.

ST. IRENAEUS OF LYONS

Years ago I wrote *Blessings of the Daily* as a way of sharing with our friends and readers some insights into the monastic routine at Our Lady of the Resurrection. It was a quiet way of sharing with others something about our daily life here. As I look back, it seems to me I had more time to write then than I have now. Of course, that perspective could be false, for if anything might now be different it is what the years have done to our memories. Seemingly, the mind remains clear and the recollection of facts and events may be quite exact. What sometimes is not totally clear is when the precise events occurred, especially those that seem small and unimportant. One looks back at past years, and the memories are sometimes a bit vague, nebulous, especially about their precise timing. As I look back at years past, at past experiences, some afterthoughts emerge and I question myself about certain precisions. The one thing that never changes, that remains immutable, is God's presence in one's life. This gives me both great comfort and complete reassurance. At the end, only the mystery of God remains. And as St. Teresa used to love to repeat: *Solo Dios basta* (God alone suffices).

MONASTIC INDUSTRIES

New wine must be poured into fresh wineskins. [And] no one who has been drinking old wine desires new, for he says, "The old is good."

LUKE 5:38–39

Today the monastic family keeps the memorial of a remarkable abbess, St. Hildegard of Bingen. The monastery she founded in early medieval times stills remains on the banks of the Rhine, the place where she founded it. The Benedictine nuns who inhabit it continue the tradition of working the land and producing a good local wine to support themselves. This is nothing entirely unusual, for the contribution of monks and nuns to wine-growing and distilling throughout the ages is a well-known fact in Europe and elsewhere. In France, for almost 1,300 years, all the largest and best vineyards were operated by monastics. And one must not forget Dom Perignon, who discovered the secret of superb champagne through the wonderful technique of second fermentation. Even today, many sorts of wines, beers, and liqueurs are still produced in monastic houses.

Here in our small monastery, we continue to use the ancient art of fermentation to produce clean, pure organic vinegars, mostly made out of local juices and wines. The fermentation process, totally different from that of industrialized vinegars which are instantly produced, can last from six months to a year or two, until the final vinegar emerges. It is a small production, but one that is appreciated by the locals, who cherish a good artisanal product. And while the quality of our vinegars may not measure up to that of wines, liqueurs, and stouts produced in European monasteries or elsewhere, I find a point of consolation reminding myself that it was humble vinegar that was given to our blessed Lord while athirst during his last hours on the cross. He, who multiplied the wine supply at Cana and left us his own blood as drink under the species of wine, was only provided the humblest of them, vinegar, to appease his human thirst during the cruelest of hours. This event, as other Gospel ones, remains part of God's eternal paradox: "My ways are not your ways," says the Lord.

ARE MONKS USEFUL TO THE WORLD?

I have been asked more than once what use or service monks render to the world. I am not always comfortable trying to find a response to this question. A monk doesn't need a justification for his life. His *raison d'être* is that he is called by God to live in intimacy with him. His life is totally useless in the world's eyes; his only justification is that his life is in God. He lives to please God alone.

St. Benedict assures us that a man or woman enters monastic solitude to seek God alone. Yes, a monk withdraws to greater solitude and silence to seek God's face, but in seeking God's face he is mindful to pray for the whole world. He prays and weeps for the whole world, ardently asking God for his tender mercy, praying to him day and night to welcome every one of his children, saint and sinner, into his loving embrace.

SEPTEMBER 19

THE PRAYER OF THE MONK IN THE TEACHINGS OF ST. SILOUAN

According to St. Silouan of Mount Athos, it is not for the monk to seek to please the world or try to explain the mystery of his life to others. That is for others to do, such as teachers and historians. In general, people—even the most solid of Christians—allot little time for prayer in their daily lives. Monks, however, try to pray constantly. While the rest of the world may forget God, monks strive at all times to be mindful of him. Monks pray unceasingly for the world. And through the prayer of monks and others like them, by God's mercy, the world continues to exist. If constant prayer were to stop in the world, it would simply perish and cease to exist, said St. Silouan.

SEPTEMBER 20

SUMMER'S END

God is more anxious to bestow his blessings on us than we are to receive them.

ST. AUGUSTINE

As we hastily take leave of summer until another year, I think of all the blessings received during the season. I thank the Lord for the inestimable gift of life and for all that was and is good during our summer days: lovely mornings and evenings, sunshine and rain that multiplied our crops, the fruitfulness of mother earth, good weather during the vinegar festival, the many visits from friends and strangers....All of it and more made our summer days a continuous blessing. As I emerged this morning from singing Lauds in the chapel, I took a long look all around: the gardens, the trees, our farm animals, the clear blue sky, the path leading to the town road and to the guesthouse, and I uttered simply, "*Deo gratias*!"

AUTUMN'S ARRIVAL

Rejoice, my dearest brothers, because you have reached the quiet and safe anchorage of a secret harbor....Many wish to come into this port, and many make great efforts to do so yet do not achieve it. Indeed many, after reaching it, have been thrust out, since it was not granted to them from above.

ST. BRUNO

Today the calendar marks autumn's official entrance. Summer's exuberance seems to be slowly waning. It is still hot, and the gardens still need watering, but new planting has come to a halt, except for a few salad greens, arugula, and spinach that seem to thrive with the cool weather. Autumn coloring is beginning to emerge, and the white clematis, usually called paniculata, is starting to bloom with the arrival of cooler weather. The purple asters and the goldenrods are still showing their bright colors on our country roads, silent witnesses to a dying summer. In the monastery we are slowly beginning to bring indoors, right into the greenhouse, some of the pots and plants that need protection from a future frost. This we do slowly since we can't bring them all at once. The fading beauty of summer is now slowly moving away and getting transformed into another beauty, an autumnal radiant one. In the flower garden around the Lourdes grotto, the first chrysanthemums are blooming and showing their lovely faces. Once again they are honoring our Lady, ever present in the grotto, with their rustic, quiet beauty. I am sure she is smiling at them.

SIGNS OF A NEW SEASON

Showering a thousand graces
he came hurriedly through these groves,
he looked at them
And in the radiance of his gaze
he left the woodland robed in beauty.

ST. JOHN OF THE CROSS

A sense that autumn has indeed arrived is felt in the crisp, cool air. It is a certain and blessed sign of the season. Last night it rained, quietly, gently, all night long, and this morning as I gazed from the porch overlooking the barn, the garden, and the distant fields, I saw the monastic land wrapped in a soft autumnal light. The sun was softly emerging from behind, awakening the earth and all its contours. I looked at our open fields filtered through this soft light from the sun. The same light rested gently on the treetops, most of them still covered with leaves; however, one noticed they were slowly beginning to turn. *What will the day bring,* I asked myself? Living fully in the countryside, in solitude and a rather continuous silence, I never cease to delight in the sights and surprises that arrive with a new season. There is always something old and something new in each of them, and they always convey something intangible, something unique about the mystery of God.

SEPTEMBER 23

THE MONASTIC FAST

But when you fast, anoint your head and wash your face, so that you may not appear to be fasting, except to your Father who is hidden. And your Father who sees what is hidden will repay you.

MATTHEW 6:17–18

Lenten fasts make me feel better, stronger, and more active than ever.

ST. CATHERINE OF GENOA

With the appearance of fall, the traditional monastic fast also makes its entrance. In fact, it officially started on September 14, on the feast of the Holy Cross, and it will last until Easter. The monastic fast is rather simple and uncomplicated. It is observed every day during this period, except Sundays and feast days. The fast teaches a monk to control and moderate his appetite. Hopefully it also assists him in other realms of his spiritual life, where he may even need more help. The way it works is that a regular main meal is served at noontime, with supper consisting of what is called a collation, something small and light, like soup, bread, and a piece of fruit. Sometimes in American monasteries, where one is accustomed to lunch and supper, the small meal is taken at lunch and a fuller or complete meal is kept at suppertime. Besides this, there is no eating between meals. As a matter of fact, I don't see much change from the way we eat habitually. Besides, smaller meals are good both for the body and the soul. They are also a constant reminder of those who are deprived and have nothing or very little to eat. I think the period of the monastic fast can be more valuable as it becomes a tool to lead us to deeper spiritual exploration, to more interior recollection, to better keeping the *memoria Dei*; that is, growing ever more mindful of God.

KEEPING UP WITH THE NEWS

Man knows mighty little and may some day learn enough of his own ignorance to fall down and pray.

HENRY BROOKS ADAMS, AMERICAN HISTORIAN (1838–1918)

Those who dislike and reject their fellow man are impoverished in their being. They do not know the true God, who is all-embracing love.

ST. SILOUAN THE ATHONITE (1866–1938)

To remain somehow informed, I usually page through, via Internet these days, basic newspapers for this area: *The New York Times*, *the Poughkeepsie Journal*, and *La Croix* in French. I mostly peruse the headlines, and when something seems important, I take time out to read the story. Not often though! Since some of the local people come to see me, they periodically inform me of what is happening in the immediate vicinity. At nighttime, especially during the cold months, I try to remain informed about the local weather. This is imperative for us country dwellers, farmers, and gardeners who need to protect our crops and animals and prepare for the following day or week.

I find it rather dreary reading the news these days. The emphasis seems to be on horrible, unnecessary wars (when is such evil really necessary?), violence, crime, greed, fear, suspicion, pride, false successes, dirty politics, and abuses of power. All of it terribly negative! The world, the country, and society at large seem to become ever more unreasonable. Only occasionally does one find something to nourish the mind and the soul. Humanity needs to be nurtured by positive news of events that speak of reason, logic, beauty, truth, peace, progress, and true charity, and not by ghastly competitive and purely materialistic attitudes, totally oppressive in my view, that find pleasure in putting others down. I am particularly distressed by the evils of war and the abuse of the poor. I may be terribly naïve, but I can't see how people who don't seem to mind using often God's holy name (endless, meaningless "God bless yous" or "God bless this or that") for whatever purpose or reason can still be proponents of violence, death, torture, and abuse of others. Recently I read an entire article on how, as a consequence of the horrible Iraq war, the Christian community in that country is rapidly disappearing. Those people, descendants from early Christian communities, are now often persecuted and massacred by the fundamentalists, and few offer them protection. This is a direct consequence of the foolish policies of our government.

The great irony of it all is that Christians were able to live safely and freely practice their faith under the previous regime, the very regime put down by our government. I often wonder, as I pray, if our present world is not running against its own survival toward a speedy explosion of a sort. If we survive at all, it is only because of God's mercy manifested in the mystery of the cross.

CONSTANCY IN PRAYER

Watching means to sit in your cell praying and being always mindful of God. This is what is meant by, "I was on the watch and God came to me" (Matthew 25:36).

ABBA JOHN THE DWARF

Praying at all times and never ceasing to pray is what Christian monastic life is all about. The monk anchors himself in prayer. He breathes, eats, drinks, and sleeps prayer...always prayer, unceasing prayer. Constant prayer is his only solace. One of the great helps in keeping this constancy in prayer is to recite over and over again the Jesus prayer: Lord, Jesus Christ, Son of the living God, have mercy on me a sinner.

This was the constant prayer of the Desert Fathers and Mothers. The monks of the desert made the Jesus prayer and that of the psalms their unceasing work. They put all else aside, they left all things behind, they gathered all their faculties, their whole being and concentrated in that one activity: the constant repetition of the holy name. In the silence of the desert, they converged and rested on the Lord Christ himself, praying continually, through the unceasing repetition of his name. And besides all else, one discovers there an overwhelming power in the repetition of the holy name of Jesus.

GOD'S TENDER CARE

To need consolation and to console is very human, just as human as Christ was.

DOROTHEE SOELLE, GERMAN THEOLOGIAN

It is late September, and we are slowly but surely moving toward a full autumn season.

The days are beginning to wane earlier, reflecting the character of the season. This is particularly so here in upstate New York. Soon the trees in the monastic land shall be converted into a tapestry of beauty. But I do not wish to rush ahead of God or myself. The Lord has his designs over Mother Nature and each of us.

Recently I was visited by a parent having serious difficulties with a son. Often, parents will come to the monastery and confide to us some of the troubles they are having with their children. All I can do is listen to them and offer some consolation by assuring them of God's tender concern for their children. Another parent who recently visited here told me his young son was in jail and refused to speak to his mother. What can one really say in such circumstances? After listening to parents with such heavy pain in their hearts, I offer to accompany them to the chapel for a few minutes of quiet prayer in God's presence. That does much more for them than anything one can say.

GOSPEL GOLD: CHARITY

Charity is the pure gold that makes us rich in eternal wealth.

JEAN-PIERRE CAMUS (1584–1652)

The person, example, and teachings of St. Vincent de Paul—whose memory we honor today—reminds me that a great deal of the Christian ascetical life consists in the true grasp and practice of fervent charity, a vigorous and ardent charity such as the one the Lord himself exemplified in the Gospels. The Lord lived charity in actuality, in the concrete, and diffused it all around him. He walked the path of charity, he exercised it with all those around him no matter who they were or where they came from, and he told us to do the same. He explicitly told us to see him in others, in the least of our brethren, and to treat others as we would treat him. "This is how all will know that you are my disciples, if you have love for one another" (John 13:35).

ARTISANS AND CRAFTSMEN IN THE MONASTERY

St. Benedict, in his profound wisdom, counsels all monks that they must earn their living by the work of their hands. Monks must avoid idleness at all costs, for as St. Benedict wrote, "it is the enemy of the soul." Given these facts, monks must earn their living, and they do so today as it was always done in the past, through a variety of means: gardening and farming, writing and publishing, artisanal products and cottage industries. In chapter 57 of the *Rule*, St. Benedict gives guidelines on how the arts and crafts in the monastery must be practiced:

> Craftsmen present in the monastery should practice their arts and crafts with humility, as permitted by the abbot. But if anyone becomes proud of his skills and the profit he brings to the community, he should be taken from his craft and work at ordinary labor. This will continue until he humbles himself and the abbot is satisfied. If any of the works from these artisans are sold, the salesman shall take care to practice no fraud. The salesman must remember Ananias and Sapphira unless they—or others who dispose of monastic property dishonestly—wish to suffer the death of their souls as well as their bodies. In pricing the objects, they should never show greed, and should sell things below the ongoing secular rate. Thus, God shall be glorified in all things.

GOD'S MESSENGERS: THE ARCHANGELS

The perfect peace of the holy angels lies in their love for God and their love for one another. This is also the case with all the saints from the beginning of time.

ST. MAXIMUS THE CONFESSOR (C. 580–662)

It is a long tradition in the Eastern Church that the choir of angels and archangels was the first to witness the resurrection of Christ. Thus during Sunday Vespers, the day in the weekly cycle assigned to honor the resurrection, the choir sings this particular stichera accompanying Psalm 140, the "Lord I Call Upon You":

With the Archangels, let us praise the Resurrection of Christ.
He is our Savior, our Redeemer!
And he will come again with awesome glory and mighty power,
To judge the word which he has made.

THE DISCIPLINE OF DAILY WRITING

These writings bring back to you the living image of that most holy mind, the very Christ himself speaking, healing, dying, rising, in fact so entirely present that you would see less of him if you beheld him with your own eyes.

DESIDERIUS ERASMUS (1466–1536)

St. Jerome was a great writer, and he wrote constantly. He left Rome, and out of love for our Savior he moved to Palestine, to a grotto into the outskirts of the tiny town of Bethlehem. There, near the Judean desert, he prayed, read, wrote, and translated daily the sacred Scriptures into Latin, the version called Vulgata (the then-vernacular of the Western world). He worked assiduously at this. For St. Jerome, the ever-old yet ever-new art of writing was indeed an enduring principle of monastic discipline, something that had to be done daily no matter what uncertainties the day brought. I am mindful of this myself, for I often feel the temptation to skip daily writing, yet deep down I am totally convinced of its value as discipline, even within the context of my human limitations. The bit of writing I do daily I see as true discipline, as an integral part of monastic living and always within the limitations of the monastic schedule in its daily rhythm. Sometimes, maybe even often, one is inspired to write something or not to write at all, one must yet sit down and face the fact that the writing must continue even if only in small amounts. This is most important in my case, both as needed discipline and as a humble way to support myself. Writing also provides the occasion to transcend oneself, to practice humility, simplicity, clarity of mind, and to place oneself totally into the hands of the Holy Spirit.

OCTOBER

OCTOBER 1 · *St. Thérèse of Lisieux*

TOUT EST GRACE: ALL IS GRACE

Behold, my servant whom I have chosen,
My beloved in whom I delight.

MATTHEW 12:18

Our daily labor is intensive enough during this period of the year—gathering and piling wood for our three stoves; harvesting, freezing, and canning vegetables for the long winter haul—that one hardly notices October's arrival. It almost went unnoticed until I realized today we keep St. Thérèse's memorial. St. Thérèse's feast is a good start for the month of October. In spite of her young years, she was endowed with that special wisdom to sense the work of grace in her at all times. For most of us that type of recognition takes years and years of monastic living or whatever our lifestyle may be. As one gets older, there is sometimes a sense that one's life moves as if it were floating in a sea of grace. As we move on, spiritually, mentally we discover the presence of grace at every corner, every turn, and with every step we take. We are inundated with the presence of grace in our lives. Grace is nothing other than the life and action of God in each of us. What is different now is the constant awareness of it. We slowly discover that life is, as Thomas Merton wrote, "full of paradise without knowing it."

OUR GUARDIANS AND PROTECTORS

For he commands his angels with regard to you, to guard you wherever you go. With their hands they shall support you, lest you strike your foot against a stone.

PSALM 91:11–12

Psalm 91 is one that nearly every monastic who lives under *The Rule of St. Benedict* knows by heart. The father of monks assigned Psalms 91, 4, and 134 to the daily Compline recitation. There is a certain pedagogy in the way St. Benedict assigned individual psalms to certain times of the day and places in the structure of the Daily Office. The three Compline psalms get repeated every night, and monks can almost sing them by heart in their sleep. As the years go by, one finds a certain inner rest and a mysterious sense of tranquility as one experiences the daily repetition of what is familiar to us. I know from my own experience how one physically feels at the end of the day, most of the times rather exhausted, when it is time to sing Compline, and yet I also feel a complete sense of relaxation, an inner liberation, singing night after night what is totally familiar to me. I particularly feel a great deal of comfort singing the section of Psalm 91 where we are reminded the Lord charged his angels to look after each of us and keep us safe in all instances. St. Bernard, in one of his sermons, says these words from the psalm should fill us with respect and devotion, and instill confidence in each of us because our guardian angels are there to render us living service and grant us their protection.

THE HOLY SPIRIT

God gives the gift of the Holy Spirit and then man becomes free. Where the Spirit of the Lord is, there is liberty.

ST. SILOUAN OF MOUNT ATHOS

We live, move, and are possessed at all times by the Holy Spirit. There is no life outside the Holy Spirit. Jesus breathed the Holy Spirit into the apostles, into each of us. The Spirit's perpetual presence in each of us is the power that sustains our lives at all times. In our intimate prayer, we sometimes dialogue with the Father, most of the time with the Son—Christ, our Savior—and occasionally directly with the Holy Spirit, or sometimes with the three at once. But no matter which of the three divine persons we are conversing with, deep down lies a realization that the soul perceives this divine presence only in the Holy Spirit. It is impossible for us to know God, to apprehend the Lord Jesus, except in the Holy Spirit. Possessed by the Spirit, our souls remain totally silent, in quiet wonder before God's infinite compassion, in total awe of his majesty and might. Through the inner promptings of the Holy Spirit, the Lord mercifully teaches the soul his personal designs for her, that at all times he is near us, if only we make the effort to keep his remembrance or memory alive. The Holy Spirit is so present in us that we can only know and love the Lord by the knowledge and love he instills in each of us. The grace of the Holy Spirit has the power to transform our souls into the likeness of him, as we daily try to follow Christ, our Savior.

POOR AND LOWLY: A GOSPEL WITNESS

Blessed are the poor in spirit, for theirs is the kingdom of heaven.

MATTHEW 5:3, FROM THE BEATITUDES

St. Francis, whose memorial we keep today, was above all a man of great humility, a lover of peace, a reconciler, as was Christ, his Lord and Master. He abhorred intellectual pride or any form of attention to himself. He sought the last place in all instances. His particular form of expressing his love for Christ consisted in the very imitation of the Lord's actions and a continual striving to abide by his words. The holy Gospels were alive and continually present to him, for through them the Lord revealed himself, his message, and the full measure of his grace.

St. Francis was poor and loved the poor, as did his Master. He entered paradise "a poor man," as the lovely antiphon of his feast states. Every year, when we repeat the antiphon, I am particularly struck by the power of the words: "Francis left the earth a poor and lowly man; he enters heaven rich in God's favor, greeted with songs of rejoicing."

Love of the poor is essential to our Christian vocation, for love and preference for the poor simply signifies love and preference for Christ, who was poor, crucified, and who entered paradise as a poor suffering servant. One thing that makes me sad in our time is the way we look and treat the poor and lowly of the world. How far are we from imitating the Lord's own example, and from the example of Francis of Assisi!

IMPROVING LOCAL COMMUNITY

Through the night of doubt and sorrow
Onward goes the pilgrim band,
Singing songs of expectation,
Marching to the Promised Land

SABINE BARING-GOULD, ANGLICAN PRIEST

As someone who has lived in the Hudson Valley for many, years—though in a certain monastic solitary seclusion and silence—I have always been concerned about the direction the local community is heading. I happen to love the valley and the local people. They are very much part of me, as I am part of them. They may not always be as spiritually oriented as one would like them to be, but I can always say they are *in via*, on the way, seeking God, sometimes without even knowing it.

There are many ways we can improve our community quality of life simply if we put the effort into it. Every person in the community can make a difference if he or she truly searches for common-sense solutions to community problems. When our volunteers, who are generous with their time and gifts, occasionally ask me about this, I always tell them, "Above all, avoid the extremes of fanaticism and remain grounded in good common sense. Get involved," I tell them, "in getting to know your neighbors and in working together to solve common problems." God will do the rest.

MONASTIC SOLITUDE

We are not in need of anything else,
except a vigilant, watchful spirit.
ABBA POEMEN, DESERT FATHER

Today we feast St. Bruno, a great lover of God and also a great lover of monastic solitude. From the earliest Desert Fathers and Mothers, such as St. Antony and St. Paul the Hermit, St. Syncletica and St. Mary of Egypt, to St. Benedict, St. Scholastica, and St. Seraphim of Sarov, all these monastics cherished their desert solitude, the sort of solitude so helpful in their ascetic striving and contemplation of God. It was the experience of deep desert solitude that unfolded for them the ultimate truth and purpose of all human life: the unique journey into the mystery of God.

Pseudo-Dionysius, an early Christian writer, says in his *Mystical Theology* that the goal of all human life is to reach the state where we are free from thoughts, emotions, sensations, and distractions so that we can dwell permanently in union with God. To reach this blessed state requires solitude, constant asceticism, and complete renunciation of ourselves. A medieval mystic, Angela of Foligno, describes beautifully the experience of those who reach this blessed state of union with God in solitude: "The eyes of my soul were opened and I beheld the plenitude of God, whereby I did comprehend the whole world, both here and beyond the sea, and the abyss and all things else; and therein I beheld naught save the divine power in a manner assuredly indescribable, so that through excess of marveling the soul cried with a loud voice, saying: 'This world is full of God!'"

A PRAYER TO OUR LADY

I was taught that every contemplative soul to whom it is given the grace to look and to seek will see Mary and pass on to God through contemplation.

JULIAN OF NORWICH

When I gaze at your beloved icon,
I sense your presence, O Mother of God,
And feel your strong love surrounding me.
I know you love all your children
Of every time and place and age,
For after all, we were all entrusted to you
By your Son in those last moments on the cross.
Therefore moved by his words,
I come to you with confidence.
I bless and praise you,
And beg you to always be my Mother.
O Mother of God,
You are the Queen of heaven,
The glory of all angels and saints.
You are also the holiest
Among all human beings,
The gentlest,
The loveliest of all God's creatures,
Mother of God,
Mother of divine grace,
Be always my Mother.

GOD'S UNENDING LIGHT

Christ, my light, my life, my all
Lead, kindly Light, amid the encircling gloom.
Lead Thou me on! The night is dark,
And I am far from home. Lead me on!
Keep Thou my feet; I do not ask to see
The distant scene, one step enough for me.

BLESSED JOHN H. CARDINAL NEWMAN

The light that shines from the face of Christ raises our poor, human, sinful condition to a truly godlike condition. The light of Christ, resplendent in our innermost, makes us true bearers of the Holy Spirit. And it is the Holy Spirit who helps us discern and understand better, more profoundly, Christ's own words: "I am the Way, the Truth, and the Life."

We are children of the light if we abide by Christ's word, for he is the Light of the World, in whom there is no darkness. As we look at the face of the Lord on the icon, we discover a resplendent light bestowed on him by the Father. That special light that subtly emerges from his face is the divine light, the light that existed from all eternity and that symbolizes the uncreated energy of his divinity. God alone is pure light, and it is only by his abundant mercy that we become sharers of it. "Christ, my light, my life, my all!"

LUMEN CHRISTI

O gladsome light of the Holy Glory of the Immortal Father—
heavenly, holy, blessed Jesus Christ.

"PHOS HILARON," SECOND-CENTURY HYMN SUNG DAILY AT VESPERS

The natural light during these autumn days, particularly at dawn and sunset, is exceedingly beautiful. There is a quality to it that is not always present at other times of the year. It is impossible to take it for granted and not become intoxicated with its ravishing magic. And of course, the perception and awareness of this light quality brings one back to the reality of Christ, the true Light of the World. In reading one of the great Greek Fathers, St. Gregory of Nyssa, I found an enlightening passage appropriate to the theme:

> When we consider that Christ is the true Light, having nothing in common with deceit, we learn that our own life also must shine with the rays of that true light. Now these rays of the Sun of Justice are the virtues which pour out to enlighten us so that we may put away the works of darkness and walk honorably as in broad daylight. When we reject the deeds of darkness and do everything in the light of day, we become light and, as light should, we give light to others by our actions.

THE STRUCTURES OF MONASTIC LIFE

The desert is a place of revelation and revolution. In the desert we wait, we weep, we learn to live.

ALAN JONES

Sometimes a monk may question the value of the *Rule,* or the monastic tradition, or the purpose of the structures of the monastic life. It is perfectly human to do so. When questioning an older monk on this matter, he would probably reply like the Desert Fathers:

> The purpose of the monk's life is to achieve continual watchfulness over his mind and heart. When, after long years of struggle, the heart becomes more sensitive and the mind through continual weeping becomes strengthened, then a peaceful prayerful state emerges, in the heart of the monk, making his prayer unceasingly and developing in him a feeling of God's presence, both powerful and overwhelming. Thus is the way of the monk: silent, ordinary, often dry, but overwhelming with passion for the presence of the living God.

SILENCE

An elder said, "Lack of anxiety, keeping silent, and silent meditation bring forth purity."

THE DESERT FATHERS

No one can deny the particular charm of this season, especially those who live in rural areas like us, surrounded by such exquisite beauty at every turn. During these fall days, the scenic beauty of the New York-New England landscape is simply dazzling with those vibrant, unforgettable autumn colors.

Fall is a time for many heartwarming activities: for hiking outdoors and renewing old friendships, for harvesting and preparing succulent dishes with the fruits of the harvest. And fall, with its particular quiet beauty, is also a time for reflecting and listening. The invitation to listen to the Lord in our innermost reverberates deeply in the silence of our hearts. The more we attune ourselves to the silence of the season, the easier it is to cultivate the art of listening. The stillness and quiet of nature is simply a reminder of the quiet and silence we must make in our own hearts to make space for God, who only speaks and allows himself to be heard in deep, deep silence. It is only in silence that we can apprehend the word and listen to the divine voice.

SHORTER DAYS, LONGER AND DARKER NIGHTS

It is good to give thanks to the LORD,
to sing praise to your name, Most High,
To proclaim your love at daybreak,
your faithfulness in the night.

PSALM 92:2–3

As our days in the Hudson Valley get gradually cooler and shorter in daylight, all of nature becomes keenly aware of the subtle transition taking place, first of all in us, and then all around us. Light, that precious commodity so taken for granted, begins to fade earlier and at a faster pace. Our minds and feelings all converge at the stark reality that winter is truly on its way and not far off. While pondering all this with typical monastic sobriety, I found these lines from an English Benedictine that illustrates what Mother Nature herself is whispering these days in the intimacy of our hearts:

Autumn
A time of transition
As the leaves die.
There is beauty in the
Leaving. Leaving a
Sacred space for God
A time to consider the holly,
Evergreen,
His abiding presence
Through all transition.

DAME LAURENTIA JOHNS

A PRAYER

O Most blessed Virgin Mary,
Most Holy *Theotokos*
And Queen of the most holy Rosary,
You designed to show yourself
To the small shepherds from Fatima.
To them you revealed a tenderness
In a maternal message.
We implore you, O Mother of God,
Inspire in our hearts a fervent love
For the recitation of the Rosary.
May we learn to meditate daily
On the mysteries of your redemption.
And as we recall them,
May we obtain the grace
To imitate your virtues
Which so pleased the Most High
As to choose for the Mother
Of his eternal Son.
I humbly ask this of you,
Through the merits of Jesus Christ,
Your beloved Son and our Redeemer.

OCTOBER 14

MINDFULNESS OF GOD

When one's whole mind and heart is in God,
the world is forgotten.

ST. SILOUAN OF MOUNT ATHOS

For St. Silouan, a monk truly possessed by God, pure prayer draws the mind and the heart—in fact a person's whole being—into one. With the mind thus descending deep into the heart, all earthly images, illusions, and fantasies are put aside. The soul then, free from human passion, is capable of striving continually toward God through unceasing prayer. During prayer, the soul is enlightened to see himself or herself in God's own light and thus is stripped bare of all nonessentials.

At this point, the Holy Spirit enters into the inner activities of the soul. Through Spirit's grace and the experience of utterly simple contemplation, the soul rises up to God in a moment of humble submission and surrender. It is now God's work to make the soul one with him, as the soul prays and weeps for the world that denies him.

A TEACHER OF PRAYER

The man of prayer finds his happiness in continually creating, searching, and being with Christ.

BR. ROGER DE TAIZÉ

Monastic spirituality, a prolongation of the tradition received from the Gospels, is in its essence all about unceasing prayer. It cultivates and feeds in the soul an immense desire for God, so that at all times the monk lives for and desires God alone. God ultimately is all he wants. This single-hearted desire for God transforms his entire being and draws him into that intimate communion with Christ and the Father, in the Holy Spirit. St. Teresa of Jesus, whose memorial we keep today, was masterful in the art of prayer. Prayer was her only *raison d'être*. She taught her disciples that if one is serious about prayer, one must daily make time for it and be willing to stand in the divine presence with an attitude of complete trust. Prayer, she would say—as did the early Desert Fathers and Mothers—consists in allowing the heart to reach freely toward God, thus entering into a loving relationship with him. During prayer, St. Teresa says, we simply call upon him who loves us and thus continue a loving dialogue with the divine Guest of our souls.

A POTATO HARVEST

And gives bread to all flesh,
for his mercy endures forever.
Praise the God of heaven,
for his mercy endures forever.

PSALM 136:25–26

Recently we harvested our annual potatoes from the garden. The weather has been so mild until now that I waited for a day when we had sufficient help to do it. The Lord who, in his goodness, always surpasses our expectations, sent us six young people for the day who were willing to dirty their hands and knees while digging for the potatoes. Three youngsters were Vassar students and three were from a farm in Cape Cod who paid us a friendly visit. As a result, the monastery benefited from their help, and we all had a wonderful experience working together as a team. I deeply admire these youngsters, whose main concern is to protect the earth the Lord has given us by using it wisely and then savoring its produce the way the Lord intended for all of us. This principle, of course, applies virtually to all aspects of life. The concept of sustainable farming, much in vogue these days, fits perfectly with that of St. Benedict, who outlined in his *Rule* the idea that each monastery must be as much as possible totally self-sustainable and grow its own food. St. Benedict's wisdom has always been evident to me and a source of great joy. There is nothing like tasting the first strawberries of the season, picking a perfectly ripe tomato in the peak of summer, of savoring our tender handpicked potatoes in the fall. It simply doesn't get better than that. *Deo gratias.*

AN AUTUMN REFLECTION

Autumn in the Northeast is all about glorious foliage, luminous days, chilly nights, and the harvest from the bounty of our gardens, farms, and orchards. This is a busy season in our kitchens, where cooks and apprentice chefs try to savor the taste of locally grown food and now have ample opportunities to do so. While laboring in the garden picking the choicest fruits from the harvest, I often reflect on God's goodness placing such abundance at our disposal. The earth belongs to the Lord, and he makes it fertile and beautiful for the sole benefit of us, his children.

THE HOLY SPIRIT AND THE EARLY CHURCH

You will receive power when the Holy Spirit comes upon you, and you will be my witnesses in Jerusalem, throughout Judea and Samaria, and to the ends of the earth.

ACTS 1:8

The Book of Acts in the Bible, attributed to St. Luke, gives us a glimpse into what the life of the early Christian community was like, particularly that of Jerusalem, so influenced by the presence of the apostles and the outpouring of the Holy Spirit. It is an account worth reading and meditating upon again and again, for we often carry with us a conception of Church structure more in keeping with what has historically come after, centuries later, rather than the simpler and more evangelical one the apostles left behind.

There is a huge difference between the two, like day and night. I often wonder, were the apostles to return today, would they recognize what the present Church structures have become through the passing of the ages? What I imply in this applies to all Christian churches across the board. The author of the Book of Acts refers to each local church community as the "church of God," for indeed each individual community represented the Church in its fullness. The Holy Spirit dwelled in each of them in his unfathomable fullness. During these early stages of the primitive Church, there was no one supreme authority over the whole of them, certainly not a monarchical system or model to follow, as we find it today in the Western Church. Each community was centered on the Eucharist, or "breaking of the bread" as they call it, bonded by charity and the application of the word of God, and presided over by an overseer or elder. To these elders the author of Acts addresses in the name of the Apostle Paul the following: "Keep watch over yourselves and over the whole flock of which the holy Spirit has appointed you overseers, in which you tend the church of God that he acquired with his own blood....From your own group, men will come forward perverting the truth to draw the disciples away after them. So be vigilant and remember that for three years, night and day, I unceasingly admonished each of you with tears. And now I commend you to God and to that gracious word of his that can build you up and give you the inheritance among all who are consecrated" (Acts 20:28, 30–32).

As we reread the Book of Acts, privately or in the liturgy, we are prompted by the Holy Spirit to rediscover the true nature of what the Church is meant to be. These individual "churches of God," dwelling in various localities worldwide, are each the full body of Christ, not just a part of it. We need to rethink the true nature of ecclesiology and place greater emphasis on the local church, in the light of what the Holy Spirit accomplished in those early Christian communities, and see them as the Gospel model of what the Church of Christ as a whole must become or be like. I don't think one can surpass the Holy Spirit or create a better model of what he did in our midst after Jesus' ascension into heaven. As we honor St. Luke today, we must express our gratitude to him for the clarity of his teaching, for his Church vision, and we must beseech the Holy Spirit—he who renews the face of the earth—to refashion Christ's Church on the original model he left us to follow.

IN GOD'S IMAGE AND LIKENESS

For you make me jubilant, LORD, by your deeds;
at the works of your hands I shout for joy.
How great are your works, LORD!
How profound your designs!

PSALM 92:5–6

The early Greek Fathers never ceased to remind us that, at the inception of human life, each of us is created in the likeness of our Creator, and they add that through the sacrament of baptism we are refashioned into the same divine image. And just as Adam, the first man, failed to live up to the standards of the divine image, God the Father sends his Son the Word—the second Adam—to raise us up to the standards expected by God.

St. Peter Chrysologus, one of the early fathers, paints the picture beautifully: At baptism, we are reborn into the divine image and adopted by God as his children. He counsels his disciples, "Let us put on the complete image of our Creator so as to be wholly like him, not in the glory that he alone possesses, but in innocence, simplicity, gentleness, patience, humility, mercy, harmony, those qualities in which he chose to become, and to be, one with us."

THE BEAUTY OF THE TREES

Artists lift the veil from their eyes in order to see and show to others the garden of life, where everything turns toward God.

MAHMOUD ZIBAWI, AUTHOR

On a luminous day such as today, we contemplate ecstatically the beauty of our trees and all of nature all around us. I am reminded of a passage by Thomas Merton in *Seeds of Contemplation*: "A tree gives glory to God first of all by being a tree. For in being what God means it to be, it is imitating an idea which is in God and which is not distinct from the essence of God, and therefore a tree imitates God by being a tree. The more it is like itself, the more it is like him." O trees of the Lord, bless the Lord.

COLDER WEATHER

May you have warm words
On a cold evening,
A full moon on a dark night,
And the road downhill
All the way to your door.

IRISH BLESSING

The cold weather almost subtly arrived here in the Northeast. Our daytime is still clear, often warm and invigorating. However, once the sun goes down, we begin to feel the chill of the season. Every evening after Vespers are sung, I now light the wood stove in our modest monastic kitchen. It is well-located in the northwest corner of the room, and so the stove counterbalances the cold with the heat it radiates. Above the stove, in the wall, a large icon of the Christ Pantocrator stands up and watches over all of us, including our cats and dog that seek warm shelter near the stove. The Lord, in his unique and quiet majesty, seems to be looking directly at us. We, in turn, gaze at him with trust and confidence, placing all of life's concerns at his feet. He rules our lives and takes care of us daily, even when we are unaware.

THE SPLENDOR OF DIVINE LIGHT

Let me shine with the light of Jesus.
Let my eyes see the beauty all around.
Never let me turn my nose up to others,
And let my mouth share the good news I have found.

IRISH BLESSING

This Irish blessing and the one on the preceding page arrived this week in the mail. They were sent to me by someone I don't know but who felt inspired to write to me while reading *Blessings of the Daily: A Monastic Book of Days.* From time to time I receive mail from readers who seem attuned to the few scribbles I write occasionally. They sometimes arrive at the monastery from far distances and tell me how some of the writing has touched their lives. I am always at a loss trying to understand them in the light of the Gospel. Personally, I have nothing to offer anyone. A monk is perfectly comfortable with his own nothingness, his own inadequacy, and with taking the last place in society. If he sees any light at the end of the tunnel, it's nothing that emerges from him but rather the light of Christ, our Savior, who transforms our daily darkness into light.

THE DALAI LAMA

O God, make us children of quietness
and heirs of peace.
ST. CLEMENT OF ALEXANDRIA

Early this morning I listened to an interview with the Dalai Lama. I must confess I don't always keep up with all the news. I usually read some of the local news online, I glance quickly at certain articles, and of course I read more extensively when there are some real-world catastrophes such as the earthquakes in Haiti and Chile. It is impossible not to be profoundly affected by the suffering of these people.

The interview with the Dalai Lama was refreshing to listen to. He was asked questions about complicated situations in today's complex world. I was delighted by his thoughtful responses, with his customary simplicity, common sense, and compassion. He responded with profound insights. He is a gentle, affable, positive man. He seems to enjoy the moment and lives it to the fullest. It is obvious he loves life and cherishes each moment. What really impressed me were his profound insights, which spring from a deep-seated wisdom. He integrates and weaves together a natural, positive attitude, simplicity, common sense, and compassion, and thus arrives to that unique depth of wisdom—which, after all, is a gift from the Holy Spirit. What a contrast to the tiresome and inadequate approach of many of our political and religious leaders today, whose speeches are filled with facts, data, and just pure rationalism. How cold, calculating, and simply empty they usually are, no matter how well-spoken they may be. It speaks to the limitations of reason, of the mind itself.

I don't know the last time I heard someone speak with the eloquence and profundity I witnessed this morning; someone really saying something and touching listeners deeply. One can see the Dalai Lama doesn't come prepared with the now usual "talking points." He listens to the question and looks seriously, as if somehow searching for something inside himself in order to find the adequate response. It usually emerges from the wealth of his life experience. His answers to problems resonate with the rest of us, for they are not purely rational ones but instigate something deeper in all of us: the need to search through life's journey and manifold experiences for the wisdom and meaningful answers that can truly satisfy our innermost.

THE HOLY SPIRIT: THE SOLE GUARANTOR OF OUR FAITH

With all humility and gentleness, with patience, bearing with one another through love, striving to preserve the unity of the spirit through the bond of peace: one body and one Spirit, as you were also called to the one hope of your call.

EPHESIANS 4:2–4

We are witnesses of these things, as is the holy Spirit that God has given to those who obey him.

ACTS 5:32

Guard this rich trust with the help of the holy Spirit that dwells within us.

2 TIMOTHY 1:14

All Christian life, according to St. Seraphim of Sarov, consists in the acquisition of the Holy Spirit. Daily, as we try to imitate Christ (or "put on Christ," as St. Paul describes it), we can only do this under the direct action of the Holy Spirit. We must learn to live consciously by the Spirit. That is to say, we must ask the Lord for the grace to be constantly aware of the Holy Spirit's personal presence in our lives.

The Holy Spirit is a person, as are the Father and the Son, so our relationship and daily dealings with him must also be personal, as it is with Christ and the Father. Moreover, the Holy Spirit is the only one who can teach us the mysteries of the faith, the mysteries of God's life in us, for he is the Spirit of truth, the one who unfolds for us the most arcane details of God's own life. On earth, only the Holy Spirit is the guarantor for the mysteries of the faith. It was necessary for Jesus to ascend to the Father, for then they sent us the Holy Spirit. And it was the Holy Spirit who came to reveal to us God's life present in us and made possible by the Lord's sacrifice. This is indeed a great, awesome mystery, how the operations of the Holy Spirit work in our world, in time, according to God's mysterious designs. I am always totally in awe of this! When praying and meditating on this mystery, one reaches the point one can't go beyond. The one certainty we are left with is that the Spirit of God, as promised by Jesus, is with us always. It is he who prays in us and guides our steps to follow the Lord's life example and teachings. He opens before us the mysterious spaces of the life of God, and he leads us directly into a loving communion with the Father and the Son, of whom he is the binder and sole guarantor.

AN EASTERN-INSPIRED PRAYER FOR EVENING TIME

Creator of the Light and fashioner of the night,
Thou, life in death, and light in darkness,
Hope unto those who wait,
And forbearance unto those who doubt.
Thou, who with thy skillful wisdom,
Turnest the shadow of death into morning;
Thou unending dawn,
Thou sun without setting.

ST. GREGORY OF NAREK, ARMENIAN SAINT

OUR DAILY SPIRITUAL ENEMIES

God be in my head,
And in my understanding;
God be in my eyes,
And in my looking;
God be in my mouth,
And in my speaking;
God be in my heart,
And in my thinking;
God be at my end,
And in my departing.

ANONYMOUS

The early Desert monks asserted that all spiritual life is a struggle, a combat. Our spiritual enemies are many: self-illusion, self-complacency, fantasies, selfishness, self-centeredness, pride, self-satisfaction, and so on. Once a disciple inquired about this from one of the elders. In reply, the elder monk said to the disciple: "The monk ought to struggle until death against the demons of illusion and negligence, especially during the time of prayer. And if, with God's help, he succeeds in this, let him turn his attention to combat against the temptation of self-satisfaction, self-complacency, self-centeredness, and let him say: 'Except the Lord builds a house, those who build it labor in vain' for 'all men are but dust and ashes' and let him recall also that 'God opposes the proud and the conceited but gives grace to the humble.'"

Unfortunately, we humans—including some who live in monasteries—can quickly give in to the temptation and evil of self-complacency. It is so easy to bow to the allures of the evil one and succumb to pride, self-glorification, and self-idolatry. I have seen this phenomenon occur again and again in some monasteries, especially in ones where those who live there see themselves as mirrors of what others should be like: They keep all the externals of the monastic observance, they claim to have new recruits, they are often in the news, and they just think themselves superior to everybody else. The idea of monastic humility, as conceived by St. Benedict and the early monastic fathers, is just not part of their value system. The Gospel teaching about always choosing the last place and being despised by others is even further away from their thinking. Success in a worldly manner is what really counts for them: They have talented members in their communities and they often get recognized for their talents. The Gospel light of humble repentance, so cherished by our early Desert Fathers, is unheard of or plainly discounted in their midst. Unfortunately, this phenomenon is manifested in such a subtle manner and gets clouded by other attitudes in such a way that it is often not perceived by the general public. I was gratified to read recently that this attitude was acknowledged by a superior general of one of those communities in France, where an attitude of superiority was obvious not only to me but to many others. In the French case, the community had to acknowledge the discovered failures of the founder and in the process they became aware of their own deceptions and perilous attitude. I could only wish that many other communities suffering a similar malaise could come to terms with their own self-deceptions.

But of course this is not easily achievable. It demands true conversion, lowering oneself to the humility levels that Christ preached and lived himself, and that is not always pleasing to those who think of themselves as mighty, important, and superior to others. True humility is never easy. Indeed, we can only truly embrace it by a pure gift from God. Our Lady did it thoroughly and became totally pleasing in God's sight. We can, therefore, have recourse to her and beg her to teach us the ways of utter humility, the type of humility that reaches, touches, and pleases the heart of God.

OCTOBER 27

GOD'S PROTECTION IN THE DAILY

God is our refuge and our strength,
an ever-present help in distress.
Thus we do not fear, though earth be shaken
and mountains quake to the depths of the sea....
The LORD *of hosts is with us;*
our stronghold is the God of Jacob.

PSALM 46:2–3, 8

It is a humble monastic custom to beseech God's protection at all times and in all instances: when we rise and before we go to sleep, before our meals and before we get involved in a particular type of work, before undergoing a trip or voyage, even when simply leaving the monastery for a short distance and for a short while. The monk always prays and trusts to be protected, shielded by God's presence at all times. Time and again I have felt—as I also do now—the power of God's protection, at times vividly, and certainly concretely. This was especially true in moments of danger where things could have turned deadly if not for his loving presence surrounding and shielding me from harm.

One of the things I treasure most in this life is the constant awareness of being protected by God. It is a not a simple belief but rather a sober, often substantiated experience. It is a subtle but real type of experience, the type one can't prove to others (and there is no need for proof either); nevertheless it is as true as the light of day and the shadows of nighttime. Every time the Lord makes his holy protection strikingly tangible, it humbles one to no end. One feels like a child, small and frail, yet totally secure in God's arms. With the psalmist I repeat daily: "The LORD is my light and my salvation; whom should I fear? The LORD is my life's refuge; of whom should I be afraid?" (Psalm 27:1).

WISE COUNSEL FROM THE MONASTIC DESERT

These are the seven rules of a monk:
Firstly, as the Scriptures say,
"Love God with all you soul and all your mind."
Then, love your fellow human beings
as you love yourself.
Fast from evil.
Never pass judgment on anyone, for any cause.
Never do evil to anyone.
Discipline yourself and purge yourself
from material and spiritual evil.
Cultivate a modest and gentle heart.
If you can do all these things
and see only your own faults, not those of others,
the grace of Our Lord Jesus Christ
will be with you.

SAYINGS OF THE EGYPTIAN FATHERS

PRAYING THE PSALMS

The psalms are the true garden of the solitary.

THOMAS MERTON, *THOUGHTS IN SOLITUDE*

There is something that never changes in the ordinary routine of the monk, and that is psalmody, the daily chanting or recitation of the psalms. Day after day, the psalms are sung in the monastery or hermitage unceasingly, lovingly, reflectively. The psalms are the daily nourishment of the monk, for in them the monk meets the Lord daily. There is nothing more precious to the monk than this daily encounter with God in the stark reality of the psalms. I can attest to this myself, ascertaining that I could not really overcome many obstacles in my daily monastic routine or make sense of them without the assistance and sustenance I receive from the psalms. They are my daily support, my daily bread, and no matter what state of mind or heart I may find myself in at the moment, the psalms are always there to redirect me, to center me again and again in that unique and eternal reality that is God.

St. Benedict wisely arranged the daily monastic schedule around the recitation of the psalms, which he called the "Work of God." For St. Benedict, as well as for the ancient monastic fathers, the psalms were not so much a method of prayer but instead a profound inner experience of God while at prayer. In the Book of Psalms, the monk meets the living God, the God of Creation and of the Incarnation, the God who upholds his daily life with tender love and endless mercy, and vice versa. Through the psalms, God reassures the monk of his promises and constant fidelity. *Quoniam in aeternum misericordia ejus.* Psalmody, then, becomes the ordinary way of the monk, the vehicle through which he approaches or encounters the mystery of God in the solitude of the monastic desert. With the psalmist we dare to proclaim daily: "I will sing of your mercy forever, LORD, proclaim your faithfulness through all ages" (Psalm 89:2).

OCTOBER 30

THE RHYTHM OF THE MONASTIC LIFE

Wim Haan of Holland relates the impact the discovery of the monastic rhythm had on his own life:

> Twice a year a group of employees from the Vrije Universiteit in Amsterdam travel to the small Belgian town of Brecht for a short stay at Nazareth Abbey, a monastic community of Trappistine nuns. For most of us this is the first introduction to life in a monastery. It is an introduction not only to a different belief structure but also to a completely different lifestyle, a life with different priorities, with its own rhythm and focus. The time spent there, from late Friday afternoon to Sunday afternoon is short but leaves a deep impression on many of us. Afterward, some of us often decide to return a second or third time, and sometimes, some individuals decide to stay for a few days longer by themselves.
>
> In the monastery people find something which they seem to have lost in their hectic everyday lives. As a guest in the monastery you are confronted with an elementary way of looking and dealing with life. Core words are simplicity, austerity, peace, and quiet.
>
> Paradoxically, a growing interest in monastic life has come at a time when an increasingly aging population has led to big problems in many communities. Their ability to support themselves is being put under increasing pressure. For a number of monasteries, the end is near.
>
> I myself experienced some mixed feelings during the various times I stayed in a monastery. The peace and tranquility of a monastery is often so contrary to my own life that the silence prompts a great deal of turmoil within myself. The wavelike rhythm of monastic life does make the day more productive, however. It sounds strange, but still I noticed time and again

that the balance between work and prayer increased in me both clarity and concentration.

It is sometimes difficult in a monastery to switch off one's own alarm clock, one's perspectives, or to ignore one's small imperfections, such as the wrong tone in the singing of the psalms or the clumsy recitation of the texts. But there is never a visit without a moment of poignancy, when the small things that are rare and different on the outside simply happen naturally in the monastery: the attention and care one receives, the friendliness and awareness of the monks and nuns, the simplicity without airs, the positive monastic attitude, the unusual, sometimes mysterious combination of enterprise and calm. Time does not drag in a monastery. The opposite is true. Every time I am surprised how quickly my stay comes to an end. Before you know it, one is saying goodbye to the guest sister.

THE MONASTIC MYSTERY

Wim Haan introduces comments by two writers who spent time as monastery guests.

I will leave you with two authors who, in my opinion, have done a good job in articulating the somewhat mysterious nature of monastic life. I start with Henri Nouwen: "Why did I go to the monastery? Because there was an inner necessity, which I answered positively. And why did I stay? Because I knew I was in the right place and nobody said otherwise. And why was I there? I am not exactly sure yet. Perhaps I won't know until I come to the end of life's road. Still, I can say that they are unbelievably valuable memories which influence all that I do and plan to do. I cannot live without being reminded of that glimpse of God's mercy I caught in my loneliness, of that light ray which broke through my darkness, of that soft voice which spoke in my silence, and the soft breeze which touched me from behind. Still, this experience does not only bring back rich memories from the past. Again and again it gives me new insight into present-day events and leads me in my decisions for the future. These memories are always present, in my compulsive behavior, in my passion, my illusions and unreal visions, they unmask the false dreams and point me in the right direction."

Karen Armstrong writes the following in the epilogue of her book *Through the Narrow Gate*: "In the monastery I discovered that we are complex beings and that the spirit, soul, and body are constantly involved in a bloody battle. One of the most important things I learned in the monastery was the relative impotence of the human will. This realization is good but it does humble you. It is also liberating in a way. I am a better nun now than I ever was in the monastery. You can be so fearful of loving other people more than God that you become loveless. Ironically enough, now I sometimes see within myself the characteristics of detachment and independence which I had such problems acquiring when I was a nun."

NOVEMBER

NOVEMBER 1

ALL SAINTS

I saw a vast crowd of countless numbers from every nation, standing before the throne.

VESPERS ANTIPHON OF THE FEAST

I have always loved All Saints Day, lovingly called in French "*la Toussaint*" a feast that evokes closeness, familiarity, intimacy. La Toussaint is a family feast, for the saints, both canonized and uncanonized, are each and all God's dearest friends, God's collaborators, and always our trustworthy, faithful intercessors. The saints are real to monks, for they plead and intercede for us daily. At the threshold of our monastic journey, each monk receives the name of a saint, who then becomes a cherished companion on the road, a friend, a protector, and a model of perseverance. As Christians, we believe the saints, close to God as they are, never cease to intercede for us, to offer us help from above, and to answer in one way or another our supplications.

As we remember all of them, I become mindful that today we really celebrate the great mystery of the communion of saints. This mystery, in the daily life of a monastery, is somehow real, personal, comforting. In the chapel, in our cells, and all around the monastery we are surrounded by icons and images of the Mother of God and these dear friends. They serve as reminders that as we daily walk our monastic journey, we are never alone, for our closest friends—the saints—are always by us, guiding our steps toward the Lord and pleading unceasingly for our sake.

ALL SOULS

Our rational nature had become dead through wickedness,
but Christ raised it to life again....
This is the meaning of that text from St. Paul:
"It is our belief that if we have died with Christ,
so we shall also rise and live with him."

EVAGRIUS PONTICUS

With the arrival of All Saints and All Souls Days, we gradually make a smooth transition into November. The month often portrays different faces, different tonalities; thus it creates diverse types of moods in people. At times it is gray, cloudy, rainy, and cold. That's usually the case on All Souls Day. Today, however, is warm and hazy, the type one could describe as an Indian summer day. Outdoors, we can breathe a sort of pleasant balmy and seductive soothing air, a vague recollection of bygone summer days and a reassurance that future summer days shall return once again. November invites us all to draw into our personal solitude, to learn again to treasure quiet and silence, to avoid useless distractions such as being in a hurry, and certainly to give up silly fears about future life uncertainties. After all, we are always in God's hands, and that is a good place to be.

Today, as we keep All Souls Day, it brings to mind past memories of the same days and times in France, when we visited our ancestors in the village cemetery, cleaned and decorated their tombs with fresh flowers, thus expressing our enduring affection to those who preceded us. It is a custom that comes from antiquity, and often the French cemeteries look more like a garden in bloom on All Souls Day. It is a cherished, intimate tradition, one that everyone adheres to lovingly. All Souls Day reminds us not only of those who have gone to God ahead of us but also of our own mortality. Ah, the mystery of eternity suddenly reappears once again in the human horizon, right before our own eyes. It is inescapable! God dwells in his eternal home, and our earthly journey is one that is heading in the same direction: eternity with God forever.

COMMUNION OF SAINTS

God alone is pure goodness by nature,
and only he or she who imitates God
can be good in moral terms.
Such a person has only one aim in life:
never to fall away from the only goal that matters,
which is our God himself.

ST. MAXIMUS THE CONFESSOR

During these early, often gray November days—right after commemorating the festivals of All Saints and All Souls—I continue to ponder the beautiful mystery of the communion of saints. It is a pity that such a mystery is often forgotten, neglected, or not mentioned at all these days, except briefly during the celebration of the divine liturgy when we profess it as part of the Nicene Creed. This afternoon, while laboring at some of the seasonal tasks outdoors, I was reminded of an episode that happened many years ago in Paris. It taught me a great deal about this poignant mystery. A friend living in Paris went to visit a woman who was a humble hermit, dwelling in total isolation on the top floor of a semi-abandoned building. She was a Russian Orthodox faithful, a pious and ascetic person who took her hermit life seriously in spite of the problems of living in a crowded and noisy city such as Paris. Nothing seemed to disturb her, and she was solicitous about protecting her beloved solitude and the quality of her silence. When my friend asked her if she was lonely living in such isolation—all alone on the top floor of a depressing, abandoned building—she replied with a gesture. With her hand she pointed at the many icons hanging on the wall. There one could see the Lord, the Mother of God, and saints. She quietly said to my friend, "I want you to know that I am never alone, for I am always surrounded by the company of all these dear friends, always comforted by their presence. They are always here with me, always present indeed, and I know I am always with them."

DAILY CONTACT WITH MOTHER NATURE

Climb the mountains and get their good tidings. Nature's peace will flow into you as sunshine flows into trees. The winds will blow their own freshness into you, and the storms their energy, while cares will drop off like autumn leaves.

JOHN MUIR, NATURALIST

One of autumn's lovely gifts is that it provides all of us with endless possibilities to taste the blessings of the season. Autumn is a special time in upstate New York and New England. It is a cherished season for all those who love keeping close to nature and enjoy the benefits of rural country life. In the country, we are always surrounded by various aspects of nature from all sides: the Berkshires and Catskill Mountains, the Hudson River, the creeks, the lakes, the forests, the dense wooded areas, the verdant fields and pastures of our working farms, and the rolling hills all around us. In a unique way, Mother Nature, with her ever-spacious outdoors, provides us with occasions for recreating ourselves, for reestablishing our spiritual priorities, for rediscovering our inner centers, and also for finding inspiration, peace, and tranquility in our daily lives. There is something healing and beneficial that takes place during this intimate contact with nature, with the mystery of the outdoors, especially when this contact takes place in a profound silence. Often people convey to me how peaceful they feel after a few days here in the country, in the tranquility and silence of the monastery, just by taking a long hike in the woods, by breathing deeply the clean country air, or just by coming in contact with our farm animals. They feel rejuvenated! The calming quality of Mother Nature often penetrates our very bones, always aiming at the deepest recesses of our souls. Often, too, Mother Nature—with that simplicity and nurturing quality so unique to her—helps restore a sense of balance and tranquility sometimes missing from our otherwise busy, agitated lives.

On Prayer

From the moment you start praying,
raise your heart upward
and turn your eyes downward.
Come to focus on your innermost self
and there pray in secret to your Father in heaven.

APHRAHAT THE PERSIAN

Recently I had a long conversation on prayer with someone who was visiting us. During the talk, the person asked me what was the best personal preparation one could make for entering into the state of inner prayer. My reply was a simple one: Empty yourself and let the Holy Spirit do the rest. The greatest obstacle to true prayer is us, ourselves. The more we are filled with the self, the less space we provide for God. And God likes to take over when he enters into the soul. He usually captures the entire territory. Jesus gave us the best example of the type of prayer that is pleasing to God. He praised the prayer of the publican as an example to us all. The Pharisee demonstrated that he was full of himself as he was addressing the Lord, thus not reaching or touching the heart of God during his prayer. The poor publican, in contrast, never ceased expressing a true, humble, and repentant spirit. The attitude of humble repentance is usually the best way to undergo the self-emptying process. Only then can the Holy Spirit pray freely in us.

MIRACLES IN DAILY LIFE

Give thanks to the LORD, for he is good, his mercy endures forever.

PSALM 118:1

The quiet stillness we encounter in our November days is an invitation to look at certain things often taken for granted, such as the daily miracles that sometimes go unnoticed.

In the Bible we often read about the Lord's big miracles, and often we forget the small ones the same Lord performs daily in our midst. Miracles don't always have to be connected to events of large proportions, such as the resurrection of Christ or the changing of water into wine. Miracles can be small, everyday occurrences, such as a kind deed performed by a total stranger, or discovering a person with a beautiful and kind mind, or the simple show of affection we receive from our pets. These seemingly small events I consider to be tiny, everyday miracles, for they carry within the power to help us transcend our own limitations at a precise moment in time. In doing so, they connect us to a divine person: a loving Father, who—as the Gospel tells us—watches for even the smallest details in our lives.

Discovering these small blessings or miracles in our daily can become a great source of spiritual comfort and inner peace for each of us. In monastic life, I find that one can usually abide in a state of steady and constant peacefulness by simply remaining mindful of God's wonders in the present moment, of the small blessings he bestows on us at a given time in our lives. As we pray the psalms several times daily, we are constantly reminded of God's good deeds in our lives. Today, for instance, since the leaves are down and our trees are bare, I was anxious to get into the garden and do some much-needed raking, but then I remembered the weatherman had last night prognosticated a rainy and windy day. Surprisingly, the day turned out to be sunny and mild, a perfect day for putting in a few hours of work outdoors. With a smile I said, "*Deo gratias*," for the small miracle of unexpected good weather. "You are my God, I give you thanks; my God, I offer you praise" (Psalm 118:28).

THE JESUS PRAYER: A DOUBLE MOVEMENT

Pray night and day.
Pray when you are happy
and pray when you are sad.
Pray with fear and trembling,
and with a watchful and vigilant mind,
that your prayer might be acceptable to the Lord,
for as the Scriptures say:
"The eyes of the Lord are on the righteous,
and his ears are open to their appeal."

THEODOROS THE GREAT ASCETIC

The Jesus prayer is a dependable, faithful companion to the monk at all times. It becomes a home to us everywhere, wherever we may be, and it always travels well. It is a rest, a solace, and at all times a point of convergence. The prayer, always short and to the point, presents in stark simplicity the reality of our inner life. Anyone who wishes to pray it can do so at all times, even sometimes when falling asleep. The fact that the prayer gets repeated over and over doesn't make its recitation mechanical. If it were so, it would lose its intrinsic value as prayer. There is a double movement in the prayer, and they are both fundamental to it. First, we address ourselves directly to our Lord Jesus Christ, and we acknowledge him as God and Savior, the all-merciful one. We breathe deeply and rest there, in his presence, counting on the power of his name to make up for our insufficiencies and sinfulness. This is the incipient and first movement of the prayer, one to which we return over and over again. The second movement concerns us, the reality of who we are and the state in which we find ourselves while praying to God: poor sinners in dire need of God's abundant mercy. Jesus is the infinitely merciful one, and we must become a living replica of the repentant publican from the Gospel. The prayer, as it gets repeated over and over, becomes an interplay back and forth between these two movements, one from which we never wish to leave. Gradually, the prayer takes over as it takes complete hold of us. Then it goes on day and night, no matter what activity or state we may find ourselves in. It goes on even while we are tired, fatigued, and ready to fall asleep at night. As we fall asleep with the prayer deeply grounded in our hearts, we are aware that in the early morning the invocation of the holy name will be the waking sound on our lips and in our hearts as we once again start our daily routine: "Lord Jesus Christ, Son of the living God, have mercy on me, a sinner...."

LOVE'S FIRE

The love of God is fiery by nature,
and when it descends in an extraordinary degree
onto a person,
it throws that soul into ecstasy.

ST. ISAAC OF NINEVEH

One of the unique pleasures of our cold evenings is to light the wood-burning stove in the kitchen and keep steadily warm by it. This is a daily task in the monastery, where we often have three wood-burning stoves going at the same time. During the stretch of a long winter night, as I continue adding more wood and feeding the stoves, in deep quiet I marvel at the magic of the flame, at the soothing comfort that emanates from the fire. There is an aspect deeply nurturing about this daily ritual, and one often feels overwhelmed by the intensity of the fire. As I enjoy these tranquil, long winter night hours in front of the stove, the imagery and rich symbolism of fire somehow becomes real. I am reminded of St. Paul's words, "Our God is a consuming fire," and that the sole purpose of our Christian lives is the attainment of the Holy Spirit, who himself is pure fire, pure love. It is no wonder that Abba Joseph, an early desert monk, used to repeat to Abba Lot, "You cannot be a monk unless you become like a consuming fire." He would add, "If you will, you can become all flame."

STRETCHING THE GARDEN VEGETABLES FURTHER INTO THE SEASON

Now leeks are in season, for pottage full good,
And spareth the milchcow, and purgeth the blood.

MEDIEVAL ENGLISH PROVERB

These early November days are often taken up with continuous work in the vegetable garden. While most gardeners put away their tools and garden work after a severe frost in October, in the monastery we make an effort to extend our garden season until sometimes December. It is true that most of the crops are finished now, but there are still some vegetables such as leeks, turnips, beets, chards, kale, and others that continue growing late into the season. This is also true of the salad greens that were planted toward the end of summer to provide us fresh greens for the table all the way to Thanksgiving or even maybe early December.

For late fall-growing vegetables, the timing of the planting is the key to success. To achieve a good crop for later in the year, one must plant the seeds sometime in early September, well before the first frost. Here in our New York-New England region, where our first frost usually arrives around St. Michael's Day, we are sure to plant them at the latest by mid-September to give the plants time to germinate and grow before the frost arrives. We are so blessed by the Lord of the harvest who continues to sustain us daily with produce and crops grown from our own land. Every evening, before Vespers, I make my way once more into the garden to gather the greens for a bowl of fresh salad for dinner. After accomplishing that, I cover the raised beds with a long sheet of plastic to shield them from a possible night frost. The plastic serves as protection for the crops, and it prolongs their lives for a few more weeks. Invariably, on Thanksgiving Day, we can still delight in some fresh produce from our own garden. This is one more reason to express gratitude to our Creator and Provider. *Deo gratias!*

THE REWARD OF MONASTIC HOSPITALITY

The patriarch Abraham
undertook the labor of hospitality
and sat by his tent door welcoming passersby,
and his table was open to all comers,
even to the uncouth and the unworthy,
for he set no limitations.
This is why he was counted worthy
to be present at that most wondrous feast,
when he entertained angels and the Master of All.
We too should love to practice openhearted hospitality
so as to welcome not only angels
but even the Lord himself as our guests,
for it was the Lord who told us:
"Insofar as you did it to one of the least of these,
you did it to me."
How good it is to be kind to all,
especially those who are unable to repay you.

THEODORUS THE ASCETIC

A PACIFIST FOR CHRIST

Today we honor the memory of a cherished, personal friend, St. Martin de Tours. From early childhood on, I have learned to love St. Martin, and he has always been a faithful companion on the road to God. He is a most inspiring monastic father, one whose influence in France is felt to this day. Inspired by the example of St. Antony, he was one of the pioneers of the monastic movement in Poitiers, in France, where he established several monasteries and where to this day thousands of churches are still dedicated to him. He was also an ardent pacifist, renouncing every form of violence. He firmly believed that to be a true follower of Christ, a "soldier of Christ" as he called himself, one must renounce any recourse to violence. While reflecting on St. Martin during my morning reading, I found a passage from Macarius the Great that, in my view, could aptly be applied to St. Martin:

> Sometimes the soul finds rest in the deepest quietness,
> and joy and perfect peace in perfectly focused spiritual delight
> and ineffably deep repose.
> At other times the soul is stirred up by grace
> and taught lessons in ineffable wisdom and understanding
> and knowledge of the spirit,
> in ways that pass beyond all our ability to speak of them....
> Manifold are the patterns of grace,
> and most varied are the ways it leads the soul.
> Sometimes, as God decides,
> grace gives rest to the soul.
> At other times it puts it to work.

READING THE SIGNS OF THE TIMES

When the spiritual intellect is stripped of its obsessions,
it discovers the Holy Spirit.

THALASSIOS THE LIBYAN

Today is one of those typical gray November days, almost gloomy. It is getting late in autumn, and all the outward signs in nature seem to whisper of winter's proximity. It has already gotten quite cold outdoors, so I usually have to wear a sweater or a coat while doing my chores throughout the property or while working with our farm animals. By midafternoon, it sometimes gets a bit warmer, and one can enjoy the crisp autumn air, always refreshing as well as purifying to our lungs. While piling some of the winter wood close to the monastery, I noticed a flock of Canadian geese flying south. *One more sign of the season,* I said to myself. It reminded me of the Gospel passage where the Lord mentions to be attentive to the sign of the times...at all times.

It is easier somehow for us to notice the signs of a changing season; it is altogether another thing to notice and read the signs of the times in the cultural events that are daily taking place in our world today. Many people feel a sense of insecurity watching our world being transformed daily, almost drastically. Technology alone is evolving at such fast a pace, making previous technology almost irrelevant. And the social sciences—such as psychology, sociology, and even anthropology—are uncovering new understandings of human nature, of what it ultimately means to develop all of our human potential. It is up to us, people of faith, to follow the Lord's exhortation to be attentive to the signs of the times. We must have complete trust that God is still in charge. We must not fear the new perceptions of reality, newer understanding of human nature presented daily to us. Like the Lord, we must keep an open mind and be eager to learn, remaining always alert to the evolutionary process in which we are all caught. The future, uncertain as it may be, is always in God's hands, and that is enough for me to trust its outcome.

THE LIGHT OF MOUNT TABOR

Truly, your disciples at Mount Tabor were instantly dazzled by the brightness of your uncreated light, and looking at one another with fright, fall on their faces to the ground, worshiping You, O Master of all.

BYZANTINE OFFICE OF THE TRANSFIGURATION

As we slowly begin to move from the autumnal light toward the winter one, I notice the extraordinary changes taking place daily in the natural light. Very early, in the almost predawn hours, I am always taken by the calm, soothing, beautiful, first signs of light that appear in the horizon, peacefully announcing a new day. Later on, just before dusk, I am struck by the dramatic changes in the sky, as the last rays of the sun set over the Catskill Mountains. There is a sublime, mysterious light quality at this time of the year. It is something that I witness almost daily and enjoy it. And no, I never take it for granted. As I reflect on the light quality during this transitional period, I am reminded of the early monastic fathers' deep appreciation for what they called "the light of Tabor." For them, the sole aim of monastic life was to enter into the mystery of this divine light and dwell permanently there.

St. John of Damascus wrote:

> Why did Christ lead his disciples onto a high mountain when he was transfigured in light before them? It was to show that when disciples arrive at the summit of love, they stand out of themselves and perceive the Invisible One. Such a person flies over the obscuring clouds and comes out into the clear sky of the soul and so is able to look more acutely into the sun of righteousness, although the perfect vision of the Godhead always transcends our capacities. On that day, pray in solitude. For stillness is the mother of prayer, and prayer is the revelation of the glory of God.

INNER-RECHARGING WITH THE SEASON

Just to be is a blessing.
Just to live is holy.
RABBI ABRAHAM HESCHEL

It is mid-November, and we are full swing into the fall season, reaping the last fruits from the harvest and heading definitely toward Thanksgiving. Many people in our area begin to push themselves into high gear for the upcoming holidays. It is a well-known experience around here that holiday time is often full of stressful moments. There is just too much excitement built around it and not enough helpful restraints to calm it down.

I often noticed how much time and energy people spend in planning the holidays, the gift-giving preparations, and on other endless busy details about the season. It is often the case that while we find ourselves terribly occupied with our social preparations, we often forget the deep influence winter itself has upon all of us. The sudden changes in the light and temperatures deeply affect our body and its psycho-rhythms. The cold weather directs us somehow to slow down our activities, gently suggesting we seek a quieter daily pace, concentrating instead on replenishing and nourishing our inner spirits. When we choose to do this and indeed settle for paying deeper attention to our inner needs, a bit of winter wisdom is being conveyed to all of us. Each season, with its own particular gifts and peculiarities, has so much to teach us. All we need do is to become sensitively attuned to them. As the colder season progresses, all of us are given the choice either to rush into the chaos and compulsion the upcoming holidays bring, or to retreat a bit and instead embrace a more harmonious life rhythm, something deeper and more in tune with the inner needs of our own souls.

ADVENTUS DOMINI

The eyes of human pride shall be lowered,
the arrogance of mortals shall be abased,
and the Lord *alone will be exalted, on that day.*

ISAIAH 2:11

Today, in a quiet and calm manner, we make our unofficial entrance into the observance of Advent, the so-called *Adventus Domini*. In doing so, we opt deliberately to follow the tradition of the Eastern Churches which established early in the history of Christianity a forty-day period of preparation for the solemnity of Christmas. I wrote about this extensively in my book *A Monastery Journey to Christmas*. In both Churches, that of the East and the West, the Advent season is looked upon as an ascetical and prayerful spiritual journey that intentionally serves to prepare us for the commemoration of the Lord's birth and ultimately for the transcendent event of his second and final coming in glory.

Advent, as it arrives on the threshold of winter, provides us the occasion to examine the aspects of darkness and gloominess in our own lives and in our world today. The purpose of Christ's coming is to free us from the terrifying power of darkness over our lives. As we await the Lord's coming, we plead to him daily to be liberated from the uncanny fears and shadows that spring from darkness and instead fill us with the light, hope, and peace that shine from his face. As we struggle during our Advent journey with tension in our lives between the forces of darkness and light, fear and trust, despair and hope, we ask the Lord to triumph in us by the mysterious power of his grace. The Holy Spirit of God is with us at every moment, at every step throughout the journey, and if we don't forsake him along the way, he will make sure that we arrive safely at our destination, well-prepared to receive the gift of God at Christmas: Christ, our Savior. "Come, Lord, do not delay. Free your people from darkness."

CONVERSION OF MANNERS

Whoever sits in solitude and is quiet has escaped from three wars: those of hearing, speaking, and seeing. Then there is only one remaining war to be fought to the end: and that is the battle for your own heart.

ABBA ANTONY THE GREAT, SAYINGS OF THE EGYPTIAN ELDERS

Conversion of manners is rather crucial in the thought of St. Benedict, so much so that he makes it a requirement, a vow, for those embracing the monastic life. It is important, however, to duly study and understand how this process of conversion takes place. It doesn't happen suddenly, simply because we wish to be converted; and it is not a negative process, as it is often portrayed by a secular world. We can only begin the process of conversion, the humble process of changing ourselves, as we try to imitate and follow the humble Christ of the Gospels.

True conversion only takes place as we put on Christ, as we try to assimilate into our own lives the teachings and examples of the Lord's own life. That, indeed, is a life task, and thus conversion is a lifelong process. The only thing that matters is not that we change ourselves but into whom we are changing. The more we imitate and incorporate Christ into our lives, the more we become Christlike: a new being much in the image and likeness of God. And this new self, or "new creation" as St. Paul calls it, is none other than the clear and visible manifestation of Christ in our lives. For indeed, by the power of the Holy Spirit, Christ becomes our life. Then and only then we can say with St. Paul: "I live, but no longer I, for Christ lives in me."

NOVEMBER 17

A REFLECTION ON RELIGIOUS FANATICISM

The Spirit is light, life, and peace.
If you are illumined by the divine Spirit,
your life will be established in peaceful serenity.
NIKETAS STETHATOS

Tonight I am occupied doing my usual Advent evening reading, simply enjoying the quiet hours of a long November night. I am also listening to a Beethoven quartet as background music. The quartet does not distract from my reading. It actually helps my concentration. Often, this time of day is also a time for deeper reflections on current events. Lately I have been thinking a lot about a persistent phenomenon that seems quite prevalent in our days, at least in certain sections of our society. It is the phenomenon of religious fanaticism. It is incredible to see how far some people carry their so-called religious convictions. Not only that, they go even further and wish to impose them on everybody else. They continually pass judgment on those who think or act differently. This phenomenon is found in all religious and political persuasions. One sees it in Muslim, Jewish, Protestant, Catholic, Orthodox, and other denominations. They go as far as burning other religions' sacred books, and their blogs and websites are often filled with one-sided propaganda that contain no depth or wisdom at all. They see the world through their own lenses, *optique*, as one says in French. It is a typical one-sided view of the world.

I am reminded by my reading that such people have existed throughout the ages, that they were present during Jesus' time and were often rebuked by the Lord. Some of these people, more often than not, emerge from circles with extreme one-sided views that often wish to cultivate or push similar attitudes among others. They tend to confuse a legalistic interpretation of the law with true fidelity to the Lord. True fidelity, according to the Gospels, is never fanatical. On the contrary, it is usually humble, nonjudgmental, peaceful, noncontentious, and, above all, it never seeks to impose its own religious or political ideas on others. This type of fidelity is inspired by the Spirit of God, the Spirit who dispenses both knowledge and wisdom and keeps the soul humble, objective, tranquil, selfless, serene, and peaceful at all times.

Often, by recognizing these signs in someone, we are able to detect those who act as the Lord's worthy disciples. St. Paul, in his Letter to the Ephesians, exhorts us to a truly balanced Christian life, thus avoiding the perils of extremism and fanaticism: "And do not grieve the holy Spirit of God, with which you were sealed for the day of redemption. All bitterness, fury, anger, shouting, and reviling must be removed from you, along with all malice. [And] be kind to one another, compassionate, forgiving one another as God has forgiven you in Christ. So be imitators of God, as beloved children, and live in love, as Christ loved us..." (Ephesians 4:30 to 5:2).

A LIFE CHOICE

Restore our captives, LORD, like the dry stream beds of the Negeb. Those who sow in tears will reap with cries of joy.

PSALM 126:4–5

Recently we received the visit of a young diocesan priest who shows up at our doors from time to time. He is an eager and sincere person, seeking to find out God's will for his life. He has been interested in monastic life for a few years now, and he asked me where or in what monastery could he sincerely give his life to the Lord. He has visited so many monasteries that at this point in his life he has a hard time deciding which would be the best place to suit his needs. What a hard a choice to make, he commented. He enumerated the qualities, geography, and practices of many of the monasteries...and he happened to be attracted to quite a few. He asked me squarely what one should look for, fundamentally, as a positive sign to make a choice. I responded simply: "Look for a community deeply rooted in humility, the most humble among all of them from every angle, practice, and reputation, the one which has nothing good to say about itself yet serves the Lord in truth, with joy and peace, one where the monks pray from the bottom of their hearts and yet make no claim upon themselves. If you find it, join it and follow in their steps."

LET GO OF YOURSELF AND LET GOD IN

Who else is good apart from God?
So, entrust all your life to him
and all will be well with you.
EVAGRIUS OF PONTUS, MONK

During this early Advent period, we plunge ourselves into a spiritual quest for the Lord's presence and what it means to prepare oneself for his coming at Christmas. With this in mind, we sojourn into an empty desert where we can attune our ears and our hearts more attentively, so we can listen to his word. Intuitively I know the rugged reality of the desert is the right place to be at this time, for its emptiness and physical bareness is a strong invitation to let go of all that is superfluous in our lives and instead heed God's word, God's message for personal conversion and repentance. Undertaking the humble work of conversion and repentance is the best preparation we can make for the Lord's coming and, in my view, it is what Advent is all about.

As I ponder these thoughts in my mind, I am reminded of the words of a dear friend who was crippled most of her life but still got to live to her late nineties. She suffered immensely and couldn't manage to do much for herself at the end, physically or otherwise, not even the simple act of walking. Yet she accepted her condition as coming from a loving Father in heaven, never complaining about it or feeling sorry for herself. Whenever I asked her how she managed to do so and preserve her inner peace, she simply replied, "I let go of myself and I let God in." She concluded: "It is all about letting go and letting God."

LIVING TRADITION

Oh, that today you would hear his voice: Do not harden your hearts as at Meribah....

PSALM 95:7–8

A living monastic tradition, concretely speaking, consists in the Holy Spirit at work. It is he who renews the face of the earth, of the world, of the Church, and ultimately, our own hearts daily, making it possible to communicate the divine life again and again to every new generation.

I am one of those monks who is deeply attached to and deeply grateful for the early monastic tradition. I see myself not only in the tradition and continuity with St. Benedict, but also with all those early monastic fathers and mothers from primitive Christianity, especially the Desert Fathers and Mothers. Our early monastic parents received this tradition directly from the Gospels, and from there they handed it over to subsequent generations. The Gospels are the source, the living waters received, accepted, lived, and then transmitted by tradition. The monastic tradition is nothing else but this living continuity with the reality of the Gospels. It is the "living water" of which the Lord spoke about.

Unfortunately, tradition is often confused with a nostalgia for certain forms from the past, and there are some monasteries, monks, and nuns who idealize and interpret tradition as such. For them, the movement of history ends at a certain point in history and nothing new since then is acceptable to them. In my view, this is a naïve and rather static understanding of tradition. For tradition to be relevant at any time, at any present moment, it must become incarnate in the peoples and cultures of our present times. Psalm 95 reminds us: Today, if "you hear his voice, do not harden your hearts." It is the today of God that matters, not the yesterday of our sentimentalities. Tradition, the living fresh waters that spring from the life-giving source of the Gospels, must always become actualized in the present moment, otherwise it is dead. Recently, I read in a French blog a paragraph that expresses this concisely:

Nostalgia is a sin, a form of sloth, and engaging in it enervates discipleship and devotion. But tradition is different; tradition is not the dead faith of the living but rather the living faith of the dead, as Pelikan said. To live within and out of tradition is not to daydream about days gone by that most of us never experienced anyway, but rather to ride the crest of the wave of God's redemptive story as we live out our own stories within its broader plot. We have no other time than the present in which to live; all of us were called for such a time as this, this time, here, now, Today, as long as it is called Today, wherever and whenever we are.

PRESENTATION OF THE *THEOTOKOS* IN THE TEMPLE

On November 21, we celebrate the unique event in the life of a young maiden, Mary, her entrance into the Temple, and her total consecration to God. In the Eastern liturgy, Mary, the *Theotokos* ("God-bearer" in Greek), is seen and celebrated as a "living temple of holiness," for it is she who shall one day bear Christ. Again and again she is praised as the "dwelling place of the Almighty," who "contains the Word that cannot be contained." So the young maiden enters into God's Temple and is seized by the Holy Spirit, the same Spirit who later shall work the great mystery of the Incarnation in her. Her parents and God's ancestors, Joachim and Anna, carry her into the Holy of Holies, knowing somehow that God has already marked the maiden's future.

In time and by the action of the Holy Spirit, Mary is to become the living temple of God. The memorial feast we keep today quietly bears witness to that fact. It saddens me somehow that this feast has lessened in character lately in the Western liturgy, for there is so much to learn from the story, and appropriately so, as we ourselves journey on our way to Christmas. Our Lady, as she becomes God's own and unique temple, is a living example for us all. Like her, we also are called to become "living temples" of the Holy Spirit, for—as St. Paul reminds us—"whoever is joined to the Lord becomes one spirit with him" (1 Corinthians 6:17).

There is a profound connection between this particular feast and the approaching mystery that shall be revealed at Christmas. Thus, today for the first time we hear during the night vigil allusions to the Nativity of the Lord. From now until Christmas, the beautiful Christmas canon composed by one of the early fathers shall be sung on the vigil of major feasts and Sundays. The canon, as it is sung, becomes a loving invitation to prepare and be ready for the Lord's arrival. "Christ is born; glorify him! Christ comes from heaven; go to meet him. Sing to the Lord, all the earth! Praise him with joy, O people, for he has been glorified."

FORM VERSUS SUBSTANCE IN LITURGICAL PIETY

Thirst for Jesus alone, so that he may inebriate you with his love.

ST. ISAAC OF NINEVEH

Remember the prophet: "Serve the LORD *in fear" (Psalm 2:10) and "Sing his praises with understanding" (Psalm 47:7) and also "In the sight of angels I will sing praise to you" (Psalm 138:1). Let us consider, then, how we ought to behave in the presence of God and his angels, and let us stand to sing the psalms in such a way that our minds are in harmony with our voices.*

THE RULE OF ST. BENEDICT, CHAPTER 19

Recently I was visited by a married couple who, in previous months, attended liturgical services, both the divine liturgy and the offices, in diverse monasteries around the country. They were more than willing to share their experiences with me. We had an interesting exchange, and I eagerly listened to their comments. The wife happened to be a musician, so she added her own insights into the matter. The range of monasteries visited were from very traditional ones where everything is observed as "once before" to a whole variety of contemporary ones, where liturgical piety has evolved with the new insights provided by the council, patristic, biblical, and liturgical studies. The conversation was a long one, and there is no time here to recount all that was said. However, I was particularly struck by one of their insights. This concerned the differentiation they made between form and substance in liturgical piety.

In their view, the so-called more "traditional" monasteries attached greater importance to the preserving of a certain worship form from the past, while the more open/evolved monasteries aimed more at substance in their worship. This was palpable, the wife related, in the singing or recitation of the psalms. She noticed that monasteries where the entire offices were done in Latin, the singing or recitation of the psalms was rather mechanical, a bit cerebral like a good performance, almost "like a Broadway show," she commented. In contrast, at the monastic communities who prayed the psalms in the common language of the people, their offices seemed more low-key, restrained exteriorly but with a prayerful quality unlike the others. It was noticeable to the couple that in these monasteries where the psalmody was understood, the words were digested and sung meaningfully, not in mechanical fashion. Besides, they said, there were pauses after each of the psalms to reflect and pray silently. The same was done after the short or longer reading of the Scriptures, where there was a prayerful pause to digest the words. The couple made other comments, such as the endless minutia they noticed in ceremonies, rituals, and pirouettes performed by these so-called traditional groups during the celebration of the liturgy, which, the couple mentioned, could often be more of a distraction than an aid to prayer. Monastic prayer, liturgical or otherwise, I told our friendly visitors, should be simple and stripped of nonessentials, worship done "in spirit and truth" as the Lord commands us, so that it can be free to concentrate totally in the mystery of God. The Lord does not seek to be honored by trivia or the superficial exterior of ceremonies, but more by the humility, simplicity, sincerity, and depth of our prayer. *Kyrie eleison.*

NOVEMBER 23

LORD, IT IS GOOD TO BE HERE

O God, restore us; light up your face and we shall be saved.

PSALM 80:4

One of the paradoxes Christians confront during their Advent pilgrimage leading to Christmas is the experience of a deep hunger for Christ mixed with the trap of the materialism and consumerism of our times. We are surrounded by a materialistic culture from all sides, and its allures continually attack all our senses. How difficult is it sometimes to remain totally spiritual during the days preceding Christmas—and sometimes even more so during the holidays themselves. One must seek continual recourse to prayer, to quiet, and hunger for his mystery. Personally, the Lord's icon is of great help to me. I simply gaze at him, sometimes losing all sense of time, and find in his presence a state of contentment and well-being. I look at him and I know he's looking at me, and when our gazes join, I feel enveloped in the tranquility that shines from his face. I feel totally captivated by his unassuming majesty. I am transported again and again to the scene of the transfiguration, where in his presence I can hear Peter humbly uttering the words: "Lord, how good it is to be here." *Ecce, quam bonum!*

WE CONFESS CHRIST, OUR GOD

O Christ, the true light who does enlighten and sanctify every man that comes into the world, let the light of your countenance shine upon us, that in it we may see the divine unapproachable light; and direct our steps in the observance of your commandments.

THE FIRST HOUR, BYZANTINE OFFICE

Today, on this day on which we keep the memorial day of the monk St. Columbanus, I am reminded of an attitude that makes the monastic witness somehow unique in our present times. It is the clear and undisputed confession on the part of the monk that Christ alone is true God and true man. From the times of the apostles to the era of the martyrs, Christ followers paid the ultimate price with their life and blood for the privilege of confessing Christ. Their confession of Christ as true God/true man was more than just paying lip service to a doctrine. They went beyond that and beyond a routine profession of faith such as the one we make every Sunday when we recite the Nicene Creed, beautiful as this may be. Confessing Christ-God was personal to them. It meant to be ready to give one's life for attesting to this.

After the persecution of Christians came to an end during the reign of Constantine, thus ceasing in actuality the witness of the martyrs, the Holy Spirit prompted a group of fervent Christians to continue carrying out this specific witness of confessing Christ in a new way. The Spirit of God inspired some Christians to withdraw to the harsh solitude of the desert, be it of Egypt or Palestine, and testify there by the witness of their lives to the truth of Christ, true God and true man. How did they accomplish this type of witnessing? By continual prayer, humble repentance, and an asceticism that implied complete fidelity to the teachings of the Gospel. Living the totality of the Gospel teachings in an authentic manner, daily, all of them without exception became the new way of confessing Christ to both other Christians and pagans alike. The monastic movement had as humble origin and sole purpose the continuation of confessing Christ to the world, the dark pagan world of its time, not unlike that of our own.

CHRIST, OUR ADVENT LIGHT

For with you is the fountain of life,
and in your light we see light.
PSALM 36:10

It is getting late into the fall season. Thanksgiving, our harvest feast, was just celebrated and it somehow marked the end of a lovely period. We are slowly but steadily proceeding with our Advent journey, which takes us right into winter itself and into Christmas. Before we say our goodbyes to autumn, I wish to acknowledge once again how much I treasured the particular blessings of the season. Our lives are deeply affected by the reality of each of the seasons. This is particularly true of fall, which touches the core of who we are. Here in the countryside, we all enjoy autumn's brisk changes in the air, its earthy fragrance, its intoxicating quality, especially during our long chilly nights. The rich colors from our trees are now gone; only the fallen leaves remain throughout the property, a reminder of what a few weeks ago made our region picture perfect. Every evening at Vespers time, we sing the "*Phos Hilaron*" while the last rays from the sun make us behold an exquisite, radiant, golden light. "Now that we come to the setting of the sun and behold the light of evening, we praise the Father, Son, and Holy Spirit God," to quote the "*Phos Hilaron.*" It is truly the time to give thanks to the Lord for his gift of light. It reminds us that Christ is our Advent light that dispels and dissipates the fear of darkness from our lives, the light that traces and directs our path into the ways of peace. Late autumn light stirs deep sentiments in our souls, and its memory continues to linger long after the season is over. We pray, "All thanks and praise to the Father, Author and Source of light, to Christ, Light from light, and to the Holy Spirit, the Giver of light!"

A STRANGE AND WONDERFUL BEAUTY

There is no excellent beauty that hath not some strangeness in the proportion.

FRANCIS BACON, PHILOSOPHER

I have learnt from the Prophet, who foretold in older times the coming of Emmanuel, that a certain holy Virgin should bear a child. Now I long to know how the nature of mortal men shall undergo union with the Godhead.

BYZANTINE MATINS OF THE ANNUNCIATION, CANTICLE

These early Advent days inspire us, as they should, to dig ever more deeply into the mystery of the Incarnation. I am awestruck by the ever-strange beauty of the mystery, its majestic power to overwhelm us. I can't let go of it. Everything about the way the Lord went about accomplishing his mystery is totally beyond human comprehension. Only faith can give us a glimpse into that abyss. Basically it all has to do with the Father's plans to send his only Son into a world he created. He assigns the Holy Spirit to accomplish this in a humble virgin, and she is told of the mystery to be realized in her during a visit from an angel. Gabriel proclaims good news of hope and salvation to the world through the Holy Spirit's action in Mary. The strange and awesome beauty of the mystery is that humanity and divinity are now joined in Mary's womb. At the crucial moment of the Incarnation, human history changes its course forever: the Word is made flesh and he dwells among us!

"THE MIGHTY ONE HAS DONE GREAT THINGS FOR ME"

Behold, the time of our salvation is drawing near. Make ready, O cave, for the Virgin is drawing nigh to giving birth. Be glad and rejoice, O Bethlehem, land of Judah, for from you the Lord shall shine forth at dawn. Hearken, you mountains and hills and all you lands around Judea: for Christ comes in his love for humanity, to save humankind, which he fashioned in his image and likeness.

BYZANTINE VESPERS FROM FOREFEAST OF THE NATIVITY

Today the Church that is in France, particularly that of Paris where the apparitions took place, keeps the memorial feast of Our Lady of the Miraculous Medal. Since our Lady, the *Theotokos*, is Advent's most important figure after that of Christ, her Son, it is fitting today that we take time to honor and reflect on the role she played on those days preceding Christmas. We read in the Gospels that her cousin, Elizabeth, called her "blessed" because she bore in her womb the Son of the Most High. Mary was praised by Elizabeth, as she was previously praised by the angel Gabriel, because she was chosen by the Holy Spirit to carry the Word of God, the second person of the Trinity. As Mary uttered her *Magnificat* in response to Elizabeth's praises, she glorified God for all he had done for her, in her. She attributed all good things to God alone, and because of her great humility she was able to experience the magnitude of favors the Lord had bestowed upon her. The time for God dispensing grace and great mercy upon Israel had arrived, and this he chose to do in using Mary as a vehicle. "The Mighty One has done great things for me, and holy is his name. His mercy is from age to age to those who fear him" (Luke 1:49–50).

CHRIST, THE DOOR

I am the gate. Whoever enters through me will be saved....

JOHN 10:9

...I have left an open door before you, which no one can close.

REVELATION 3:8

Here in the monastery, we move rather hastily with our winter preparations and, yes, we also continue vigilantly our Advent journey to Christmas. We are particularly mindful that this journey is one that hopefully will bring us closer to the Lord. During these Advent days, I use different images of Christ provided to us in the Scriptures, particularly in the Gospels, to feed my inner prayer. One of the images that is very personal and speaks volumes to me is the one of Christ the door, the keeper of the gate. Very often when I pray or meditate gazing at the large icon of the Lord in our chapel, I get a clear and distinct understanding that Christ is truly the door through which we must all pass to come to the Father. As I focus on that precise icon day after day, I see an open door through which I must go through to enter deeply into God. In the icon, the Lord remains totally still in his mystery, his majesty, inviting me lovingly to come to him, to enter into him so to speak, so that he may show me the Father. He gently reminds me again and again that "he who sees me sees the Father" for "I and the Father are one."

CHRIST, OUR ADVENT HOPE

May the God of hope fill you with all joy and peace in believing, so that you may abound in hope by the power of the holy Spirit.

ROMANS 15:13

Advent is a season of hope. During our Advent days, we are invited to relive the hope of ancient Israel as it waited and longed for the Messiah, for him who would bring deliverance to God's Chosen People. The sacred Scriptures, especially the writing of the prophets, inspire us to enter into that expectant hope that nurtured the faith of the people of Israel. Hope is a theological virtue, a gift from the Holy Spirit, one that fills our souls with joyful anticipation for the desired one of our hearts. In the midst of the gloom, greed, and deadly materialism of our present times, we await in hope, for we know the Lord is truly coming, and he shall free us from personal despair and slavery, as he once did for the Israelites.

During our Advent days, we delight in rediscovering that the source of our hope is a person, Christ the Lord. Hope is not an abstract attitude, belief, or virtue. St. Paul tells us it is Christ who is the source of our hope, and we know that he is all love, all goodness, all mercy, the pure reflection of God's glory. Furthermore, through the grace and action of the Holy Spirit, Christ lives and acts in us, and it is hope that makes us more alert, more vigilant, somehow fully awake and ever grateful for his Real Presence in our lives. Jesus the God-man is the sure anchor of our hope, our hope of glory, and he promised to be with us always until the end of time. *Christus, spes nostra.* In the words of one of the seasonal antiphons: "Eagerly we await the fulfillment of our hope, the glorious coming of our Savior."

THE APOSTLE FIRST CALLED

As he was walking by the Sea of Galilee, he saw two brothers, Simon who is called Peter, and his brother Andrew, casting a net into the sea; they were fishermen. He said to them, "Come after me, and I will make you fishers of men."

MATTHEW 4:18–19

The feast of the Apostle Andrew falls appropriately during the period of our Advent journey, for Andrew was one of the first among the apostles to recognize Jesus as the expected Messiah. After first encountering Jesus, Andrew goes in haste to communicate the good news to his brother Peter: "'We have found the Messiah,' (which is translated Anointed)" (John 1:41). The great St. John Chrysostom, the "Golden Mouth," comments in one of his homilies: "Andrew's words reveal a soul waiting with the utmost longing for the coming of the Messiah, looking forward to his appearing from heaven, rejoicing when he does appear, and hastening to announce so great an event to others." It was Andrew's task to bring his brother Peter, and hence others, to the source of light: the Lamb of God who takes away the sins of the world. It is our task now, following in Andrew's steps, to point others to the same Lamb of God, to him who alone offers salvation to the world.

DECEMBER

DECEMBER 1 · Blessed Charles de Foucauld, Modern Desert Father

THE HOLY SPIRIT

Come, let us rejoice in the Holy Spirit!
Let us sing endless praises to Christ our God!
Let us celebrate the joy of Joachim and Anna,
The conception of the Mother of God,
For she is the fruit of the grace of God.

VESPERS HYMN FOR THE CONCEPTION OF THE *THEOTOKOS*

During these peaceful and calm Advent days, there is a mysterious presence felt in our prayers and readings, a presence of whom little is spoken. It is the subtle, mysterious, almost incomprehensible presence of the Holy Spirit. We know through faith that from all eternity, in the intimate council of the Holy Trinity, the Holy Spirit was assigned the work of the Incarnation. It was by his mighty power that the Son of God became incarnate in the Virgin Mary. The Incarnation of God's Son, willed by the Father long before the ages began and totally assented by the Son himself, is the particular and unique operation of the Holy Spirit.

The more we immerse ourselves in the work of prayer, the more we come to discover something about the Holy Spirit's presence in our lives. "It is one thing to believe in God," Staretz Silouan used to say, "and another to know him." It is in prayer and by the direct action of the Holy Spirit that we come to understand something of the mystery of the Incarnation, of the two natures of Christ: divine and human. Only the Holy Spirit can communicate to the praying believer something of that splendid divine union of two different natures and two wills. Infused divine knowledge is a gift from the Holy Spirit, and it is his divine power that opens our hearts and minds to this type of knowledge. It is through experiencing the Holy Spirit interiorly, deep, deep within our souls, that the mystery of Jesus Christ is revealed to us. The Holy Spirit confers on us both faith and grace to arrive at this divine knowledge. Advent is a special time to keep close to the Holy Spirit (though we know through faith that all times are his and belong to him). But Advent and Christmas are periods of abundant graces that flow from the inner life of the Blessed Trinity. These graces are channeled into our hearts through the power and grace of the Holy Spirit. Humbly, patiently, the Holy Spirit pursues each of us, gradually revealing his divine presence in us, eagerly preparing our hearts to become a worthy manger for the Savior.

A RADIANT LIGHT FROM THE EAST

People look East, the time is near
Of the crowning of the year.
Make your house fair as you are able,
Trim the hearth and set the table.
People look East and sing today:
Love, the Lord, is on the way.

EIGHTEENTH-CENTURY CAROL

From ancient times, monastics in general have kept the venerable custom of praying with their eyes gazed toward the East. This was not based on simple preference or personal devotion but on sound biblical tradition. As we read in the Gospel of Matthew: "For just as lightning comes from the east and is seen as far as the west, so will the coming of the Son of Man be" (Matthew 24:27).

The mystery of Advent tells me that Christ became incarnate in time and revealed to us what lies beyond time, awaiting all of us. The vision holds a promise that, at the end of time, when the Lord of glory appears from the East as Savior and Judge, we, his disciples, shall hear the glad tidings from his mouth: "Come, you who are blessed by my Father. Inherit the kingdom prepared for you from the foundation of the world" (Matthew 25:34). These words from the Gospel are particularly consoling to hear during our Advent days, filled as they are with earthly cares and busy Christmas preparations. They bespeak of the *beata pacis visio*, the "blessed vision of peace" promised to all of us in the new Jerusalem, where God's kingdom will be fully realized. "Our Savior, the Dayspring from the East, has visited us from on high, and we who were in darkness and shadow have found the truth: for the Lord is born of the Virgin" (Exapostilarion Matins of the Nativity of the Lord).

DECEMBER 3

THE ADVENT DESERT

What did you go out into the desert to see?...
Why did you go out?

MATTHEW 11:7, 9

It was in the desert that Israel had come to know God.

CARL R. KAZMIERSKI, *JOHN THE BAPTIST: PROPHET AND EVANGELIST*

Advent, in a subtle way, plunges us directly and without hesitation into the desert experience. The desert is not a sentimental or romantic place to dream about; it is bare, austere, empty, and desolate. There is no place to hide in its confines. It is just what it is: the desert. Advent, similar to Lent in many ways, implies—and really requires—a sojourn into the depths of the desert. Like John the Baptist, God asks us to journey into the desert for a specific purpose: to prepare the way for the Lord. More than ever, we need to find ourselves in an empty place, in the bare reality of the wilderness. We are too busy otherwise—like Martha, "worried about many things"—to adequately provide our undivided attention to "only one thing." The desert helps us to strip off all unwarranted necessities and face squarely our own sinful reality, our naked and broken humanity in utter need of redemption.

The desert is also the place for pursuing the patient waiting attitude that God demands from each of us. This patient waiting attitude is similar in many ways to that "patient endurance" counseled by the Apostle Paul. It demands true patience, and it also means hard work. This patient waiting attitude is inspired by deep faith and trust in God and is the work of constant prayer under the guidance of the Holy Spirit. During this time of patiently waiting for the Lord's arrival, he asks from each of us complete trust and openness to his particular designs for our lives, complete and total cooperation with that which he wishes to accomplish in us. When Christmas, the Lord's day, arrives, we shall then discover the truth of the prophetic words: "The wilderness and the parched land [of our hearts] will exult; the Arabah [desert] will rejoice and bloom" (Isaiah 35:1).

ADVENT LONGING

Be thou my vision, O Lord of my heart,
Naught be all else to me save that thou art;
Be thou my best thought in the day and night,
Waking or sleeping thy presence my light.

EIGHTH-CENTURY IRISH CELTIC POEM

The shorter days of late autumn make the Advent reality a stark and reflective one. It turns us inward, as it intensifies our hope, our longing, and our patient waiting for the Messiah. Through active faith and much prayer, we struggle to purify and cleanse our desires, for we wish to be properly prepared and in good form for the arrival of the Lord at Christmas. We simply can't take for granted this most unusual gift of God's imminent coming to us. An arrival never dreamed of in olden times, an arrival that shall change the course of history forever. Through the mystery of this divine/human birth in our midst, God's own personal visitation to our world, the face of humanity is transfigured, redeemed, and changed forever. Nothing will ever be the same!

Advent is an evocative time to reflect and cultivate a deep yearning, a most passionate longing for the Lord, so that he who is to come doesn't come in vain: He wishes foremost to be born in the innermost of our hearts. St. Anselm, in his *Proslogion* (a discourse on the existence of God), expresses beautifully the sentiments that we should make our own at this time:

> Enter into your mind's inner chamber. Shut out everything but God and whatever helps you seek him; and when you have shut the door, look for him. Speak now to God and say with your whole heart: I seek your face. Lord, I desire you. Teach me to seek you, and when I seek you show yourself to me, for I cannot seek you unless you teach me, nor can I find you unless you show yourself to me. Let me seek you in desiring you and desire you in seeking you, find you in loving you and love you in finding you.

THE HUMBLE WITNESS OF THE *CRÈCHE*

The hinge of history is on the door of a Bethlehem stable.

RALPH W. SOCKMAN, PASTOR

The Christmas season is rich in manifold traditions that spring from 2,000 years of lived Christianity. Throughout the centuries, people were inspired to paint, compose music and poetry, and sculpt Nativity sets in order to tell the Christmas story. These traditions continue to our present day. One of the dearest and most enduring among these customs consists in recreating the Christmas scene, or *crèche* as it is commonly called in French, *pesebre* in Spanish, *presepio* in Italian.

The French word *crèche* simply means "crib," and it is commonly used to depict a classic Nativity scene with figures of people, animals, a star, angels, and a stable as portrayed in the Gospel story of the birth of the Savior in Bethlehem. There is an endless diversity of these Nativity scenes or *crèches* created and invented by artists and artisans from all around the world. The Christmas story, the mystery of the Incarnation, has a timeless, universal appeal not only for well-trained artists, sculptors, and painters, but also for the humble, sometimes illiterate artisans who feel seized by the mystery of Christmas and wish to express it somehow.

In Europe—particularly in France, Spain, and Italy—starting in early November they conduct the annual Christmas fairs (*la foire de Noel*) all across the towns, villages, and monasteries where the local people get together to buy the traditional figurines and decorations needed to assemble the family *crèche.* It is a well-known custom that one buys a few figures at a time and that one continues building the *crèche* collection throughout the years. This is particularly true in Provence, where the native *crèche* consists not only of the classical Holy Family figures, shepherds, and animals but also includes other personages called *santons*: the three kings, the local baker, the farmer, the seamstress, the priests, the banker, and all the villagers. Using the theme of the Nativity, the Provençal people recreate the image and life of their own villages. The *santoniers*, as are called those who make the traditional clay figurines that are part of the *crèche*, find a particular joy in representing their rural people in a variety of forms standing at the scene of Jesus' birth.

Like the European festivities, our monastery's annual Christmas fair is held every year during the first and second weekends of Advent. It provides to many the occasion to admire and perhaps purchase some of the beautiful *crèches* collected from all over the world, lovingly put together by Vassar students, former students, and friends of the monastery. We have a variety of *crèches* to choose from. They come from countries such as Bangladesh, the Philippines, and Sri Lanka, as well as those closer to home, such as Mexico, Honduras, and Peru, plus those from Germany, France, Italy, Scandinavia, and China. This year the monastery is also offering some antique Italian, French, and German *crèches* that are more than 100 years old. Besides the *crèches*, items from the monastery kitchen and garden, plus monastic cookbooks and Christmas cards, are also available to the public. The monastery's tiny St. Joseph Atelier becomes almost a beehive of activity during the days of the fair. People sometimes travel long distances to attend our annual event, often in spite of bad weather. And they always come in the peace and joy of the season, eager to participate in what has become a yearly Advent ritual. *Benedicamus Domino!*

ST. NICHOLAS

St. Nicholas, the most human of saints, was always ready to help where need existed. By his very humanity, the saint reflected popular hopes and fears. He changed because human needs changed.

MARTIN EBON, *ST. NICHOLAS: LIFE AND LEGEND*

Early in Advent, a season that speaks to us of hope and of the great efforts we must make to lead honest Christian lives, today we celebrate the feast of St. Nicholas. His feast is an important pause on our Advent journey, a time to reflect and ponder on St. Nicholas' admirable example of Gospel living. There is much in his life that Christians of all times and places can learn from.

I can't help but think how appropriate it is for Christians today to reflect on the humble example of St. Nicholas. His life, a rather ordinary one, was given entirely to prayer and good works. He was not a monk, writer, or teacher, but he preached daily to his people the word of God, and he lived by it. He battled for the rights of the poor and oppressed and vigorously defended the rights of widows and orphans. One could easily describe St. Nicholas today as a saint with a certain social conscience. Like Christ, his Lord and Master, St. Nicholas was a good shepherd to his flock, exercising special compassion and mercy toward the outcasts, the poor, the undesirable of his time, and all those who were in distress in one form or another. His gentle goodness and exemplary life radiated beyond the limits of his own diocese of Myra, attracting pagans and unbelievers to the revelation of Jesus Christ, the Messiah.

THE LORD WHO COMES, THE SAVIOR WE AWAIT

Hope in God begins to disconnect our spiritual intellect from all material obsessions, and when our intellect is finally liberated, it will finally possess the love of God.

ST. MAXIMUS THE CONFESSOR

Advent is all about the coming of God in our midst. This sense of Christ's approaching as the Savior of all is what gives Advent its distinct and special character. Of course we know indeed that Christ already came some 2,000 years ago, but what Advent does is to renew the awareness of his presence among us. The grace of Advent also intensifies our longing for the Lord, for our full communion with him.

Each year, Advent helps us relive anew the mystery of the Incarnation, of Christ coming into the womb of Mary his Mother—and later, on Christmas Day, to the world at large, so now he comes again to be reborn in our hearts. Through the grace of the sacraments, especially the Eucharist, he penetrates our innermost selves. Advent also brings to mind that other coming of the Lord, his final coming in glory, reminding us that we must become like the vigilant servant of the Gospel, always ready for Christ's return. We anticipate this Second Coming in joy, praying, as the first Christians did: "Come, Lord Jesus, come."

OUR LADY OF ADVENT

When his mother Mary was betrothed to Joseph, but before they lived together, she was found with child through the holy Spirit.

MATTHEW 1:18

As Christians, we can learn much from the example of Mary about how to approach our Advent days. She is a living image for how to prepare oneself for Christmas. The presence of the Mother of God can be felt quietly in our hearts as we make our tiny efforts to walk the Advent journey in her company. Our Lady is the perfect companion in the journey toward meeting Christ, her beloved Son, for she is the humble servant who now carries him within. From the moment she received the good news from the Archangel Gabriel about the mission God intended for her, she accepted her role with utter humility and simplicity. She does not attribute anything to herself. She simply obeys God's plan for her and submits entirely to the work of God's Holy Spirit. When Gabriel arrives at her modest home in Nazareth, he finds a humble maiden waiting, ready to accept whatever the Lord's design holds for her.

Our Lady of Advent is without any doubt a unique model of how to embrace and love the true Advent spirit as we continue on our road to Christmas. She lived her own Advent for nine months, a longer period than our short four to eight weeks. She also lived it with greater intimacy, for he whom we expect to come dwelled within her, and she nourished and cared for him with unsurpassed love. The lowly, prayerful, humble, quiet, waiting attitude exercised by our Lady during her own Advent exemplifies what all our Advent days should be like. In the midst of the noisy and often chaotic Christmas preparations we encounter in today's world, the example of the Mother of God stands apart from all that is false, haughty, glittering, selfish, or superficial. Mary's presence in our midst, radiating a serene beauty through her silence, her acceptance, and total submission to God's plan, speaks volumes to each and every one of us.

What profound lessons we can all learn from her. Like the *Theotokos,* each of us is also called to accept God's personal plans for our lives and to surrender to him. Like Mary, we, too, are called to better our lives not once, but many times as the Lord reveals his will in our daily lives. Like our Lady, we must live our own submissions to the Lord with complete simplicity, humility, and trust in his plan for each of us. "Most Holy *Theotokos,* save us!"

ADVENT VIGILANCE

Christ our Judge commands us to be vigilant. We wait expectantly for his holy visitation, for he comes to be born of a virgin.

COMPLINE, PREFEAST OF THE NATIVITY

The practice of inner vigilance puts us in a perfect Advent mood. There is nothing closer to the true Advent spirit than a vigilant attitude. Indeed, vigilance is a Christian, monastic virtue. The monastic day starts with the praying of vigils. Early in Advent, one of the Church readings reminds us of Jesus' words: "May [the Lord] not come suddenly and find you sleeping. What I say to you, I say to all: 'Watch!'" This admonition from Mark 13:36 is a strong reminder of the need for constant vigilance. To cultivate an inner, vigilant attitude means to remain continually on the alert for all those signs the Lord provides us daily. They encourage us to persevere in our Advent resolutions and seek his presence in all of life's circumstances. Be alert, be vigilant, be on guard: This means keeping our hearts in a state of constant readiness. We know, as he himself reminds us, sometimes the Lord comes "like a thief at night." Advent vigilance challenges us to be ready at all times for his coming. Vigilance urges us to be prepared, for the Lord is close at hand. Vigilance is central to a humble, prayerful, and meaningful Advent observance. We keep vigil and patiently wait as we beseech the Lord to come and fully enter into our lives. It is true that Christ comes to us not only at Christmas, but even at all times, daily. Nevertheless, his coming at Christmas is special, for at Christmas we are filled with the intensity of our desires, the longing for our redemption, and full of grace and joy. Our Advent vigilance reminds us often that Jesus, the Messiah and our Savior, is indeed near us and that, likewise, we are also near and dear to him. *Veni Domine, et noli tardare.*

ENTERING INTO GOD'S MYSTERY

Rather the L*ORD* *takes pleasure in those who fear him, [in] those who put their hope in his mercy.*

PSALM 147:11

In all wisdom and insight, he has made known to us the mystery of his will in accord with his favor that he set forth in him.

EPHESIANS 1:8–9

Advent reminds me daily that throughout each of the liturgical seasons, the Church encourages us to move forward on our spiritual journey and enter ever more deeply into God's mystery as manifested in the great events of Christ's earthly life: his Incarnation and birth, his Epiphany and theophany in the Jordan, his transfiguration on Mount Tabor, his passion and resurrection in Jerusalem, his glorious ascension into heaven and his sending of the Holy Spirit at Pentecost as he promised, culminating all these celebrations with the mystery of mysteries: the Blessed Trinity. From the early days of the Christian communities, the faithful were invited to nurture their faith by continually meditating on the sacred events and mysteries of the Lord's earthly life. The liturgical seasons and celebrations provide us precisely an occasion to relive the mysteries of Christ's life, and furthermore to receive the graces imparted by them. For it is Christ, our Lord, who alone has access and can introduce us to the Father. And it is the Holy Spirit who stirs and nurtures Christ's life in us, Christ's presence in our hearts. It is by the Spirit's actions alone that we are reminded of all Christ said and did during his earthly years. It is also the Holy Spirit who ultimately illumines our souls with Christ's light, inspiring us daily to put the Master's teachings into practice. Our Advent days provide a timely opportunity to journey profoundly into God's mystery through the deepening of our faith, through growing in humility and love, and through assiduous recourse to prayer. "Come, Lord, and set us free!"

THE ANCESTORS OF THE LORD

And he said to them, "Oh, how foolish you are! How slow of heart to believe all that the prophets spoke! Was it not necessary that the Messiah should suffer these things and enter into his glory?" Then beginning with Moses and all the prophets, he interpreted to them what referred to him in all the scriptures.

LUKE 24:25–27

We are experiencing the sharp, cold weather expected from the season. I have no doubt that winter has arrived on our shores in full force. One of the joys provided by these wintry days is to be able to descend into the fruit/vegetable cellar and find there firm, juicy fruits and vegetables to keep us going throughout our winter months: apples, potatoes, Jerusalem artichokes, squash, carrots, turnips, onions, and even some lovely beets. I delight heartily in being able to choose for our evening meal from the fruition of our own harvest. Summer and fall are now behind us, but the memories of the gardening season linger. In monastic life, there is always this sense of continuity among the seasons. The seasons contain a logic all their own. They have a blessed, mysterious rhythm that progresses and paces itself daily under God's wings. We can't always explain this mysterious rhythm, only experience it.

A special grace I attribute to Advent is that it plunges us deeper into the Old Testament, helping us rediscover in its pages the drama of our own waiting for Christ here and now. This suffices for me to treasure ever more so that section of the Bible. It is like falling in love with the word of God all over again. Some Christians of our times have lost touch with or interest in the Old Testament. I even once overheard someone saying, "Now that we have the New Testament, we don't need to waste time with the Old." And yet to fully understand the mystery of Christ, we must make recourse to those who preceded him: the patriarchs, the prophets, the entire history of the people of Israel. Furthermore, we must make their deep longing for the Messiah, for the arrival of God's kingdom, our own.

It is important to study and honor the beloved ancestors and prophets who foretold the Lord's coming, among them Abraham, Isaac, Joseph, Moses, David, Elijah, Daniel, Isaiah, and Jeremiah, as well as Joachim and Anna, parents of Mary and grandparents of the Lord. Their example, attitude, and message must be assimilated by us as we also long for the coming of the Messiah. Through prayer and deep faith, we join today the assembly of those Old Covenant holy men and women who patiently awaited the Lord's arrival, the Savior and Redeemer of both the old and new Israel. "O Shepherd of Israel, lend an ear....LORD God of hosts, restore us; light up your face and we shall be saved" (Psalm 80:2, 20).

JUDGE NOT

Do not make any judgment before the appointed time, until the Lord comes, for he will bring to light what is hidden in darkness and will manifest the motives of our hearts, and then everyone will receive praise from God.

1 CORINTHIANS 4:5

Everywhere we go these days, we hear people groaning about the present hard times bestowed upon all by bad news from the economy. People mention their financial and investment losses, the lack of jobs, the falling wages, a paralyzed economy. It is almost depressing to hear these constant complaints and be unable to help or find solutions that could help others. In my case, all I can do is include these concerns in my daily prayer and mention people's immediate needs to the Lord. Although life itself is often hard and awfully brief, the rough times linger on and extend themselves into an almost permanent state of anxiety and fear for many. Some of these people just never manage to emerge from their trials and tribulations; they sometimes fall into a state of self-pity and begin to pass harsh judgment on others. Judging others, under any circumstances, is never an answer to our personal problems. This is what I sometimes tell those with whom I have direct contact. Furthermore, the Lord admonishes us in the Gospel never to judge others so that we ourselves may avoid being judged. Blaming and judging others for our misfortunes is as old as the world itself, but it never solves any problems. The Desert Fathers, taking seriously the Lord's words, always refused to engage in any type of passing judgment on others, hard as this sometimes was. They vehemently stuck to the Gospel teaching, reminding their disciples, "If a man is possessed by humility and poverty, and he does not judge others, the fear of God will come to him" (Abba Euprepios). Advent, as we await the Lord's return, is an appropriately good time to pray and beseech the Lord to acquire a nonjudgmental attitude toward others. "Come, Lord Jesus, Come!"

CHRIST: THE LORD OF HISTORY

Behold, I make all things new.

REVELATION 21:5

Advent is a season with a special message. It points us directly to Christ, our Savior, the Lord who is to come. He is the Alpha and the Omega, the beginning and the end, indeed the Lord of history. The ages, time, and the seasons were created by him and for him alone, for at the appointed time the Father sent his only begotten Son to rule over all. When we confess Christ, our God, we confess the reality of the Mystery that was intended by the Father from all eternity: the glorification of his beloved Son as the Lord and Master of history, in time and for all eternity. We Christians live in the here and now, but we are already caught in the movement and progress of time that looks to its ultimate consummation, the end point, when all things will converge in Christ. St. Paul reminds us that all nations, each of us, were made and are called to belong to Christ alone; therefore we must place all our hope in him alone. Our finite, time-limited existence is caught in that patient waiting for the mystery to be revealed at the end in all its fullness. This is why Advent not only references Christ's first coming in history, but even more so to his ultimate one at the end of the ages, when he shall appear in the clouds as our Judge and Savior, and when history will again be reshaped and made new by him, the Lord and only purpose of all history. "Behold, I make all things new."

ATTACHMENT TO CHRIST

Withdrawal from the world means two things:
the withering away of our obsessions
and the revelation of the life that is hidden in Christ.
THEODORE THE ASCETIC

Advent is all about getting closer to the Lord and about the deepening of our life in Christ. Christ is the starting point of our Advent journey, the in-between, and the end point toward which our steps and energy must be directed. St. Benedict, in his wisdom, is a good teacher pressing the disciple to prefer nothing to Christ and his mystery, letting him or her know that he alone is the source of our faith and the true nourishment of our souls. For St. Benedict, the love of Christ is both the only goal and sole purpose of a Christian monastic life. From day one in the monastery, the disciple is invited to realize that, without Christ, his monastic life offers no meaning and makes no sense. Daily, little by little, the early monastic is urged to discover who this Christ is, what his teachings and life on earth were like, and slowly begin to imitate him. And of course, the Gospels become the fountain from which the disciple learns to drink in order to assimilate into his life Christ's own life. In the prologue of the *Rule,* St. Benedict makes this teaching clear to the disciple: "With the Gospel for our guide, may we deserve to see him who has called us to his kingdom."

Through every aspect and particle in the *Rule*, St. Benedict wishes to transmit to the disciple his own deep attachment to the person of Christ, thus energizing the disciple to build up his own bond with the Lord. St. Benedict often cites St. Paul throughout the *Rule*, and this should not be a source of surprise to anyone. The Christocentric character of St. Paul's teachings conveyed an appeal for St. Benedict equal to none, except for the Gospel itself, the words and example of the Lord himself. St. Benedict certainly made St. Paul's word his own: "For me, to live is Christ." For St. Benedict the only thing that mattered at all times and all occasions was to be found "in Christ." This continual and inseparable communion with Christ was St.

Benedict's only aim and goal, the only one he proposed as a model to the disciple. During these last days of our Advent pilgrimage, let us ask the *Theotokos*, our Lady of Advent, to increase in us a tender and loving attachment to the person of her Son, Christ our Lord and Savior. *Mihi vivere Christus est.*

JESUS, THE MESSIAH, LOVER OF THE POOR

Have among yourselves the same attitude that is also yours in Christ Jesus, Who, though he was in the form of God, did not regard equality with God something to be grasped. Rather, he emptied himself, taking the form of a slave, coming in human likeness.

PHILIPPIANS 2:5–7

During the years of Christ's public ministry, one theme that appeared frequently in his teaching was that of embracing real poverty, a self-emptying state. "Blessed are the poor of spirit," he often said to his disciples. In another context he reminded them, "The poor you will always have with you," as if to say, "In the poor you will always have me, find me." Christ's own example and admonition was a challenge to the disciples then, as it is for today's Christians who often overlook this hard-to-take teaching from the Lord. It was hard to accept it when Jesus reminded the rich young man that he must leave all his wealth aside to follow him, and it is hard for us to accept it now, slaves as we are of a materialistic, greedy culture, too attached to our worldly possessions. Jesus, the Messiah, paved the way by his own example and teachings, the only way we can travel safely into God's kingdom. From the first moment of the Incarnation, we learn from St. Paul, the Word of God emptied himself of his divine attributes and embraced human poverty, taking the form of a servant for our sake.

If Christ had chosen the wealth of an earthly kingdom, he might have fulfilled the expectations of many of those who surrounded him. Instead, by rejecting worldly possessions and power, he vindicated and validated the lot of the poor and the lowly of his times, the vulnerable and dispossessed of today and of all times, who, according to his wisdom, remain always with us. Jesus lived the mystery of his earthly life in a continual act of total surrender to God, his Father, and he did this by choosing a lifestyle contradictory to that of the world, one of simplicity and poverty, one of total self-emptying.

It is in the example of that life that we are to seek the truth of his message, especially during these late Advent days while we eagerly await his arrival. The poverty, abjection, and self-emptying of the Lord are for us both the example and the means by which we follow closely in his footsteps. The people of Jesus' time expected a powerful, triumphant Messiah; they knew he would be coming, and they longed for his arrival. Christ knew what was expected of him, what signs the people were looking for, yet he came instead in disguise and challenged them with the truth. The Lord was meant to be born and live as a poor man and one day die crucified as a criminal. That was a contradiction to all expectations! He challenged his disciples, as he challenges us now, to leave behind their and our own preconceived ideas of what the Messiah must be like. If we keep our eyes and ears open to his message, we shall discover that he chooses a poor stable as a birthplace and embraces poverty, hardship, sacrifice, and great simplicity as his lifestyle. It is only by doing likewise that we can understand the mystery of his life and assimilate the true meaning of his message.

ADVENT/CHRISTMAS WRITING

Behold, I proclaim to you good news of great joy that will be for all the people.

LUKE 2:10

Daily writing, for most people, is both a discipline and an exercise of the creative process. For a monk, however, it seems to be a way of grounding oneself more concretely in the divine mystery. After all, the writing seems to emanate somehow from one's daily spiritual experiences: prayer, reading, meditation, liturgy, work, or just simply observing the events of the daily. As a monk, we pray, work, chant, and read daily. And it is in this daily repetitive routine or exercise that we are called to enter into the mystery. Entering into the mystery doesn't immobilize our faculties or forms of expression; it rather activates them, allowing one to convey something of that otherwise totally wordless experience.

Something like that happens in the writing done during this blessed Advent/Christmas period. And this is true not only about creative writing, it can be about any writing, including simple letter or Christmas-card communication, which is what I will do today and tomorrow. Advent/Christmas writing inspires us to go out of ourselves and communicate with others, and this always happens in the context of the mystery into which we are plunged. It is a reflection of it. It is the experience of the mystery that inspires us to sit down, take our pens, and just write. The mystery recharges our minds and our hearts, it makes us eager to try to convey something of its experience. Sometimes we fail, but we still try. The experience of the mystery reinvigorates our daily life, and thus our writing is included in it. Somehow, we move forward and write with greater trust, because from within we intuitively know the mystery cannot be totally contained. As the angels did on that first Christmas night, we too must communicate to others the glad tidings that Christ is to be born again in our midst.

DECEMBER 17

O SAPIENTIA (O WISDOM)

O Wisdom, O holy Word of God,
you govern all creation with your strong yet tender care.
Come and show your people the way to salvation.

VESPERS ANTIPHON OF THE DAY

Our Advent journey has spiraled, and here we are at Christmas' doorstep in no time. After having made notice of the ups and downs of the Advent journey, seemingly short as I look back at it today, I think I may take notice for next year and try to improve a bit with a more spiritually restrained instinct and wisdom. Next year, or the year after that, I shall make a point of pacing myself a bit more slowly, perhaps more thoughtfully—more prayerfully for sure—as I approach these most solemn days commemorating the Lord's birth.

O Wisdom of God, God's one and only begotten Son! God spoke one word, and that was he, Jesus, the Word incarnate and our Savior. In his great mercy, the Lord has bestowed upon me, us, a delicious, almost irresistible taste for words. How do I dare then approach and try to discern this all-surpassing appetite for the uniqueness of his Word, his only begotten Son? This is all new to me, to us. Suddenly, they are no longer human utterances, they all cease and only a word remains, the Word of God! Come, O Lord, O Word of God, and show us the way of salvation.

O ADONAI

O sacred Lord of ancient Israel, who showed yourself to Moses in the burning bush, who gave him the holy law on Sinai mountain: come, stretch out your mighty hand to set us free.

VESPERS ANTIPHON OF THE DAY

The sharp cold weather has officially made its entrance here in the Northeast, into upstate New York and New England. Geography and topography don't always differentiate borders, which are mostly a result of human historical arrangements. There has been little snow so far, but hints of it are daily and all around. One of the joys of these wintry days is to anticipate what is in store: long hours by a heart-warming wood stove, quiet time for music, reading, contemplation, and the assertion not to give in to boring thoughts and attitudes, not by rejecting all positive living, but by not living and praying enough. Inner prayer is always the key that opens the doors into a mysterious, yet real, world. And real prayer these days is all about expectation, about the nearness of a certain coming, about someone who comes to free and liberate us from ourselves and from all other forms of bondage. Our liberator once manifested himself in the mountains of ancient Sinai. Today he is much closer: the Catskills or the Berkshires or simply the Hudson Valley continue to reveal him. There we find him daily, always stretching out his mighty hands to save each of us!

DECEMBER 19

O RADIX JESSE

O Flower of Jesse's stem, you have been raised up as a sign for all peoples;
kings stand silent in your presence;
the nations bow down in worship before you.
Come, let nothing keep you from coming to our aid.

VESPERS ANTIPHON OF THE DAY

Last night the snow fell silently, almost majestically, in the Hudson Valley. Some would call it an anticipation of a white Christmas. It was so quiet, without a breath or sound of wind outdoors. This morning the rural countryside was clad in spotless, clean white. It was calm and it was beautiful. Our winter nights are long now, for the sun rays don't begin to break until almost 7 a.m. The sharp winter weather is an invitation for turning inward into serious spiritual matters as we attentively await an arrival. It is not too long now, for the Savior is almost at our doorstep. This evening at Vespers time, while singing the *Magnificat*, we are reminded powerfully of the rich symbolism of the flower that once bloomed on Jesse's stem. This beautiful flower is none other than Christ, our Savior, a flower from a Virgin Mother. As the O antiphon reminds us, Christ shall blossom from Mary at the time of his birth in Bethlehem and there be raised as a sign of salvation for all peoples. All nations then, all of us included, shall gratefully acknowledge the Father's infinite gift to us and worship him together with his only begotten Son, our Lord Jesus Christ, and the Holy Spirit. We are reminded by this that at all times the glorious mystery of Christ's Incarnation involves the participation of the entire divine Trinity.

Behold, a rose of Judah, from tender root has sprung.
A rose from root of Jesse, as prophets long foretold.
It bore a flower bright
That blossomed in the winter
When half-spent was the night....

O CLAVIS DAVID

O Key of David, O royal Power of Israel,
controlling at your will the gate of heaven:
Come, break down the prison walls of death
for those who dwell in darkness and the shadow of death;
and lead your captive people into freedom.

One of the most memorable experiences for anyone in Germany, France, or Austria at this time of the year is savoring the winter holiday season at one of the country's multiple Christmas markets. The colorful fairs, embellished by glittering lights, are held in most towns and cities during the four-week Advent season leading to Christmas. The scents of roasted almonds, gingerbread cookies, and savory snacks such as fried bratwurst and potato pancakes intermingle with the steam rising from mugs of hot wine (or cider) as people stroll through the cozy markets choc-a-bloc with cute wooden booths and stalls. Locals and tourists alike shop in these "cities of cloth and wood" for Christmas ornaments, statuettes for the family *crèche*, and traditional handicrafts from nutcrackers, wooden figurines, straw stars and smokers, to textiles, Christmas cards, toys, and glass or tin tree ornaments.

Ringing in the holiday season, cities across the United States are also beginning to imitate and celebrate in imitation of the traditional European Christmas market. Not unlike the Christmas markets in Germany, Switzerland and others, each American Christmas market carries a flair that is unique to the city or region where it takes place. There are several right here in our own New York State and throughout New England. And while the Christmas markets are spreading holiday cheer among their customers and attendees, in the quiet of the monastery we pursue our prayerful vigil and eager waiting for him who is to come. Our preparations for the holy night's arrival is more of a spiritual nature, and as it intensifies it requires silence, stillness, the quieting down our senses so that we may concentrate on the mystery that is to be revealed.

Today's O antiphon makes direct reference to the ancient messianic titles the prophets used to describe the expected Messiah, he who would come to set Israel free. This Messiah, a descendant from the house of David, is the only one with access to the key that shall one day unleash Israel's power. He himself is the key, the one who shall unlock for all of us the doors to God's kingdom. The eternal Father bestows all power upon his beloved Son, and it is through him alone that we are given access to the Father. In his infinite love, the Father provides us a Savior, his own Son, to liberate us from our state of captivity and the shadows of death. Tonight, as we complete Vespers, our Evening Prayer of praise, we pray with the words of one of the seasonal carols:

Makes darkness pass away,
True God, true Man, we pray,
Help us in every sorrow,
And guard us on our way.

DECEMBER 21

O ORIENS

O Radiant Dawn,
splendor of eternal light, Sun of Justice:
come, shine on those who dwell in darkness
and the shadow of death.

VESPERS ANTIPHON OF THE DAY

Today we enter officially into winter, for the calendar marks the date of the winter solstice in our hemisphere. Today is commonly known as the shortest day of the year. The day hours seem fewer and the night hours extra long, seemingly darker and ever more intrusive, almost mysterious. It is hard to explain the power darkness holds over us. The long winter darkness, almost always gloomy, makes this reality somehow tangible for all of us. Sometimes during these prolonged winter nights, I try to stimulate and encourage myself by sometimes repeating: "We are children of the light and darkness has no power over us," or by making recourse to the words of Psalm 91:5–6: "You shall not fear the terror of the night nor the arrow that flies by day, nor the pestilence that roams in darkness, nor the plague that ravages at noon." During those moments of prayer, I feel only the power of God can overcome that of darkness. I am not comfortable with the experience of darkness, and I know some cases where people can be terrified by it. Fortunately for us Christians, there is hope in the fact that Christ is our light. He himself once affirmed, "I am the Light of the World." He is the splendor of that eternal light that shines from the Father's face. Through him, we are invited to enter into fellowship with God, where the divine light shines forever. He, the Sun of Justice, has overcome the darkness and the power of death, and from now on—by sharing in his fellowship—we are forever illumined by the Light that no darkness can ever touch or consume. I am often comforted, strengthened by the words in one of the psalms: *Deus illuminatio mea et salus mea.* "The Lord is my light and my salvation."

O REX GENTIUM

O King of all the nations,
the only joy of every human heart;
O Keystone of the mighty arch of man,
come and save the creature you fashioned from the dust.

VESPERS ANTIPHON OF THE DAY

Advent and Christmas are unique times for experiencing the joy of praising the Lord in song. From the Gospels we learn that the first thing the angels did on that first Christmas night was to joyfully praise God, singing, "Glory to God in the highest and on earth peace to those on whom his favor rests." It was with song that they thus announced to shepherds in the surrounding Bethlehem fields the good news of the Lord's birth. I always find that our Advent and Christmas music, the chant, or others such as Bach's seasonal music, are full of hope and prayerful joy, the sort of hope and joy that intensifies in our hearts the desire for the Lord's arrival. Music and singing enhance our spiritual celebration as we begin to experience what our faith tells us is going to happen during these final days of the journey. Music is part of all of life and a natural vehicle for our fervent prayer on these last steps of the Advent/Christmas pilgrimage. Praising the Lord in song is nurturing and restorative to our own inner spirits. It is amazing the sense of sheer release, healing, depth, and freedom we feel as we intone and sing the last beautiful O antiphons. Tonight we sing, ponder, and pray on one of the final ones, "*O Rex gentium*," which I loosely translate as, "O King of all the peoples and nations." Yes, Jesus is the king knocking at our doors, bringing salvation to his people, to all of us. He is the desired one of all of us and the one who comes to fulfill every desire of ours. As he knocks at our personal doors, at the heart of each of us, he infuses new life into us, a new life of grace and peace. Our response in song is a humble way of showing him our gratitude and love, for he arrives for the sole purpose to save the creatures he once fashioned from the dust. With our Lady, the *Theotokos*, we praise God in glorious song: "My soul proclaims the greatness of the Lord; my spirit rejoices in God my savior" (Luke 1:46–47).

O EMMANUEL

O Emmanuel, king and lawgiver,
desire of the nations, Savior of all people,
come and set us free, Lord our God.

VESPERS ANTIPHON OF THE DAY

It is hard to believe, but here we are at the threshold end of our Advent journey. Tomorrow, as we prepare for the official announcement of the Lord's Nativity, we shall sing, in the words of the Invitatory: "Hodie, today, you will know the Lord is coming, and in the morning you will see his glory." These words from the Invitatory have always carried throughout the years deep personal sustenance for me. In many ways, it is an arrival point. After tomorrow, there is no more waiting time. Advent, for a monk, for every Christian, is a faith journey. It's a journey with a beginning and a conclusion, a journey full of questions, sometimes perplexities about life's issues and so on—ultimately sometimes one even questions the validity of undertaking the journey. Without faith, the journey would make no sense. Thankfully, the Lord is present with us, by our side all along the way, and sometimes during moments of quiet prayer he pieces together a response or provides us a spiritual intuition to the perplexing questions that arise in our souls during those life-questioning moments. By the power of God's grace, we then arrive to a deeper awareness and appreciation of the sole purpose for the journey. Sometimes, while feeling a bit down and under dark shadows, in our own search for light or for an answer, it can help us to recall the inner disposition of the prophets and the people of the Old Testament, as they too, sometimes in a gloomy state, waited in faith and hope for him who was to be their liberator.

As we arrive to this last day of the journey, I realize more than ever that not everything during that space of time was all light, peace, and serenity, as one often assumes. No, there were also moments of darkness and doubt, moments of weakness and fear, but precisely because of all of it, all that is positive and sometimes negative in life, we appreciate even more our desperate need for salvation, for the liberation the Lord brings to our lives through his coming. Today at Vespers, we shall call upon him for the first time with the name the angel gave him: Emmanuel. It means: "God with us." To call this child yet to be born, this God-man-child Emmanuel means to accept gratefully the grace of our own destiny as children of God. From now on, our own lives shall be forever marked by the reality of God's infinite fidelity to his people. God is indeed faithful to his promises, and on Christmas Day he shall reveal himself to us as Emmanuel, that is, God with us! The path through life's mazes may not always become simple and easy to follow. Life's seasons, from winter and spring to summer and autumn, are not always a smooth tonic or breath of fresh air, but from now on we shall be able to walk life's path with the firm conviction that he is Emmanuel, God with us! We may still feel the fragility and weakness of our human nature but also know that God, by embracing it, turned this fragile nature into a source of grace and salvation, giving us all a total new life. In the words of the antiphon sung during the Christmas octave *O admirabile commercium*: "Marvelous is the mystery proclaimed today: man's nature is made new as God becomes man, he remains what he was and becomes what he was not. Yet each nature stays distinct and for ever undivided."

HOW FAR TO BETHLEHEM?

Break out together in song,
O ruins of Jerusalem!
For the LORD has comforted his people,
has redeemed Jerusalem.
The LORD has bared his holy arm
in the sight of all the nations;
All the ends of the earth can see
the salvation of our God.

ISAIAH 52:9–10

An old Christmas carol echoes the sentiments that should be ours today. In the carol, visitors, probably the field shepherds, ask the local people, "How far is it to Bethlehem?" These dear visitors—full of warmth and thanksgiving, joy and good fellowship—are eager to arrive at the scene of the manger and behold there God's wonder in the flesh. Early today, during the Morning Office, we heard the solemn announcement of the Nativity, and with grateful hearts we sang in response the troparion for the prefeast of the Nativity:

Prepare, O Bethlehem,
For Paradise has been open to all.
Adorn yourself, O Ephrata,
For the Tree of life blossoms forth
From the Virgin in the cave.
Her womb is a spiritual paradise
Planted with the divine fruit;
if we eat of it, we shall live forever
And not die like Adam.

As we proceed with the rest of our monastic day, laboring at the tasks that comprise our daily routine plus other duties encompassing last-minute preparations for the upcoming festivities (first Vespers of the Nativity, the eucharistic celebration), we keep the eyes of our hearts fixed on one point only: our final destination for tonight and tomorrow is Bethlehem. Tonight, tomorrow, in the Bethlehem of our hearts, Christ wishes to be born once again as he did once in Bethlehem of Judah. Our task now consists in preparing a warm, humble place to welcome him, a manger to be born again, this time right in the center of our hearts.

DECEMBER 25

CHRISTMAS: THE *DIES NATALIS*

Come, brethren, let us behold the Son of the hidden God, reveal himself to us in the flesh, while hiding his mighty power.

ST. EPHREM THE SYRIAN, HYMN

Christmas, in a unique way, is the celebration of God's tenderness for his people. The Incarnation of the Son is a totally incomprehensible mystery, unless we accept it unconditionally as a sign of God's pure love for humanity. How else can we explain it? On Christmas Day, the all-powerful and immense God, hiding his divinity, appears before human eyes under the guise of a humble and tiny child. O impenetrable mystery, *mysterium magnum*, indeed! Christmas is truly the revelation of this otherwise totally hidden God, as the prophet Isaiah rightly calls him: *Tu est verus Deus absconditus* ("You are truly a hidden God"). To accept the truth and reality of Christmas means to accept the mystery of the Incarnation and ultimately the mystery of God. The Lord confounds us by his strange actions, but in the midst of them we find the truth!

I often think that part of the reason the Lord appears to us as hidden is not so much the fact that God wishes to hide himself from us, but more the result of the inability and limitation of our human mind to comprehend God. Our minds, by their nature, are not equipped to go beyond their limits. Of course, the Lord was well aware of this, since he created us. Yet he still wished to communicate with us and share our lives, so he found a way of making himself available and comprehensible to our eyes through the mystery of the Incarnation. This meant the splendor and mystery of his divinity remained hidden from our eyes, while appearing in human form as a tiny and helpless child. The mystery of this self-emptying of God, this kenosis of the Son of God, where his divinity remains hidden from sight and only his human nature appears, is what the incomprehensible mystery of the Incarnation is all about, and it is what Christmas unveils before our eyes today. St. Irenaeus of Lyons explains it in clear terms: "God became man that man may become God." The Lord, in his own unique way, by assuming our humanity, gave us a direct entrance into his divinity.

Tonight, after singing the second Vespers of the feast, I gaze and prolong my prayer before the *crèche* in the chapel and before the icon of the Nativity. The words from some of the old carols rise spontaneously in my mind. One from ancient Slovenia has a special charm and resonance as I keep repeating the words:

In the grotto of Bethlehem
It is both night and day,
And from the arms of Mary
The Child-God smiles at us.
Sweet Child, all my love,
You came down from heaven
To give me your love and to be with me.

THE FLOW OF HUMAN HISTORY AND RECKONING TIME

Time itself has been illumined by the Light which the darkness cannot dispel.

AN ORTHODOX THEOLOGIAN

Once again we have completed our Advent journey and reached our destination, our goal. We are now at Bethlehem, and the Christmas season is all around us. As we repeat the journey year after year, we are confronted once again with the mystery of time. Recently a friend sent me a text so appropriate for the season, which I decided to paraphrase here. We begin the reckoning of time from the moment of Christ's birth. This is a fact accepted from long ago but unfortunately today a mere convention for many. Seldom does one recall and acknowledge the unique event from which we begin to count time. In so doing we betray our insensitivity to history. In ancient days, time was computed from the Incarnation of God the Word. This means we live in a world that has been made new, redeemed, and sanctified already, that even now we live in the realm of grace and reckon the years by this total newness. Time itself has been illumined by the Light that darkness cannot dispel. In a new and higher sense, God is with us from that mysterious day forward, from that holy night in Bethlehem when God "was manifested in the flesh" (1 Timothy 3:16). Ever since, we continue to plunge ourselves daily in the worship of the God who on that night descended down from heaven. That is truly the mystery of Christmas, the mystery of the holy night. And now we keep it yearly among our most treasured memories. On the holy night we remember not only what happened on that same night long ago, but also that which has come to fulfillment now. And ever since, we continue the reckoning of time, the years of grace of our Lord and Savior Jesus Christ, for God did show us on that night how much he loved the world.

A CONTINUATION FROM YESTERDAY

Yesterday's meditation is continued here.

St. Paul tells us that in the fullness of time God sent into the world his only Son to be born of a woman. In a precious instant, the Son of God became the Son of Mary, the Virgin. Here lies the assurance of our faith and the beginning of our salvation, the guarantee and source of eternal life. This is why both those on earth and those in heaven rejoice today: The mystery of God-made-flesh is revealed to us, and all of us can rejoice in the splendor and glory of the Incarnation. The kingdom of God began its manifestation, its revelation in history, and became recorded in the mystery of passing time, summarized in the meekness and humility of a simple child. The star of God's eternal covenant stopped at a precise spot in the universe, shining brightly and pointing to a lonely cave in Bethlehem. The humbleness and obscurity of the cave testifies that the kingdom now revealed is not one of this world. Though this sacred event happened long ago, during the days of King Herod in the tiny city of Bethlehem, this "then" is, in a true sense of the word, an everlasting "now." It was truly a beginning, the starting point of something new...the opening page of the good news of the Gospel. History recorded the event in those first chapters of the Gospels of Luke and Matthew, and thus the good news of this New Covenant was revealed, the good news that continues "today," until this very day. The ancient prophesies of old, the predictions from the prophets, all came true on that first Christmas holy night.

Today I am spending part of the day, as I do most days, tending to our small flock of sheep, a flock that goes by the name *le petit troupeau de Bethlehem* ("Bethlehem's little flock"). In the barn where our flock finds refuge from inclement weather, the sheep enjoy the presence of their own *crèche*. From a protected corner in the barn, a rustic terra cotta statue of the Baby Jesus looks pleasantly at the sheep, smiles at them, and accepts their homage. I am sometimes pleasantly stunned seeing the sheep take their time looking curiously at the small baby.

O wonder of wonders, I tell myself, *even these simple beasts are able to recognize their Creator hidden under the form of a tiny baby.* It is not altogether a surprise they were among the first invited to come over with the shepherds, their masters, and behold in the stable the birth of the Son of God.

O blessed and humble beasts—chosen to be among the first to witness the divine, luminous event taking place in an obscure cave in the midst of a dark night—hear heavenly singing from the angels on high.

In a stable, dark and dreary,
Who will be the first to kneel?
At the crib where Christ is sleeping,
Who will be the first to kneel?
Wake, ye shepherds, seek out your King!
Bring your flock and loudly sing,
Till the air with echoes ring!

SIXTEENTH-CENTURY POLISH CAROL

A HOMILY ON THE NATIVITY OF THE LORD BY ST. GREGORY PALAMAS

So now God
not only forms human nature anew
by his own hand
in a mysterious way,
but also keeps it
near him. Not only
does he assume
this nature and raise it up from the fall,
but he inexpressibly clothes himself in it
and unites himself inseparably with it
and was born as both God and man:
from a woman, in the first instance,
that he might take
upon himself the same nature
which he formed in our forefathers;
and from a woman
who was a virgin,
in the second,
so that he might make man new.

THE NATIVITY CRIB: THE *CRÈCHE*

For the grace of God has appeared, saving all.
TITUS 2:11

For God so loved the world that he gave his only Son.
JOHN 3:16

The Christmas season is always full of various joyful customs, events, and traditions. There is the family Christmas tree in center halls usually surrounded by presents, the homey decorations all around the house, the fresh greens, the bright lights, the Christmas music, the Christmas candles, the greeting cards, and of course, last, but not least, the Christmas *crèche* and the Christmas icon. I must admit that sometimes I tend to think we would be better off if sometimes we did with less glitter, less materialism, less copious meals, less commercialism in general and concentrate more on the spiritual significance of the festivity. This is where I think the presence of the *crèche* and the Nativity icon are precious tools to help us recenter ourselves in what is essential: the reality of the mystery of the Incarnation.

One of my favorite Christmas stories is the one that recounts the origins of the first *crèche* scene by St. Francis of Assisi in thirteenth-century Italy. I often tell it and repeat it to children when they visit the monastery during this blessed period. The assembling of the first *crèche*, crib, or manger at Christmastime, however one may wish to describe it, is indeed attributed to St. Francis. We are told that three years before his death, Francis found himself on Christmas Day at the little Italian village named Grecio. Since it was the Lord's birthday, he wanted to do something special to honor him. The inspiration came to him to build a real living *crèche* with authentic figures, people, and beasts. He prepared a crib and placed plenty of hay all around it. He asked his friars to bring in an ox and a donkey and he accommodated them around the crib. He asked another friar to find some local shepherds and their sheep and invite to join the scene at the stable. When it got close to the time for Midnight Mass, Francis gathered all his friars, followers, and the local people carrying lanterns and singing Christmas hymns. They processed to the stable temporarily arranged inside the church and placed a real little baby, covered in swaddling clothes, on the top of the straw covering the crib. We read in the story that St. Francis was so moved by the experience that he fell into *éxtasis.* He and the people remained kneeling for hours close to the crib, seized by intense joy and a most tender feeling for the event they were reliving at that precise moment. Tears of happiness bathed their eyes, and with thankful hearts they imitated the angels at Bethlehem, singing endless praises to the Lord.

Ever since that first *crèche* was constructed at Grecio during St. Francis' time, the tradition has continued throughout the centuries to our own days. Every monastery, church, school, and Christian home honors this most lovely of Christmas customs and arranges yearly a Nativity scene in their midst. The *crèche* makes the little Lord Jesus especially present among us during the Christmas season, and those who surround him take delight in the joy, the blessing, and the pleasure of his divine company.

O holy Child of Bethlehem
Descend to us, we pray;
Cast out our sin, and enter in,
Be born is us today.

THE HOLY FAMILY

Joseph, O dear Joseph of mine,
Help me rock the Child divine,
God reward both thee and thine in paradise,
So prays the mother Mary.
I will gladly, lady of mine,
Help thee rock the Child divine.
God's pure light on thee will shine in paradise.
So prays the Mother Mary.
He came down at Christmastime,
In the town of Bethlehem.
Bringing to men far and wide,
Love's diadem.

"JOSEPH, O DEAR JOSEPH," FOURTEENTH-CENTURY GERMAN CAROL

The Christmas story is about a unique family. A humble family, one once only known by its immediate relatives in Nazareth, and yet today known all over the world. The principal member of the family is a tiny baby, the Son of God, the Most High. He enters the world in a poor, dark cave, for his parents Mary and Joseph couldn't find room elsewhere. Mary is the woman God chose to be his Son's earthly Mother. And Joseph, the humble carpenter from Nazareth, Mary's husband, is the man God chose to watch and care over Jesus and Mary. Both Mary and Joseph, truly humble people, are remarkable in the eyes of the Most High, and it is to them that the Son of God pledges obedience and fidelity. From the Scriptures we learn of Mary's deep faith and obedience to God's will. It is because of it she heard herself called blessed at the salutation from the angel. She could have never imagined in a million years God's plan for her. Obedient and humble that she was, she accepted God's plan for her and offered her total submission to him. The same could be said of Joseph the carpenter, he who in the Scriptures is described as a "just man." Joseph was preeminently a man of faith, and it was totally in faith that he accepted the role assigned to him by God: to guard, nurture, and protect this holy Child and his Mother and provide for their daily needs. Both parents, Mary and Joseph, loved with unsurpassable love the tiny Child entrusted to them. By God's unique design, they were called to be Jesus' closest relatives. He responded to their love, and they responded to his. And the world has never known love such as the one that bonded these three! And the three of them: Jesus, Mary, and Joseph—united in faith and love—lived in complete obedience to the Father, to his special plan for their lives. And as time went by, we learn from the Scriptures, Jesus grew up in wisdom, grace, and in years, in divine and human favor, under the tutelage and wise guidance of Mary and Joseph. God's unfailing plans were being fulfilled!

DEO GRATIAS: A MONASTIC YEAR'S COMPLETION

It is not your business to succeed, but to do right.
C.S. LEWIS, AUTHOR

I will sing of your mercy forever, Lord.
PSALM 89:2

This year of the Lord ends as it started, always counting on the unfailing protection of the Mother of God. I am constantly calling upon her by reciting the *Sub Tuum Praesidium* many times during the day and also during the night. Our Lady is always there by one's side, pointing at all times to Christ, her Son. She makes sure that we don't lose sight of the one essential in this life, and she never ceases to repeat: "Do whatever he tells you." Daily life goes on, following its same monotonous but healing rhythm, trying to make sense of the eternal paradox that is our Christian life: We seek Christ daily and yet we already find ourselves in him, we die daily and yet we are already living in him, hidden with Christ in God.

In our search for God, we keep looking for answers, and the response arrives saying there are no answers, only the darkness of faith and the hint of a presence. And that presence can only be perceived when we are empty of ourselves. To be filled we need to empty ourselves first. That is the daily task. God does the rest. One thing that amazes me daily is the experience of God's abundant mercy with each of us. This experience often overwhelms me. Sometimes I feel it as if it were a heavy weight, almost physically heavy. I am convinced that if our world wasn't so materialistic, our countries, churches, and communities so centered in themselves rather than being open to the mystery of God and the depth of his mercy, that they, too, would be transported to another realm by the experience of God's unfathomable mercy. It is hard to explain it and one doesn't seem to find adequate words to describe it. It is so real, so immense, and so heavy indeed! It is all in the experience, in the reality of it, and the subsequent memories that recall the experience and the feelings involved. The psalms then become my daily nourishment, my only escape. They give voice to my need for outburst: *Misericordias Domini in aeternum cantabo* ("The Lord's mercies I shall sing forever").

Translations of Phrases Found in Some Reflections

(ALL BUT TWO ARE LATIN)

January 6	*Venite adoremus:* Come, let us adore (him)
January 19	*O bonitas, Deus soli:* Oh Supreme Goodness: God alone
February 5	*Memoria Dei:* Remembrance of God
February 8	*Deo gratias:* Thanks be to God
March 9	*Veni, Sancte Spiritus:* Come, Holy Spirit
March 27	*Tempus fugit:* Time flies/Time flies away
May 1	*Ora et labora:* Pray and work
May 23	*Veni, Sancte Spiritus:* Come, Holy Spirit
June 21	*Ora et labora:* Pray and work *Laus Tibi Domine:* We praise to you, oh Lord
June 26	(French) *Le Christ, notre seule esperance:* (Latin) *Christus, spes mea:* Christ, our only hope Christ, my hope
July 3	*Surrexit Dominus vere:* The Lord is truly risen
July 16	*Regina Décor Carmeli, Ora pro nobis!:* Queen and beauty of Carmel, pray for us
July 17	*Et replevit orbis terrarum:* And he (the spirit) fills the whole world *Veni, Sancte Spiritus:* Come, Holy Spirit
July 21	*Gloria Dei, homo vivens:* God's glory is man alive *Gloria a Patri, et Filio, et Spiritui Sancto:* Glory to the Father, to the Son and to the Holy Spirit
July 27	*Benedicamus Domino:* Let us bless the Lord
August 11	*In Te, Domine, speravi, non confundar in aeternum:* In You, Lord, I place my trust, don't let me be confounded forever

August 26	(Spanish) *La paciencia todo lo alcanza:* Patience gets everything
September 4	*Deo gratias:* Thanks be to God
September 13	*O tempora, O mores:* Oh times, oh customs/O what era and what behavior
September 20	*Deo gratias:* Thanks be to God
September 23	*Memoria Dei:* Remembrance of God
October 16	*Deo gratias:* Thanks be to God
October 29	*Quoniam in aeternum misericordia ejus:* Because his mercy lasts forever
November 6	*Deo gratias:* Thanks be to God
November 9	*Deo gratias:* Thanks be to God
November 22	*Kyrie eleison:* Lord have mercy
November 23	*Ecce, quam bonum:* Behold, how good it is
November 29	*Christus, spes nostra:* Christ, our hope
December 5	*Benedicamus Domino:* Let us bless the Lord
December 9	*Veni Domine, et noli tardare:* Come, Lord, and do not delay
December 14	*Mihi vivere Christus est:* To me to live is Christ
December 21	*Deus illuminatio mea et salus mea:* God is my light and my salvation

Bibliography

St. Athanasius. *The Life of St. Anthony.* Baltimore: Newman Press, 1978.

A monk of the Eastern Church. *A Year of Grace of the Lord.* Yonkers: St. Vladimir's Press, 1980.

Burton-Christie, Douglas. *The Word in the Desert.* New York: Oxford University Press, 1993.

Beard, James. *Beard on Bread.* New York: Knopf, 1995.

Cassian, St. John. *Conferences.* New York: Paulist Press, 1985.

Climacus, St. John. *The Ladder of Divine Ascent.* New York: Paulist Press, 1982.

Cummings, Charles. *Monastic Practices.* Kalamazoo, Michigan: Cistercian Publications, 1986.

d'Avila-Latourrette, Br. Victor-Antoine. *A Monastery Journey to Christmas.* Liguori, Missouri: Liguori Publications, 2011.

____. *Blessings of the Daily: A Monastic Book of Days.* Liguori, Missouri: Liguori Publications, 2002.

____. *Blessings of the Table: Mealtime Prayers Throughout the Years.* Liguori, Missouri: Liguori Publications, 2003.

____. *The Gift of Simplicity: Heart, Mind, Body, Soul.* Liguori, Missouri: Liguori Publications, 2009.

____. *Twelve Months of Monastery Soups: International Favorites.* Liguori, Missouri: Liguori Publications, 1996.

____. *Simply Living the Beatitudes.* Liguori, Missouri: Liguori Publications, 2010.

De Vogue, Dom Adalbert. *The Rule of St. Benedict: A Doctorial and Spiritual Commentary.* Kalamazoo, Michigan: Cistercian Publications, 1983.

Desprez, Dom Vincent. *Le Monachisme Primitif.* Editions de Bellefontaine, 1998.

Dieu est Vivant—Catechisme pour les familles. Paris: Editions du Cerf, 1980.

Doubleday Christian Quotation Collection. New York: Doubleday, 1997.

St. Ephrem. *Hymns on Paradise.* Yonkers: St. Vladimir's Press, 1997.

Evdokimov, Paul. *The Struggle With God.* New York: Paulist Press, 1966.

Gaza, Dorotheos of. *Dorotheos of Gaza: Discourses and Sayings.* Collegeville, Minnesota: Cistercian Publications, 1978.

Haan, Wim. *The Monastic Rhythm of Life.* Http://www.bezinnen.nl/teksten/wim_eng/monastery_time.htm.

Hone, William. "February." *The Every-day Book and Table Book.* London: T. Tegg, 1830.

Egender, P. Nicholas. *Horologion, la priere des eglises de rite Bizantin.* Toulouse, France: Éditions de Chevetogne, 1975.

Hourlier, Dom Jacques. *Reflections on the Spirituality of Gregorian Chant.* Orleans: Paraclete Press, 1995.

Hunt, Leigh. *The Months: Descriptive of the Successive Beauties of the Year.* Whitefish, Montana: Kessinger Publishing, 2004.

à Kempis, Thomas. *The Imitation of Christ.* New York: Vintage, 1998.

Leclercq, Dom Jean. *The Love of Learning and the Desire for God.* New York: Fordham University Press, 1960.

Les Fetes et la Vie de Jesus-Christ. Paris: Editions du Cerf, 1985.

Levi, Peter. *The Frontiers of Paradise.* London: Collins, 1987.

Liturgy of the Hours According to the Roman Rite, The. New York: Catholic Book Publishing Company, 1976.

Louf, Dom Andre. *The Cistercian Way.* Kalamazoo, Michigan: Cistercian Publications, 1983.

Maria, Mother. *Sceptrum Regale.* Greek Orthodox Monastery of the Assumption, 1973.

McGuckin, John Anthony, translation and introduction. *The Book of Mystical Chapters.* Boston: Shambhala Press, 2003.

Merton, Thomas. *Contemplative Prayer.* Freiberg: Herder and Herder,1969.

____. *The Monastic Journey.* New York: Doubleday, 1978.

____. *The Silent Life.* New York: Farrar, Straus, & Cudahy, 1957.

____. *Thoughts in Solitude.* New York: Farrar, Straus, & Cudahy, 1957.

Moltmann, Jürgen. *The Church in the Power of the Spirit.* Minneapolis: Fortress Press, 1993.

Martyrologe Romain, Editions de Solesmes, 1977.

Morison, E.F. *St. Basil and his Rule.* Oxford: Oxford University Press, 1912.

New Jerusalem Bible, The. New York: Doubleday, 1985.

Philokalia, Volumes 1 & 2 (On Prayer of the Heart). London: Faber & Faber, 1951.

Rule of St. Benedict, The: Translated With Introduction and Notes. A.C. Meisel and M.L. del Mastro. New York: Doubleday, 1973.

Les Sentences des Peres du Desert, par Dom Lucien Regnault, Editions de Solesmes, 1966, 1970, 1976.

Les Sentences des Peres du Desert, par Dom Lucien Regnault, Serie des Anonymes. Solesmes-Bellefontaine, 1985.

Rogers, Samuel. *Human Life.* Publisher: John Murray, 1819.

Sophrony, Archimandrite. *Staretz Silouan.* Editions Presence, 1973.

Stevenson, B. *Home Book of Bible Quotations.* New York: Harper & Row, 1977.

Thekla, Sister. *Mother Maria: Her Life in Letters.* New York: Paulist Press, 1979.

Thekla, Mother. *St. Andrew of Crete (The Great Canon),* Library of Orthodox Thinking.

Treasury of Religious and Spiritual Quotations. The Stonesong Press, 1994.

Van Zeller, Dom Herbert. *The Holy Rule.* New York: Sheed and Ward,1978.

Vivian, Tim. *Four Desert Fathers.* St. Vladimir's Press, 2004.

Waddell, Helen. *The Desert Fathers.* Ann Arbor: University of Michigan Press, 1957.

Ward, Sister Benedicta. *Harlots of the Desert.* Kalamazoo, Michigan: Cistercian Publications, 1987.

. *The Sayings of the Desert Fathers.* Kalamazoo, Michigan: Cistercian Publications, 1975.

Woolever, Adam. *Encyclopedia of Quotations (Treasury of Wisdom).* D. McKay Publications, 1893.

Worthley, John. *The Book of the Elders.* The Systematic Collection Cistercian/Liturgical Press, 2012.